America's Original GI Town

CREATING THE NORTH AMERICAN LANDSCAPE

Gregory Conniff
Bonnie Loyd
Edward K. Muller
David Schuyler
Consulting Editors

George F. Thompson
Series Founder and Director

*Published in cooperation with the
Center for American Places,
Sante Fe, New Mexico, and
Harrisonburg, Virginia*

Village President Robert Dinerstein stands at the center of the flag presented to Park Forest by the National Municipal League in 1953. Over his right shoulder is Philip M. Klutznick, president of American Community Builders (ACB). Jack Star of *Chicago Magazine,* then of *Look Magazine,* is in the fedora. He is behind and to the left of Dinerstein. At the far left is Edward Waterman of ACB and Frank Norris, an early trustee of Park Forest. The woman to Waterman's left is Rose Waterman. The man in the lower right is Bernard Blumenthal; the woman to his right is Friedl Blumenthal. The man with the fur collar is Edward E. Cohn, an employee of B'nai B'rith and resident of Park Forest. *Source:* courtesy of Park Forest Public Library.

America's Original GI TOWN

PARK FOREST, ILLINOIS

Gregory C. Randall

THE JOHNS HOPKINS UNIVERSITY PRESS
Baltimore and London

The Johns Hopkins University Press
2715 North Charles Street
Baltimore, Maryland 21218-4363
www.press.jhu.edu

Library of Congress Cataloging-in-Publication Data will be found at the end of this book.
A catalog record for this book is available from the British Library.

ISBN 0-8018-6207-8

To my wife, Bonnie, who stood patiently by me
and helped me fulfill my dream

This is the American Way of Life

The crowded tenement and the smoky apartment have become symbols of our life in our great cities . . . the choking, destructive influences of such environment have relegated our essential centers of commerce to second rate places to live and work. The flight to the better places in the suburbs has met the urgings of relatively higher income families. This need not be . . . nor can it long continue without disastrous results.

Our national existence is enriched by the product of our large concentrations of populations. We must bring to those centers the opportunities of the American way of life. For those who want it, this means the advantage of size combined with the simplicity of smallness . . . It means access to the stimulating industry of a Chicago and to the open and easy living of a green town . . . It means the opportunity to labor in the fuming and belching furnaces that make our nation strong—and to live in the tree-studded, cleansed atmosphere of a smokeless town . . . It means the privilege of aiding the flow of commerce from a skyscraper and living close to the earth amidst the park blocks of modern planning.

In short it means the free man's right to seek his best work opportunity without the sacrifice of his urge to enjoy healthful and wholesome living . . .

This is the American way of life . . . To this ideal, the town is consecrated.

PHILIP M. KLUTZNICK, *President*
American Community Builders
October 1946

Contents

Preface

My earliest memory of Park Forest was watching a helicopter land in the shopping center and seeing Santa Claus arrive. It was a wonder to a five-year-old, and it would be the first of many memories that I have carried with me from that village. The death of a neighbor's son, only a few years younger than me, was my first memory of tragedy; he was struck by a car. I remember being bundled up to play in blizzards and going to get my first dog. Park Forest is memories—and that may be one reason why I am drawn back to it. With time the sharp edges have softened.

We came to Park Forest because there were apartments available to a young family from the sticks of Michigan. Fresh from Michigan State College with a degree in journalism, my father, John, had a job in the Loop, Chicago's downtown. My mother, Mary, had two young boys to manage. My parents were like 99 percent of every other new resident and family in Park Forest—under thirty, college educated, with two kids, and survivors of two wars within the last ten years. And, like the others, they were from somewhere else.

As a child, I remember calling our landlord the ABC Company. Forty years later I learned that the correct name was ACB (for American Community Builders). Even though we moved up, and, like so many other families, moved out of Park Forest, I maintained strong connections to the Village until I went away to college at Michigan State. Park Forest became for me, and for so many others, my hometown, a place of my earliest memories.

Park Forest was a product of the times. If it hadn't been built, other small towns would have been constructed in the area to fill the insatiable housing demand of post–World War II America. Millions of veteran GI's and their young families needed homes, and, because of the Great Depression and the war, few houses had been built, and even fewer were available. For ten years after the war's end not many builders would fail owing to a lack of customers. At the height of the construction of Park Forest, 3,010 apartments would be built and occupied in two years, or approximately six a day. At the peak of the single-family homes sales program, 10 homes per day would be completed.

This book is not just a history of the planning, construction, and the residential life of a GI town but an effort to tie Park Forest to the ongoing experiment of community building in the United States. It is the story of the evolution of a place. Park Forest was not just an organized collection of buildings and stores but also homes with bedrooms, kitchens, front yards, and driveways; it was filled with parks and parades, schools and learning, libraries and culture. This book presents historical examples from which the concept for the Park Forest and its community design were developed as well as descriptions of individuals who played a role in building the village—the builders and architects who had the vision, perseverance, and connections necessary and the village's early residents.

The early chapters place Park Forest along the time line of small communities that have a direct connection to the idea of the early-twentieth-century English garden city and look to the builders of the village to consider their ideas and motivations. Later chapters address the first wave of residents and the subsequent occupation of the village's single-family homes. The leaders of the young town are presented, as are the battles that were fought for the schools, the village hall, and continued growth. This is not intended to be a social history of the village, a community that faced the usual problems of urban growth: racism, economic collapse, and the social unrest of the "sixties." It is the story of the physical structure of the village—the bones, if you will. The residents provided the flesh.

My personal experience with new town planning and living began with Park Forest. Little did I know that through my research I would find out, forty-five years later, why my parents had lived in World War II barracks buildings at Michigan State, why Park Forest was more important than a place to go to school and to grow up in, and why my parents maintained friendships with our neighbors on Algonquin Street even after every one of them had moved on.

I have traveled extensively across the United States and have been involved in the planning and development of some of America's finest residential communities and neighborhoods. And, interestingly, understanding the simple buildings and special aspects of Park Forest has given me a better perspective on these other communities. Fifty years soften edges. Trees grow, building styles change, and neighborhoods age. Politics and planning go hand in hand: with great leaders, great things can happen; with mediocre leadership, opportunities are missed. In time, adversity forces a community to challenge itself and move forward. Sometimes events cause it to change. Park Forest experienced all of these phases. But it was also a product of strong personalities. One man, in particular, took on the mantle of another's dream and became the catalyst for one of the United States' greatest experiments in community building.

It is the story of young men returning from war and creating, out of nothing, a new idea for living—of families and friendships and new concepts in education and recreation, of imaginative shopping and living. And it is a testimony to the children, thousands and thousands of them, who grew up in a suburban world very different from most others in the United States.

I hope that, after reading this story of Park Forest, you will agree that it is not the design and the architecture that makes a community successful and sustainable; it is the people.

Acknowledgments

When I started this biography of Park Forest, I was unsure of the depth of the written histories available and whether anyone would even care if they were found. After a few short letters, doors opened everywhere. I found that the residents, past and present, were extremely proud of their village. This was most pronounced in the Oral History program started through the persistent efforts of Elizabeth Ohm, who in the late 1970s secured a grant that resulted in over eighty taped interviews and transcribed reminiscences by early residents and many of those responsible for the village's design and construction and growth. These documents formed the backbone of this story.

With special thanks I acknowledge Carroll F. Sweet Jr., for the use of his written autobiographies of his days in Park Forest and the memories of his father, Carroll F. Sweet Sr. I also thank both him and his wife, LaNe, for their hospitality and time during interviews. Edward and Rose Waterman offered their time, through hours of taped memories, and their support. They were the first to sign on for the experiment that was to become Park Forest.

Bernard Cunningham offered his comments and corrections and represented a gentle but firm testament of the past. Sadly, both Mr. Cunningham and Mr. Sweet passed away while the final chapters were being completed.

Others who came later to the village but greatly aided my search were Jane Nicoll, assistant reference librarian for the village. Her assistance in acquiring photographs and information and, especially, her sharp pencil were greatly appreciated. Larry McClellan supported my efforts with historical data. Magne Olson, the village historian, contributed his comments and, where necessary, corrections. Carl Stover offered his input on the history of the shopping center. John Schlossman, son of the architect for the village, was helpful by opening his archives to this research and sharing memories of his father, Norman. With help from the current village manager, Janet Munchnik, and recent village planners, the current history of the village was tied to the past. It is my hope that the story is as true as can be remembered.

To tell the story of the Klutznicks I turned to Philip Klutznick's 1991 autobiography, *Angles of Vision*, written with the assistance of Sidney Hyman. Sidney helped me to place the family both in the context of the times and in its place in the history of development in the Chicago region. Sidney was also a strong hand gently pushing me from behind and encouraging my efforts. He too believes that this is a story worth telling.

Many others contributed a comment here and there which helped me find the proper track. John Zukowsky, Curator of Architecture, the Art Institute of Chicago, helped place Park Forest into the perspective of Chicago architecture. I also thank Marc A. Weiss for his work on the FHA and postwar developers and Paul D. Spreiregen, for his biographical collection that saved the work and letters of Elbert Peets. There were many who, with a comment, helped with the context of the times.

Most important, I recommend William H. Whyte's many books on urban growth and the postwar development of the suburb. Without his book *The Organization Man*, Park Forest would have been one more forgotten village in the postwar United States. While the final editing for this book was being completed, Mr. Whyte passed away in New York. His voice will be missed.

And, last, I also want to thank all the citizens of the village, both past and present, for their part in the ongoing experiment that is Park Forest.

America's Original GI Town

CHAPTER ONE

The Builders

Peg:	What else did you ever think you wouldn't do when you were over seas?
Fred:	Well, I never had any clear idea but there were two things I was sure of . . .
	One, that I knew that I would never go back to that drug store.
Peg:	And what was the other thing?
Fred:	It was even sillier. I dreamed that I was going to have my own home. Just a nice little house with my wife and me out in the country, in the suburbs anyway. That's the cockeyed kind of dream you have when you are overseas.
Peg:	You don't have to be overseas to have dreams like that.
Fred:	Yeah, you can get crazy ideas right here at home.

—*Best Years of Our Lives* (1946)

THE unquenchable optimism of Americans for their future, after World War II, was the result of years of economic and social trials that would have torn other countries apart. Park Forest, a village on the South Side of Chicago, was born during this postwar euphoria. This village, and others like it, would change the social and physical landscape of America during the twenty years after the war more than the country's expansion had during the previous one hundred and seventy years. It unalterably changed how Americans would live and view themselves for the rest of the century.

The Depression and World War II created an environment ripe for change. In the space of eight short years, from 1925 to 1933, the country's economic collapse caused the number of new homes built in the United States to plunge from 937,000 residential units a year to 93,000. Foreclosures on private homes in 1933 reached one thousand a week. America's wealthiest could still build, but the majority of its citizens had to make due with older housing, many built before 1900. The number of new homes fell far below that of the demand. The failures within the banking industry left little capital available to private builders. The government's involvement in residential construction, through the offices of the Public

Works Administration, U.S. Housing Authority, and other federal agencies, resulted in the retail builder being effectively squeezed out of the market.

Programs initiated during the Depression by the Roosevelt Administration to build homes and create jobs fundamentally changed the relationships between the federal government, financial institutions, builders, and home buyers. The government stepped in to provide housing for the "worthy poor," as they were called, and to protect those barely hanging on. Washington agencies, by the end of the 1930s, were directly building and managing a sizable portion of American housing. These agencies also set standards that would affect private construction and financing while at the same time impacting local planning and zoning regulations throughout the country. The Federal Housing Administration (FHA) established guidelines for housing and planning which specifically supported the expansion of residential growth into the suburbs and almost summarily created an antiurban sentiment.[1]

Washington planners believed that most veterans and war workers would return to their prewar hometowns, but they were wrong. Many stayed where their wartime jobs were, others moved to the "big city," and many ex-GI's remained near their wartime bases. California's remarkable postwar growth began at this time, fueled by the appearance of transient American citizens and soldiers who were discovering the benign climate and seemingly unlimited potential for growth there.

America's greatest social challenge after the war became the housing of millions of returning veterans and their young families. Housing built during World War II supported the war effort. Being of marginal and temporary quality, it was generally located near war plants and seldom where most people wanted to live after the war. Buying a house during the war, for many, was not only a financial impossibility but was not even a long-term desire. Most of those who relocated for a job in war production rented places to live. The war's end brought great expectations, and now a new home was one of them.

The Depression, federal policies, and the war changed forever how Americans built homes, how they paid for them, and how and where they lived. The efforts of government agencies and social and economic changes were to lead to a twenty-year American "diaspora," with the suburban areas the major beneficiary.

The war in Europe was over by late spring of 1945. The unexpected death of President Roosevelt in April stunned a nation of those who had lived for four years with the constant thought that death might arrive at their own door in the form of a telegram. The death of the president was a loss grieved as heavily as the death of so many of their own husbands, brothers, and fathers. Thoughts of the end of the war and the reuniting of families were, for many, the only elements of consolation and hope in this great time of sadness.

Vice President Harry Truman, a Kansas City politician and former U.S. senator from Missouri, became president, and he was immediately faced with both foreign and domestic issues that had been kept hidden from him by Roosevelt. Meeting the postwar housing demand was one these issues. The population of the United States was 145 million people, and almost 10 percent were in uniform at the end of the war. During the first year after the war over six million military personnel were released from service, and another four million followed in 1946. Their release reunited 2.5 million families in 1945 alone. In the Los Angeles area fewer than 15 percent of the 782,000 war workers left the city. At the end of the war 98 percent of American cities reported significant housing shortages, and, when combined with the 90 percent who reported shortages of apartments, it was painfully obvious to the administration that trouble may be brewing.

The war had produced many families whose members had never lived together. Now, at the end of the war, these reunited families had no place to live. They were living with relatives and friends and in make-do structures. Some were even living in chicken coops; this was so common, in fact, that the FHA put out a booklet on how to modernize and get a loan to fix up your "coop." Some were living in mothballed bombers and others in salvaged street cars. Yet, even with this intense housing demand, the *Saturday Evening Post* reported only 14 percent of the population were willing to live in an apartment or "used home."[2]

The prewar Roosevelt Administration had shown its interest in housing through the Greenbelt community and new town efforts in the late 1930s, but these were not the successes it had envisioned. The concern for the housing of returning GI's had begun at the national level two years before the end of the war, when significant attempts at housing reforms were pushed through Congress. The most important piece of legislation was the passage of the Serviceman's Readjustment Act, or GI Bill, in June 1944. Among its important features was its guaranty by the Veterans' Administration for the larger portion of mortgage loans to veterans to purchase, build, or improve existing housing. The GI Bill's impacts on housing are comparable to those of the FHA. One significant difference was the limitation of the GI Bill to provide owner-occupied housing, a relic of the government's preference to support single-family housing.

Articles written for *House and Garden* and *Architectural Record* magazines in 1943 systematically presented how new communities should be built and where. But still there was not enough housing to meet the demand. America did not need hundreds or even thousands of new homes; it needed millions.[3]

For both practical and political reasons Truman turned to private builders. It was Truman's desire to provide housing for the twelve million military personnel soon to be released. It would be housing for those who would work, housing for the millions who would return to colleges and universities under the new GI Bill of Rights, and housing for their families. In June 1945 he called to the White House sixteen men who were directly or indirectly involved with the nation's housing programs. One of the people attending this meeting was an old friend of Truman's and the commissioner of the Federal Public Housing Authority (FPHA), Philip Klutznick.

Truman asked everyone at the meeting what their particular agency or department could do to facilitate the provision of housing for returning veterans. The FHA responded that they didn't build housing but only insured the home mortgage, and, under an FHA program, it would take twelve months to two years to get private builders the necessary insurance needed for their construction projects. Other agencies voiced similar concerns about delays and other problems. Klutznick had anticipated this question and presented the president a broad program that outlined how existing military and defense housing could be converted to private use. His agency had housed over a million people during the war, and agency conversion experiments showed how these buildings could be dismantled and moved to new locations, such as college campuses. Truman approved of the concept and, after legal and accounting issues were resolved, the program was allowed to move quickly forward. The $450 million Veterans' Temporary Housing program was launched in late summer.

The Truman Administration continued the far-ranging and social engineering beliefs of the liberal Democratic Party and the "New Deal." To calm the country he thought that it was imperative that his domestic program be presented as soon as possible after the victory over Japan. In Truman's first postwar message to Congress, on September 6, 1945, he outlined an extensive list of programs including unemployment compensation, minimum wage increases, and, most important, an extension of the War Powers and Stabilization Act. The act meant that the government would maintain control over businesses and prices. Last, he proposed federal aid to construct one million new homes a year. It was an all-encompassing socially progressive and liberal program which Truman believed could not wait four months until his first State of the Union address. He called his programs the "Fair Deal."[4]

Truman then sent to Congress a program supporting the housing industry. He wrote: "The largest single opportunity for the rapid expansion of private investment and employment lies in the field of housing, both urban and rural. The present shortage of decent homes and the enforced widespread use of substandard housing indicate vital unfulfilled needs of the Nation."[5] There would not be a repeat of the social disaster that occurred in the United States after World War I, when little assistance was offered to help soldiers move from military to civilian life. There would be no veterans' marches on Washington after this war if Truman could help it.[6]

There was a general feeling throughout the nation that it was time to make up for the sacrifices of the past sixteen years. Workers were demanding more jobs, increased wages, and lower prices. On April 1, 1946, the United Mine Workers went on strike. That summer all three automakers were shut down (at a time of unprecedented demand for cars and trucks), steel plants were closed, and freight shipments were off by 75 percent. In Chicago the use of electricity was ordered cut in half. On May 23 the railroads were struck. At one point during that summer over a million workers were marching in picket lines. And yet these dire conditions affecting labor could not alter the course the country was on. The rapid changes to the postwar economy left only 2,270,000 unemployed by the end of 1946; what is more, there were 2,300,000 marriages, mostly young marriages.[7]

It was a time of a significant change to the traditional family in America. The difficulties of the 1930s and the war broke down many family structures. A rootlessness had infected the country, a disconnection to the land and separation from the ethnic urban neighborhoods its citizens had known. Children grew up and moved from their old neighborhoods of "extended kin and community" and began to form new communities. The United States was expanding exponentially, and the growth was into the country, into the suburbs.[8] As William H. Whyte noted in his 1956 book *The Organization Man*, "In suburbia, organization man is trying, quite consciously, to develop a new kind of roots to replace what he left behind." In America it was a time of unlimited opportunities for the men and women who "left home and kept on going."[9]

Peace brought a higher standard of living and created a demand for social and recreational services never dreamed of by the nineteenth-century American family. This new affluence provided families of the late 1940s and early 1950s the opportunity to buy homes with more living space than their parents could have ever afforded. They could take vacations to faraway locations and buy televisions to entertain themselves. More leisure time meant increased demand for more parks, more swimming pools, more theaters, and more space for meeting halls and libraries. These families bought the finest automobiles Detroit could produce and contributed to the evolution from railway to highway which would forever change how communities would be designed. The private automobile and its demands would shape the American future.

It was also apparent, soon after the war, that the old urban areas of cities were doomed. They would continue to survive into the next decade but only because of the largesse of federal spending. There was a significant vesting of political power through voters and political machines in these urban areas, but even the politicians could not prevent the mass exodus of predominantly young, white, educated families from the city to the new frontiers of the suburbs. The suburbs had the one element that the inner city did not have: affordable, clean, spacious, and segregated housing. These families, from the foxholes and factories of the war effort, looked for safety and a good roof over their heads in these new lands.

The 1930s advanced a new and important source for information and entertainment: the movies. Although the medium was almost forty years old in 1946, it was the 1930s and the war years which made movies a central part of American life and culture. Often the movies reflected and influenced what Americans were thinking and feeling. In the most dramatic movie of the postwar period, *The Best Years of Our Lives* (1946), Frederick March, Dana Andrews, Myrna Loy, and Teresa Wright brought home all of the fears and desires of the returning veterans, for many of whom home would never be the same. The movie's screenplay, written by Robert E Sherwood, a prominent Democrat and speechwriter for Franklin Roosevelt, was politically charged and expressed many of the deep-seated anxieties in the country immediately after the war.

In *Apartment for Peggy* (1948) the national problem of apartment shortages was explored in a humorous yet serious manner. In the movie only with a proper apartment could William Holden get his GI Bill education. The small town, the cornerstone of America, was exalted in Frank Capra's *It's a Wonderful Life* (1946). The perception of the village, where everyone could own their own home, walk to school or town, and live among not just neighbors but friends, became a deep desire that would fuel the dreams of young families across the nation. The movie also explained in simple but elegant terms that buying a home on credit was not something to fear but was a way of helping America grow.

This return to the home and the postwar examination of the American condition would continue for the rest of the decade of the 1940s. In *Miracle on 34th Street* (1947) Natalie Wood's character's dream wasn't for a horse or a doll but for a home in the suburbs with a swing in the backyard. Her dream was not lost on the young moviegoer. And, not to forget the older dreamer, *Mr. Blandings Builds His Dream House*, released in 1948, was based on the book and adapted short story by Eric Hodgins published in *Fortune* magazine in April 1946. If Cary Grant, as Mr. Jim Blandings, could build a home in the country, so could every other veteran, even if the trials and costs were significant. As Grant's character says:

"Muriel and I have found what I am not ashamed to call our dream house. It's like a fine painting, you buy it with your heart not your head, you don't ask how much was the paint and how much was the canvas, you say its beautiful and I want it. If it costs a few more pennies you pay it and gladly. You can't measure the things you love in dollars and cents. Well anyway that's the way I feel about it. And when I sign those papers on Saturday I can look the world in its face and say it's mine. My house, my home, my 35 acres." Muriel quickly corrected, "Our house, our home, our 35 acres."

Jim and Muriel cashed in their government war bonds to buy the house.

Not all the information the American citizen received about the suburbs was positive. In a lengthy article in the July 1945 *Harper's Magazine* John P. Dean went into great detail about the pitfalls and financial difficulties of home purchasing and financing. He depicted the kind and size of housing a family would need in years to come and how buyers would be "trapped" in a home purchase. Were they ready to commit to a "permanent" home? Were they able to tackle the legal obligations, and did they understand the "real" costs of a home purchase? His article attacked the home purchase while offering an alternative that cautiously supported rentals and a new concept called "mutual home ownership," which proposed that the participants in the plan be technically cooperative owners of a housing development purchased from the federal government through a nonprofit corporation. This plan would allow the excess funds generated by the mutual ownership to be used by the resident members if they were to become unemployed or physically incapacitated. It was socialized housing at its best and worst. This was the logical extension of the New Deal 1930s thinking that all goods and services must come from the government.[10]

Additional articles in the *Atlantic Monthly* cautioned new home buyers about financing their home. *Collier's* explained the suburban life in terms that a city dweller would understand, and the *Saturday Evening Post* and *Fortune* magazine talked about the advantages of living outside the city's problems. Even with all this, the young ex-GI and his family knew the one thing they needed was a home—a home they could own.

Many of the wartime builders, planners, and bureaucrats took up the challenge of the almost unlimited housing opportunities of the postwar era. The lessons these builders learned from the three Greenbelt communities and other housing developments built by the federal government in the late 1930s proved immeasurable. New towns and communities take years to plan and build. The less government interference, the more speedily the process can move forward. Builders needed the government's help, yet they knew the government must be kept at arm's length to insure speedy construction, stable land prices, and decent profits.

New sewers, drinking water, roads, and highways to these towns must be built or expanded. Few banks had the ability after the war to fund such large-scale constructions. After the banking and financial collapses of the 1930s, the federal government had placed tight reins on the financial institutions, and ten years later the regulations were little changed. If communities were to be built, it would only be through ongoing direct or indirect aid from the federal government. The partnership of federal agencies and private capital would create new communities through innovative and creative financial structures that rivaled the planning of the new town itself.

Growth developed in outlying areas, the suburbs, and not in the cities. Urban city planners were motivated by political pressure into protecting current city values and markets. Older residents were loath to pay for the costly expansion of utilities and services for new residents, and they refused to do so. Large new communities could never be built within urban areas without an extensive uprooting of current residents. The distribution of federal political and financial support to urban areas was a direct result of the political expediency of giving in to the voter-rich central city and its demands. This dissemination of funds was done with one hand while trying to support the new towns forming around all the major urban centers with the other. It was a no-win attempt to support a dying urban center financially while at the same time giving money and services for suburban growth, which in turn was being blamed by the city dweller for the urban center's ills.

The demands of the postwar family would never be met if new communities were compelled to expand within the existing urban zoning and street patterns. Most cities were not the result of competent planning but had grown from a never-ending patchwork of urban growth, use, reuse, and self-interest. Great and even spectacular civic structures and facilities were built in the 1930s, but they rarely provided residents any improvement to their lives or those of their families. These civic facilities almost never included affordable housing or good schools, and they certainly were never built for the support and nurturing of the family. There was a belief, supported in the movies and in magazine articles, that the new towns and suburbs provided a quality of living unavailable in the old city, and this is what attracted the adventurous from the city to a new life in the suburbs.

The Chicago region was an expanding balloon of opportunity. Most transcontinental rail lines passed through the city and provided a central distribution point for most of America. Businesses, and their attendant jobs, focused on this area of the country. Chicago was the hub of the United States after the war, even with its housing problems. And there were significant housing problems. One out of eight Chicago families, in the summer of 1946, was homeless. Many families were forced to disperse their members to different parts of the city in hopes that all of them could find a roof to live under. Landlords were quick to evict tenants when the rent was overdue because new tenants brought higher rents. In Chicago 150 evictions occurred each day. Overcrowding was endemic. Public health officials wondered out loud why there hadn't been a major outbreak of serious disease.

The cause for this overcrowded condition was simple—not enough new housing—but the reasons for it were as complex as the politics of Chicago. In Chicago eight out of ten families rented, yet in the summer and fall of 1946 no apartments were under construction, none were planned, and there was no prospect for a change to this picture. Chicago needed 120,000 dwelling units for returning veteran families and thousands of additional units for single men and women. It needed homes for 200,000 war workers who came to the city for jobs and stayed after the war. Yet, with all this demand, during the previous ten years Chicago had torn down more housing than it had built.

The city was a study in extreme contrasts. To visitors staying at the tonier downtown hotels, it was a delightful and beautiful place to visit; but the trip from the South Side airport, Midway, required passing boarded-up and decayed dwellings, homes without toilet facilities, and buildings unfit for habitation. Those arriving by rail could not miss the tenements crowding the tracks. Crowding was evident not only in the slums of the city but also in the nicer North Side neighborhoods as well. Mailboxes had three and four names listed on them; friends boarded with friends, and three and even four generations lived together.

In 1946 building contractors "started" 6,500 dwellings, and, with what was started in 1945, over 14,000 units were under construction. Unfortunately, the lack of materials and the nature of Chicago politics brought 8,500 of these units to a complete halt. In addition, a lack of city funds prevented the movement of temporary shelters, movable houses, Quonsets, and trailers to areas in need of housing.

Politics and labor had been married in Chicago for almost fifty years. Graft and corruption had been steady partners since the days of the bosses and boodlers of the 1890s. Materials that could have been utilized for housing went to racetracks, restaurants, theaters, parking garages, and to the University of Chicago, for office buildings. The limited building materials available always went to public institutions, which could spend most. The home builder could not meet the going price even for nails.

The scarcity of skilled labor in the city also contributed to the inability to complete or even start new homes. In 1925 the city had 125,000 skilled building tradesmen, but the Depression reduced that number to 87,000. The war dried up the labor pool even more and significantly reduced the number of apprenticeships. Tradesmen wanted bigger factory construction projects because they paid more and provided steadier work. The seasonal home building industry could not compete.

Union work ruled in Chicago and, coupled with the zoning ordinances, provided the most important reasons why the home builder could not compete in the marketplace. Plasterers put on three coats of plaster when two were required by the code. Lathers considered thirty bundles of lath a day's job and left when finished, even if two or three hours were left in the workday. Factory-installed glass window frames had their glass panels removed and then reset. Codes prevented or restricted preassembled plumbing, cabinets with hardware, and even ready-mix concrete. The Chicago Metropolitan Home Builders' Association estimated that labor rules would keep housing completions to seventeen thousand units per year even with a demand of over a hundred thousand dwelling units. With all this in mind the city's building trades unions were only apprenticing four thousand youths.

The Chicago building codes were designed originally to protect its citizens from fire, disease, and other hazards. Yet by World War II these codes had become a barrier to prefabricated housing, new and improved materials, and modern building techniques. The *Chicago Tribune*, in a postwar article, exclaimed: "Chicago sticks to a code which is a racketeers' delight . . . It provides an easy method of serving special interests through provisions which, on their face, are designed to promote safety and health. These [codes] . . . specify certain materials giving manufacturers and tradesmen who install them a monopoly within the city, and banning their competitors." One builder, La Salle Homes Construction Company, was geared up to build three hundred homes. Land, labor, and materials problems cut his goals to thirty units, and six months later he had only finished two homes.[11]

The demands of long-term growth in the region were apparent, but it was obvious to the home builders that their opportunities would not come within the city limits of Chicago. Local builders began to look seriously to the areas just outside the city limits of Chicago. The areas along existing rail lines and near train stations became more important than before the war. To the few builders who had the foresight to look to southern Cook County, the potential for their enterprises would be realized far beyond their expectations.

It was within this transformation of America that Park Forest, Illinois, one of the earliest and best planned of the postwar "New Towns," was begun. Park Forest was created by three men who would meet this coming change. Each was from a different place and one from a different era. The crossroads of time, opportunity, and politics brought them together.

Philip M. Klutznick was born in July 1907, in Kansas City, Missouri, to Morris and Minnie Klutznick. His parents and older sister had immigrated to the United States from Poland soon after the Kishinoff pogrom of 1905. With help from the Industrial Removal Society, whose goal was to help immigrant Jews move to the interior of the United States, they were relocated to Kansas City by way of Galveston, Texas. Morris Klutznick had established himself in Kansas City as a shoe store owner by the time Philip was born. The senior Klutznick's entrepreneurial spirit was passed on to his oldest son, and that talent was to serve Philip all his life.[12]

Klutznick began to practice law in Omaha, Nebraska, in 1929, after finishing his studies at Creighton University. There he set up his practice with his brother-in-law, Sam Beber. At that time the City of Omaha was bankrupt, and Klutznick saw the newly created National Industrial Recovery Act as a means of pulling Omaha up and out of a painful financial situation. On June 16, 1933, Congress approved the National Industrial Recovery Act, which authorized the use of federal funds for slum clearance and to finance low-rent housing. With subsequent appropriations under this legislation fifty low-rent housing developments with more than twenty-one hundred units were built nationally by the Public Works Administration. Klutznick served as assistant corporation counsel to the city of Omaha in 1933 and 1934 and was instrumental in writing significant legislation that became the Nebraska Housing Authorities Act. Through the use of this recovery act funding, money flowed to the city and helped to ease its financial situation. Klutznick would later be called the "founding father" of public housing in Omaha and Nebraska and, to a large extent, in the nation. He was recruited, in 1933, as special assistant to the U.S. attorney general for public lands. His reputation quickly built as a housing expert, and in 1941 he was noticed by Ferd Kramer, a dynamic official in the federal Office of Defense Housing. Kramer decided to hire Klutznick and offered him a position that brought him to Chicago as regional coordinator in charge of building temporary housing for defense workers and their families. His friendship and professional relationship with Ferd Kramer would continue for over fifty years.

Klutznick's various federal positions required extensive contact with home builders and their associations across the United States. Those responsibilities, all in support of the war effort, had placed him in a position of putting people and resources together to build temporary and permanent housing for war industry demands. His primary concern, however, after assessing the existing housing supply, was the lack of good rental housing. Through his contacts in the home building industry he pushed for more rental units to meet the expanding need.

Small building firms expanded during the war, especially those that could obtain priority financing through the government as well as government contracts. Local builders, especially those that were willing to provide the needed war industry housing, found in the government a partner that not only supported their financial needs but filled their material demands as well. Klutznick met with these home builders and began to educate them on the short- and long-term advantages that could be gained through proper planning and marketing. Most builders knew how to build and sell a house, but few knew how to build and then rent hundreds of versions of that same house.

Fig. 1. The planners and builders of Park Forest. Seated, *left to right*: Allan S. Harrison, chief of construction; Nate Manilow, treasurer; Philip Klutznick, president; Jerold Loebl, vice president and architect; Carroll Sweet Sr., member of the board of directors. Standing, *left to right*: Carroll Sweet Jr., special assistant to the president; Israel Rafkind, comptroller; Hart Perry, secretary; Richard Bennett, staff architect; Norman Schlossman, staff architect; Charles Waldmann, member of the board of directors and utility engineer; Joseph Goldman, construction advisor; Elbert Peets, town planner; and Nathan E. Jacobs, public relations counselor. *Source:* courtesy of Park Forest Public Library.

Klutznick was a close friend of the new president, and his twenty-year relationship with Truman would redefine his opportunities. Klutznick could see, after three heady Washington years, that his position as commissioner of the Federal Public Housing Authority was going to change. Peace would create unlimited opportunities, and, if there was one element of Klutznick's personality that would never alter, it was his instinctive ability to see an opportunity and seize it.

Carroll Fuller Sweet Sr., in the spring of 1945, was living in Chicago and, like all who had been born in the last quarter of the nineteenth century, had seen the world irrevocably change. He was born in June 1877, one year after the Battle for the Little Big Horn. Now, sixty-seven years later, a war of hideous proportions was about to end and with it the birth of a bold and different world.

The road traveled to Chicago by Sweet had been a long and, at times, a difficult one. Born in Grand Rapids, Sweet was the eldest of five children and graduated from Yale University in 1899. He had been a vice president of Old National Bank, western Michigan's oldest and most prestigious financial institution. He had been founder and president of Western Michigan Tourist and Resort Association and, like so many others, had been out of work during the Great Depression. As Sweet's life moved into the difficult times of the 1930s, he became deeply involved in the New Deal politics of the Roosevelt Administration.

The Depression forced many from their homes. One of the first programs created by the Roosevelt Administration to protect homeowners successfully was the Home Owners' Loan Corporation (HOLC). This government corporation refinanced homeowner mortgages, enabling owners to keep their homes. According to John P. Dean, in his 1945 article for *Harper's Magazine*, the "HOLC acquired over a million mortgages, representing about 18% of the total mortgaged home owners in the United States, but even so, the mortgages accepted for refinancing amounted to only 34% of those who applied. Furthermore, by the end of the decade, the HOLC was forced to foreclose on about one-sixth of the mortgages accepted."[13]

Sweet, a Democrat for over thirty years, was offered and accepted the position of director of the HOLC office for western Michigan and the Upper Peninsula. During the days when loans were being made, his district led the nation; during the time when the program was in a receiving mode, his foreclosures were the lowest. He knew how to cut "red tape" and was a man who did not believe in "useless bureaucratic interference." Federal officials, on several occasions, came from the state headquarters office in Detroit prepared to fire him, and each time, after examining the facts and hearing from his outstanding staff, they left him alone.

The "challenge days" of the HOLC were over by the end of the 1930s and with them came demands for an administrator with Sweet's abilities. He was offered and accepted the job of executive director of the Michigan Real Estate Association, located in Lansing, Michigan. These were troubled times for Sweet personally; he and his wife separated, and after that he quit his directorship and headed to Chicago to look for a job that would appeal to his own personal desires. He soon found a position with the regional office of the National Housing Administration (NHA). At the start of World War II, he was the temporary regional allocator of critical materials, especially those materials needed by the home building industry.

Carroll Sweet had often been asked by Chicago developer and builder Nathan Manilow to join his home building firm. In 1944, after the strains of his

NHA job proved too much for the elderly Sweet, he was ready to accept Manilow's offer. Manilow needed Sweet in another position however, to help manage and nurture the National Convention of Homebuilders, which was relocating to Chicago from Cleveland. It was Sweet's responsibility, as executive director of the Chicago Metropolitan Home Builders Association, to see that the money-losing convention would not be a liability to the Chicago association. Through his efforts, and his idea to add suppliers of building materials to the convention, the convention would grow to become the largest of its kind in the United States. Carroll Sweet, after these responsibilities were completed, then formally joined Manilow's office.

Nathan Manilow was born in Baltimore, Maryland, in 1898. He quit school to sell shoes when he was fifteen and earned his first big money at twenty by buying six thousand World War I surplus shoes at $2.85 a pair and selling them for $4.00 each. He was pragmatic and had a knack for spotting what people needed. He was a risk taker, a promoter, and a maker of real estate deals during a time when few opportunities were open to Jews. His innate and almost instinctive ability to focus on "the deal" greatly compensated for his lack of a formal education. Manilow's capacity to learn and face challenges was almost boundless. He turned up in Chicago in 1920 building one hundred three-flat apartment houses and a $1.5 million commercial structure. Manilow realized, after this building venture, that he was on the wrong side of the borrowing business. Shifting to the lender side earned him a profit of 69 percent on his first year's invested capital, which he had lent to other builders.

The building and growth boom of the 1920s carried many up with the tide. Manilow's ability to loan money to other builders with short-term needs supported their building activities as well as his own. Having become a millionaire by 1929, the crash only changed his venue, not his viewpoint. After building three hundred apartment and commercial buildings in Detroit, Manilow moved back to Chicago, in 1939. He intuitively and soundly believed that people wanted homes, not apartments. Acting on his belief, he assembled the largest parcel of land inside Chicago's city limits, a square mile of land on the South Side near Ninety-fifth Street, and began the $25 million Jeffrey Manor, a community of thirty-one hundred homes. World War II and a lack of building materials unfortunately slowed down most construction projects, including Jeffrey Manor.[14]

Manilow could see that, with the end of the war, this situation would change. He knew Chicago's housing problems and how difficult and expensive solving these problems might be. He began to explore systematically the areas immediately surrounding the city for opportunities. He was sure that it was here that unencumbered growth would happen.

Philip M. Klutznick met Carroll Sweet while working with the National Housing Association in Chicago. A mutual friendship and respect developed between them, and, when Klutznick went to Washington as assistant administrator of the National Housing Agency in February 1942, he asked Sweet to become a "troubleshooter" for the NHA Washington office. Unfortunately, the amount of travel and time required of Sweet proved to be too much for him. He needed a less strenuous job, and he found it with Nathan Manilow. Klutznick also met Manilow during his stay in Chicago. Their casual and professional relationship during this time hardly foretold the future, when the three of them would join to form the trinity that would build Park Forest.

CHAPTER TWO

The Beginning

When I look around at what you two have got here, well I don't know.
Maybe there are some things you should buy with your heart and not with
your head. Maybe those are the things that really count.

—Bill Cole, attorney to Jim Blandings,
Mr. Blandings Builds His Dream House

DURING THE fall of 1945, soon after VJ Day, Carroll Sweet visited Philip
Klutznick in his Washington office. Sweet had come to Washington,
representing Nathan Manilow's interests, to ask Klutznick's help in acquiring some of the excess military buildings for peacetime use. Sweet and
Manilow had an idea that, if they acquired some of the surplus defense structures
available under the Veterans' Temporary Housing program, they could use them
to build a new town for returning veterans, a GI town.

Sweet had a dream. "Here I am, an old man," he told himself, "who has
never done anything for anyone but me—nothing at all for the boys of those
three wars whose victories have made my whole life possible." He had traveled
extensively about the country and had seen the palatial estates of the rich. The
thought of a town, a great new city of trees and parks, an estate for people, began
to jell. He kept thinking, "Can't anything be done to give those veterans something approximating that kind of living on a scale they can afford?" Gradually,
Sweet evolved a scheme for a town, a GI town, which would have the spaciousness and greenery of a park and affordability for all.[1]

Klutznick turned Manilow's and Sweet's housing requests down for two reasons. First, the government's housing materials could not be sold to private
builders, only to public agencies. Second, under no condition would he release
these structures for use by returning veterans. The quality was not good enough
for these men and their families. Klutznick told Sweet the idea was excellent and
sound but that his GI community should be well planned and thought out. The
materials should be as good as available, and the FPHA structures didn't meet
that standard. "I would be ashamed," Klutznick told Sweet, "to build a permanent GI village or anything else that way. If you and Nathan Manilow want

to build a GI town, make it one worthy of the men who served the country so well."[2]

Manilow's construction firm had already begun to address the issue of the returning veteran. Chicago was the second largest city in the United States at the end of the war, and many of the millions of discharged veterans would be returning to the region, thus compounding the existing housing shortage. Manilow had begun building Jeffrey Manor on Chicago's South Side before the war, and now, with peace, the sale and rental of the thirty-one hundred single-family homes and townhomes began to improve. Manilow knew there would be an end to this community and that he would soon need to start another, but there was a problem—a paralyzing shortage of construction materials.

There had been a substantial shortage in almost all construction materials for nongovernmental use for several years. Shortages in lumber, bricks, clay sewer pipes, gypsum board and wood lath, and cast iron pipe. Most shortages were the result of a lack in manpower (soldiers who didn't return to their homes), low wages that discouraged new employees, and price controls. Truman announced, in early winter 1945, the appointment of Wilson W. Wyatt as housing expediter and head of the National Housing Administration. Klutznick's Federal Public Housing Authority was grouped together with the Federal Housing Administration and the Federal Home Loan Bank Administration under the National Housing Administration. As housing expediter, Wyatt could determine price adjustments and priority ratings in the building industry and also exert a strong influence on wages.

Wyatt proposed to handle the housing shortage as if it were a war production job, and in February 1946 he announced his program. It was a lengthy list of prohibitions that would restrict commercial and industrial construction in favor of residential construction. It would channel scarce building materials to housing units that would cost six thousand dollars or less or would rent for fifty dollars a month or less. The program would increase the supply of building materials through subsidies to producers, increase prices and wages, use surplus war plants, provide some government underwriting of the risks, and guarantee a market for a struggling prefabricated housing industry. Most important, it would restore the liberal financing terms that the FHA gave to builders of war housing. The program was immediately attacked and debated. Opposition to the subsidy plan was especially strong.[3]

The government and private builders and their associations campaigned with confusing and contradictory announcements about how much housing was really needed. In January 1946 Truman said, "We urgently need about five million additional homes—now." The National Association of Home Builders, in which Manilow and Sweet were deeply involved, issued an estimate that 1.5 mil-

lion new housing units "would relieve the extreme pressure." Almost everyone
had some number that fell between these two figures. Wyatt's program was not as
fulfilling as it would first appear. The 1.2 million housing units proposed, more
than were built during the entire decade of the 1930s, would also include temporary housing (trailers and other nonpermanent types of housing) and the rehabilitation of existing residential structures. These rehabs would not contribute to a
long-term solution but did inflate the numbers. The remaining housing units
would come from new housing, but only about half of those units started in 1946
would be available for occupancy that year. As a result, the housing the government proposed would still fall seriously short of demand. Even though Wyatt's
forecast for 1947 of 1.5 million units relied more on permanent construction, his
figures had to rely on an unproved prefabrication industry to help meet the goal.
The real problem was not the number of units but the availability of materials to
build the homes—materials that were still under the firm control of the government.

Fortune magazine conducted a survey in early 1946 and found that the American people believed that the government would need to step in to help ease the
housing shortage. Americans supported home building by the government, lending money at low interest rates directly to people for the construction of their own
homes, the control of building materials for low- and medium-priced houses, and
the government's control of rents. Many of these beliefs were the result of fifteen
years of social conditioning which had fixed a belief in the altruistic and nurturing nature of the government.

Shortly after his first meeting with Klutznick, Carroll Sweet returned to
Washington, this time with Manilow. They told Klutznick they were planning to
build a new town out of quality materials as soon as the materials became available. Manilow and Sweet believed Klutznick would be a great asset in their efforts to build this new town, especially with his experience in materials, sources,
and acquisitions. Would he join them? Klutznick had been offered a number of
other postwar opportunities in New York and back home in Omaha. Their offer
would need careful consideration, and certain requirements would need to be
met before he could even think of accepting it.

Klutznick indicated that he might be interested if the town were not just another housing project or suburban development. He explained to them that the
most important aspect of such a venture was the planning of the town itself. The
planning would require locating housing areas, commercial areas, industrial sites,
parks, and other community services. It would require new utilities and roads, a
good water supply, and well-designed storm and sanitary drainage systems.
Klutznick also told them that for this town to become successful it must be more
than a collection of houses; the new town must be incorporated. The residents

must create new public institutions to govern and manage the new town or village and fully participate in the decisions that affect the community and its future. This conversation, as reported by Klutznick a bit self-servingly, seemed almost a lecture—one that Nathan Manilow surely didn't need. Manilow, being only nine years older than Klutznick, had far more experience in private home and community building than Klutznick had experience with the federal government.

It is also not hard to imagine that Sweet and, more important, Manilow offered the position to Klutznick for his influence and ability to acquire the building materials they needed for the community and for his FHA contacts. These may, in fact, have been their primary reasons for asking him to join them. It was not his experience in construction management and knowledge of Cook County politics and zoning approvals which had them travel almost a thousand miles to offer him a job.

This value of community planning was, however, a fundamental belief for Klutznick. It was based on his wartime experience and the experience the federal government and he, as an administrator, had had with the three Greenbelt towns planned and built in the 1930s. It is important to note that, even ten years after their construction, there were few supporters within the Truman Administration for these experimental communities built under Roosevelt.[4]

The new community that Klutznick described for Sweet and Manilow was a manifestation of planning concepts and designs for communities aggressively designed and built between 1900 and 1939—communities that shared many of the same planners, visionaries, and theorists. Even more revealing is that many of these new communities could trace their lineage back to the Chicago area of 1869. Five great planners would be the grandfathers of Park Forest—whose careers extended over almost one hundred years of planning for human settlements. They were Frederick Law Olmsted, Ebenezer Howard, Henry Wright, Clarence B. Stein, and Elbert Peets. All five, through their visions for new towns, would build on one another's work in an effort to create better and more successful places for people to live.

In 1868 Emery E. Childs, a Chicago developer, asked the noted American landscape architect Frederick Law Olmsted and his firm, Olmsted, Vaux and Company, to design a "suburban village" on his sixteen hundred–acre property twelve miles west of Chicago. The plan for Riverside was revolutionary in its concept and breadth and unlike anything else in the country. Olmsted and Vaux created a residential community along the banks of the Des Plains River, with a hierarchical plan of lot sizes, separated by generous open spaces and parks. Not having been designed to the current trend of the time, the grid pattern of streets in mid-American cities, Riverside's residential roads curve in generous sweeps

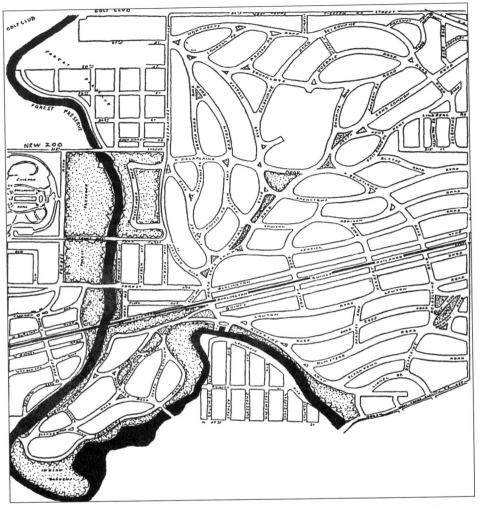

Fig. 2. The basic principle of Riverside's design was the subdivision of the site into "village-like" neighborhoods, with each area intimately connected to parks and common grounds. *Source:* redrawn from original plan by Olmstead, Vaux & Co.

and meet with soft tangents at well-landscaped intersections. The only portions of the village which did not curve were the business streets that paralleled the Burlington Railroad. "In the highways," said Olmsted, "celerity will be of less importance than the comfort and convenience of movement . . . we should recommend the general adoption, in the design of your roads, of gracefully-curved

Fig. 3. Time has treated Riverside very well; mature trees now complement the soft curves of the streets one hundred and twenty years after they were built. *Source:* author's photo.

lines, generous spaces, and the absence of sharp corners, the idea being to suggest and imply leisure, contemplativeness and happy tranquillity."[5]

Although its early days were financially troubled, the village's overall design is a testament to the genius of the concept and the thoroughness of the execution. The automobile, thirty years in the future when the plan was at last completed, has not destroyed the village. Garages are placed in the rear of the lot, driveways are narrow, and the streets not overly wide. The design is still an example of melding the plan to the topography of the land. Riverside changed one of the fundamental concepts of town design more than any other American community: the integration into the standard grid pattern of streets of curving streets with deep residential setbacks. Olmsted wrote that a well-designed suburb is "the most attractive, the most refined and the most soundly wholesome form of domestic life, and the best application of the arts of civilization to which mankind has yet attained."[6] The completeness of Riverside cannot be overlooked. It has stood unchanged in both plan and substance while, during the last hundred years, the area around it has grown, suffered, and deteriorated. The village's strongest defenders are the current residents.

In 1869, as Riverside was being planned and built, a young Englishman set out from his London home looking for opportunities in the western United States. Nineteen year old Ebenezer Howard and two friends moved to Nebraska, tried farming, were quickly disillusioned, and within a few months Howard moved on to Chicago, where he lived for ten years.

It was here in the Midwest of the United States that many of the most important ideas for twentieth-century town planning were initially formed. According to Howard, his stay in Chicago had a great influence on his life. It gave him a fuller and broader outlook on social and religious issues than if he had stayed in England. His time in Chicago helped to direct him: "greatly in the direction of perfect freedom of thought: and associated with this, a very deep sense of responsibility, and a clear perception that all values, to be rightly estimated, must be assessed mainly by their influence on the spiritual elements in our nature."[7]

Howard, court reporter by profession and land reformer by vocation, had by the end of the nineteenth century authored theories for radically reforming the community planning process. Those theories culminated in the Garden Cities movement. His experience in Chicago helped to account for the Americanism in his makeup. He believed in the American process of thought and action and that from it evolved the ideal to the real. This was contrary to his belief that in England the process went from the concrete to the abstract. This shifting of the creative process toward the ideal remained with Howard all his life. He became a stimulant and inspiration to the Garden Cities movement, and, as Dugald Mac-Fadyen notes in his 1933 biography of Howard, "If Chicago did not fill his pockets with gold it did something better: it fitted him for world citizenship."[8]

Howard's own thoughts on nineteenth-century American city planning are unknown because he wrote little of his experiences in Chicago, but his inquisitive mind would not have allowed the efforts of Childs, Olmsted, and the Riverside community to pass unnoticed. It is not hard to imagine Howard visiting the Riverside development and that the impression it made stayed with him for almost twenty-five years, gestating.

The Chicago region continued to expand during the late nineteenth century, starting soon after the Great Fire in October 1871. There was, even then, concern about the sprawl of development. One result was that Chicago and Cook County began a program of buying up swamplands, woodlands, and farmlands and setting them aside as permanent parklands. The Cook County Forest Preserve system was to have a fundamental impact on Howard's theory for Garden Cities and the use of parklands and farmlands as buffers between communities.

In his seminal book *Garden Cities of Tomorrow* Howard proposed dramatic changes in city planning. Initially published in 1898 and called *Tomorrow: A Peaceful Path to Real Reform*, it was republished in 1902 with the new name. Howard proposed that it was "universally agreed to by all men" that people must

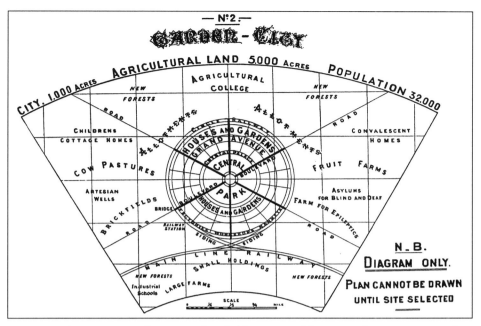

Fig. 4. Ebenezer Howard's concept for a bold new city of the twentieth century centered on organization and order. *Source:* E. Howard, *Garden Cities of To-morrow,* 1902.

be stopped from relocating into the already crowded urban areas and cities. His theory was simple: "Town and country must be married, and out of this joyous union will spring new hope, a new life, a new civilization." He believed people must be given opportunities to find better surroundings in which to live and to enjoy nature and be a part of it. This new village concept and its advantages would be a draw, or, as Howard called it, "a magnet," attracting those believers to this new life. These town-country magnets would be called Garden Cities.

The Garden City was not the idle whimsy of a Victorian romantic but a well-thought-out analysis of what would be needed to plan, build, and occupy this new form of community living. Howard developed conceptual plans and details showing how the various relationships among land uses would work. He first presented his plan in diagrammatic form: a circular design with concentric land uses spreading outward from the garden and civic core. This radiating pattern may indicate how much of an impact Mrs. Cora Richmond, a well-known Christian Science lecturer, had on Howard after he met her in Chicago, in 1876. Richmond, reputed to be a seer, told Howard that she saw his future as, "in the centre of a series of circles working at something which will be a great service to humanity."[9] He would use her prophecy in his theories.

The Garden City's diagrammatic plan had radiating roads, like spokes, which bisected the town into wards and neighborhoods. These roads interconnected the rings of development which expanded outward from the center. Commercial interests were in the first ring outside the public core, and industrial uses were closest to the railroad. Residential neighborhoods were behind the commercial areas. In the surrounding buffers were farms, woodlands, pastures, and some institutional uses. Town planning had never had this form of analysis and structure before. This "unique combination of proposals" separates Howard's ideas from all others previously offered.

The Garden City, as envisioned by Howard, is a town-country community with specific characteristics.

1. Larger than a village, substantially self-supporting, and separated from other towns by a large agricultural zone. This is not just a town "in" the country but one which is a complementary part of the country.

2. Directly accessible to railroads.

3. Limited in size to property of not more than an "area of 6,000 acres, which is presently purely agricultural, and has been obtained by purchase in the open market." This land will be divided into a central core of 1,000 acres for a town of 30,000 people, and the remaining 5,000 agricultural acres will house 2,000 people. This agricultural zone will act as buffer and control the growth of the village center.

4. Land occupied through leases and not sold to the occupants. The entire community's acreage will be "legally vested in the names of four gentlemen of responsible position and of undoubted probity and honor, who hold it in trust."

5. Managed through controlled planning. All aspects of the community will be planned before the start of construction and to allow for later adjustments as needed under municipal control.

6. Divided into equal districts or wards of 5,000 people each. Each will be a complete town within itself. (This element of Howard's proposal will later lead to the neighborhood concept in community planning.)

7. Designed to be spacious. In addition to the suggested 145 acres for a central public park, ample lands will be available for a town hall, public library, museum, theaters, concert hall, hospitals, schools, churches, swimming pools, and public markets. Howard's concern was for public facilities and for housing. His proposal would be for all people, not just a select few. There will be "ample sites for homes . . . ample space for roads . . . so wide and spacious that sunlight and air may freely circulate, and in which trees, shrubs and grass give the town a semi-rural appearance."

8. Planned so as to include the expectation of the outward expansion of industry from the older Central City into the Garden City. These industries will be located along the periphery of the town and will include factories, warehouses, dairies, and other clean industrial facilities. These industries will be both municipal and private in ownership.

9. Planned for a maximum population size of 32,000. When reached, another town center will be selected, and the additional regional growth would transfer and continue there. This new town center will, like its parent, be buffered from the old town center and grow to its predesigned size. In time these towns will encircle and support the old Central City. Howard was one of the first to understand and propose the concept of the "satellite town."[10]

Howard's ideas first took tenuous hold in the British planning fraternity. Others who shared his ideas soon joined his planning and reform group. In 1902, after an extensive search to find a suitable property, a site was found which met Howard's criteria for the construction of a Garden City. The site proved to be a third smaller than the prescribed six thousand acres but in all other aspects excellent. The property was the Letchworth Estate, located thirty-five miles north of London in Hertfordshire and on a branch of the Great Northern Railway.

Growth was exceedingly slow during Letchworth's first ten years. The town continually faced financial problems, which added to the difficulties of paying for even this limited growth. By 1919 the town had grown to only ten thousand people, but Howard would not be deterred. He believed so strongly in his Garden Cities' concept that he began another community, Welwyn, about twelve miles south of Letchworth. Even though many of the same economic problems beset this new town, Welwyn's planning benefited from what had happened at Letchworth. Welwyn's population also grew slowly, and by 1930 eight thousand people were living in almost twenty-five hundred dwelling units.

What was significant about the planning of these two villages was the strong character of the street pattern that radiates outward from the central core. Outward rings of roads, serving primarily residential neighborhoods, encircle the town center. Each village was anchored on the rail line to London. Both were placed with respect to the specifics of the site, high ground at the core, and existing roads to neighboring villages. Welwyn was highly structured and the commercial core built to surround generous open parklands decorated with fountains, flowerbeds, and colonnades of linden trees. A strong axial alignment of the roads led into and out of the village.

The principal planners for Letchworth were Raymond Unwin and his partner, Barry Parker. Unwin wrote in his pamphlet *Nothing Gained by Overcrowding* that large, open-space areas could be preserved in the centers of residential

Fig. 5. Ebenezer Howard, the father of the "Garden City" and "New Town" concepts of the twentieth century. *Source:* First Garden City Heritage Museum.

"superblocks" without adversely affecting the density and cost per lot or unit. His innovative planning ideas also included cul-de-sac streets and architectural control over the exterior design of speculatively built dwellings. Letchworth's residential density is, in its densest areas, twelve houses to the acre, and its overall average density is five units to the acre. Unwin even proposed children's playgrounds. By today's standards these design elements do not seem profound, yet at the turn of the century they were revolutionary. Significant changes were to alter the final plans over the years, and many of the stronger components of the initial plan have been lost; the radial plan still exists, but the center of Letchworth is a park, not the grand public buildings that Unwin showed in his initial plans.

Simple as these beginnings were, the new towns, Riverside, Letchworth, and Welwyn, were to have a profound impact on the concept of town planning in the United States. Lewis Mumford, the most influential urban writer and critic of the last seventy-five years, would later write, "At the beginning of the twentieth century two great inventions took form before our eyes: the aeroplane and the Garden City, both harbingers of a new age."[11]

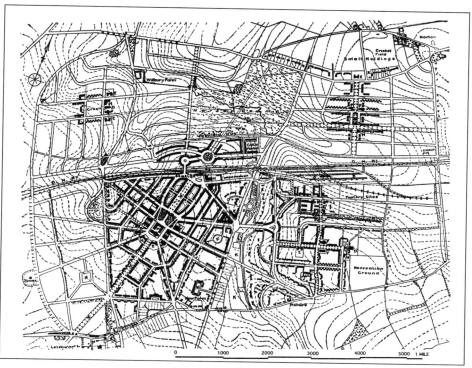

Fig. 6. Parker and Unwin's original plan of Letchworth Garden City as first published (April 1904). *Source:* C. B. Purdom, *The Building of Satellite Towns.*

Mumford also points out, in his essay "The Ideal Form of the Modern City," that Howard offered two other contributions to the form of the modern community. The first is a logical and organized division of the Garden City into six wards or neighborhood units. This division of the new town would predate the concept as it developed in the United States by almost a generation. This "self-contained" aspect of planning would be the backbone of planning for the latter half of the twentieth century. The second and possibly most important element was that these communities are never completely self-contained. They would need to be connected by rapid transportation and that the interconnections of these Garden Cities would in fact allow facilities and resources of each to be more easily supplemented by the others. By this, then, the communities would have the benefits of the larger and older "social cities" without the problems of the congested metropolis.[12]

Immediately after World War I and throughout the dynamic 1920s, Americans were rapidly building and expanding. The efforts and concepts of Ebenezer

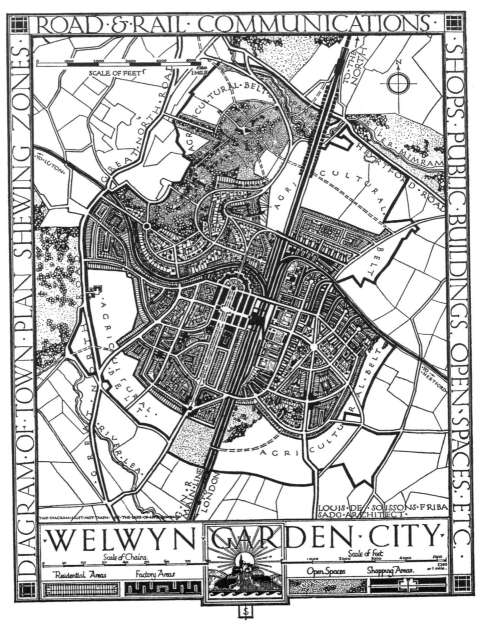

Fig. 7. Diagram of Welwyn Garden City, 1920. Plan by Louis de Soissons Fribasadg, architect. *Source:* C. B. Purdom, *The Building of Satellite Towns.*

Howard and Raymond Unwin were being restudied and applied. Among the persons intensely involved as planners and architects in the new field of town planning were two New Yorkers, Henry Wright and Clarence B. Stein. Their work on the design and construction of low-cost housing and better land-use planning, championed by their friend Mumford, was to revolutionize American community planning.

The conceptual planning by Wright and Stein and essays on urban planning and social reform by Mumford led to their formation of the Regional Planning Association of America, in 1923. This nongovernmental group, with never more than twenty members, extensively analyzed and discussed the state of planning and development in the country for ten years. It was within this group that progressive communities such as Sunnyside Gardens and Radburn were conceived, designed, and built. Within this intellectual environment ideas were cross-fertilized. The group's members could move between tasks and ideas without losing their ultimate focus of building balanced communities, reducing the urban and residential community to human scale, and establishing communities with a balanced social program. This, they hoped, would lay the foundation for ever-widening theories of national, continental, and global community planning.

This background and the efforts of one of the members, Alexander Bing (himself an experienced real estate operator), led to the creation of the private City Housing Corporation. This corporation's goal was to design and build the first Garden City in America, based on the Howard English model.[13] Correspondence between Howard and Bing, in the mid-1920s, showed their mutual interest in "launching a Garden City" in the United States, but Howard died before their goal could be mutually undertaken.[14]

The City Housing Corporation's first venture in community planning began with Sunnyside Gardens, in Queens, New York. The site was a seventy-seven-acre parcel of land acquired from the Long Island Railroad—close to Manhattan and only a fifteen-minute trip, by subway, to the Forty-second Street center of New York. Built continuously from 1924 to 1928, Sunnyside Gardens ultimately had 1,202 family units laid out in a uniform pattern of growth and organization. Using the existing network of streets, the plan evolved as a series of 200- by 900- foot residential superblocks. Two- and three-story brick apartment buildings were built facing the street and laid out to enclose an interconnected open-space park. These blocks, ten in all, were to change the standard urban pattern of development within a typical neighborhood. Not encumbered with traditional lot lines, separate housing structures, alleys, and disconnected spaces, these new residential blocks closed off the street from intruding into the large private, commonly held, landscaped open spaces. Changes were continually made, as the development grew and evolved, to these interior spaces and their use.

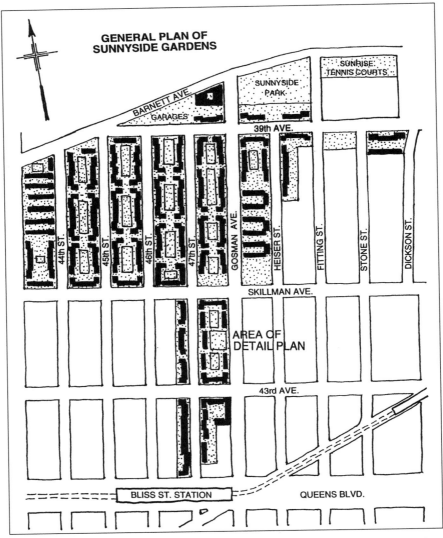

Fig. 8. The General plan of Sunnyside Gardens showing the relationship of the development to the city block street system. *Source:* redrawn from C. S. Stein, *Toward New Towns for America.*

The intrusion of the automobile during this thriving economic period was also beginning to become apparent. Sunnyside's early plans did not take into full account the automobile and its growing popularity. As the community grew, a garage was built at the perimeter, almost a thousand feet from the farthest unit. Later, a heated garage was constructed nearer to the neighborhood but proved to

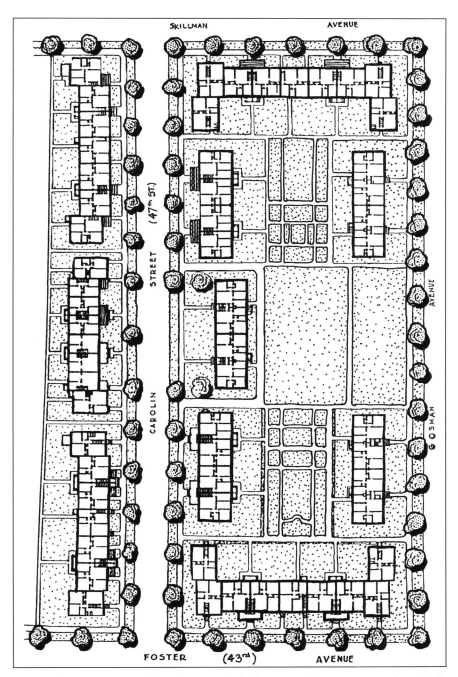

Fig. 9. The first unit complex of Sunnyside, built in 1924. *Source*: redrawn from C. S. Stein, *Toward New Towns for America*.

be too expensive to maintain with only tenant and resident support. It was later determined that the simpler and more convenient the structure, the more successful it would be. In the last phases of construction the residential buildings were turned inward and away from the existing rows of apartments, which faced the community. These courts opened out and directly accessed the street, a harbinger of the eventual parking court.

Lewis Mumford, Sunnyside Garden's most well-known resident for eleven years, says of the housing block and design: "It has been framed to the human scale and its gardens and courts kept that friendly air as, year by year, the newcomers improved in the art of gardening and the plane trees and poplars continued to grow . . . So, though our means were modest, we contrived to live in an environment where space, sunlight, order, color—these essential ingredients for either life or art—were constantly present, silently molding all of us."[15]

Luckily, the land was left zoned as industrial. This resulted in a freer design that allowed the specific type of community and aesthetic objectives desired by the planners. The varied heights and sizes of Sunnyside's buildings were in violation of the existing residential zoning ordinances. Specific heights and the massing of buildings, if the site had been rezoned as residential, would have had to have been designed to meet those ordinances and codes. Flexibility and creativity would have been lost.

The residential units themselves were a mixture of two- and three-unit structures, two and three stories high. Most units were exposed to the sun and fresh air on three and, in some layouts, four sides. They were stacked "flats" that entered from the street side, and the first-floor units had direct access to the courtyard and gardens inside the block. The second-floor units were designed with a porch that extended the unit and living space into the courtyard. The buildings had cellars or basements that, because of the designer's insistence, expanded the amount of personal storage space for the residents.

The 1920s brought on one of the greatest housing booms in U.S. history. The post–World War I depression and low numbers of homes built during the war only exacerbated the problem. The 1920s saw great changes in the character and look of America:

—Annual housing production accelerated from 449,000 units in 1921 to 937,000 units in 1925.
—For the entire period from 1921 to 1928 production totaled 6.3 million units, an annual average of 785,000 units.
—The nonfarm population increased by 2.2 percent annually from 1921 to 1928.
—Immigration, while somewhat curtailed, still continued, with 707,000 immigrants arriving in 1924.

—Average household size dropped from 4.20 to 4.00 persons.
—The average nonfarm income rose by 22 percent from 1920 to 1928.
—Automobile ownership rose from 6.8 million in 1921 to 17.5 million in 1928.

The 1920s were not known for social reforms, but concepts and advances in housing made prior to World War I at the state and local level were extended and refined. These areas included building and housing codes, city planning legislation, and zoning ordinances, and the government actively supported these actions. Local zoning was upheld by the U.S. Supreme Court in the *Euclid* case, and other federal agencies promoted the use of model statutes for city planning, zoning, and building codes.

Sunnyside Gardens, far too small to be considered a Garden City, was designed with the hope that it could create a setting in which a "democratic community" could grow. It was, in fact, a study of what a portion of an American Garden City could be. The City Housing Corporation provided the land, buildings, and equipment that supported community gatherings and activities. It encouraged a community association that was more effective than the separate "block" organizations that had evolved in other neighborhoods. When the difficult times of the Depression hit, this association provided a cohesiveness for the residents not found outside Sunnyside. Unfortunately, as time passed, and in the face of the economic problems facing the tenants, the community could not withstand the slow erosion of its unity and eventually lost much of the vitality that separated it from others. Even the difficult times of the Depression, however, could not destroy the beauty of Sunnyside Gardens.[16]

In 1927 the City Housing Corporation, after the early success of Sunnyside Gardens, believed it was now time to fulfill its dream and build a complete Garden City along the specific instructions of Ebenezer Howard. The corporation, after looking at many potential sites, settled on a location in New Jersey. It purchased two square miles of raw farmland located in the Borough of Fairlawn, near Patterson, and called the new community Radburn. The land lay on a branch of the Erie Railroad and was near a new highway that was to lead to the new bridge being built across the Hudson River into New York.

The planners, Clarence Stein and Henry Wright, separated the site into three distinct "neighborhoods" of about eight thousand to ten thousand people each—a goal that, when reached, would meet the size specified by Howard for a Garden City, thirty thousand inhabitants. Even though there would be a minimal greenbelt separating Radburn from other encroaching developments, they believed that their community would be able to stand alone and not be lost within the adjacent growth. Unfortunately, industry did not find the limited industrial lands in Radburn as desirable as other areas of the region. This eventu-

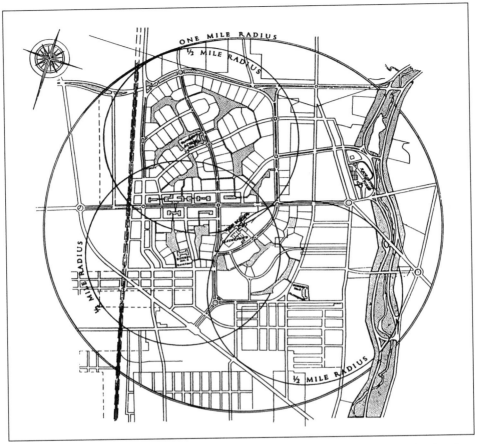

Fig. 10. General Plan of the "Radburn" concept, which centered on the high school and secondary centers of the neighborhood schools. *Source:* redrawn from C. S. Stein, *Toward New Towns for America*.

ally resulted in the village becoming a bedroom community to New York City and northern New Jersey and not the job center it was hoped to have been.

The concept of the superblock, championed almost thirty years earlier by Raymond Unwin, at last found a home in Radburn. These superblocks of housing were interconnected by streets and walks, all leading to an extensive list of recreational, business, and retail facilities. The plan, according to Stein, was based on the concept of overlapping circles, each a half-mile radius, with an elementary school fixing the center. The high school would be placed where these overlapping circles met. Each neighborhood would have its own shopping center, and the ultimate plan was to include athletic fields, tennis courts, and an extensive system of parks and open-space areas. The residential areas would be interconnected by overpasses and underpasses to separate pedestrians and automobiles. These separation structures worked so well that there was only one serious accident, a broken arm, during the first twenty years of their use.

The radical change that began with Riverside and continued with Radburn was the departure from the traditional grid lotting pattern. The plans for Radburn developed a system of streets which used the cul-de-sac and parking court as the primary residential device for clustering homes. These clustered homes would face the court for direct access from the street but also permit access to the interweaving open space that connected the whole village. It was this dual frontage that set this community apart from the usual street and alley suburban form of the times.

The homes, initially detached and then attached as the market showed its acceptance for this new style, were away from the main roads. Children, moving through the village, were not forced to cross major streets on grade but used the under- and overpasses. Footpaths connected the different residential clusters, and most sidewalks were not directly attached to the street. The planners understood, even in the late 1920s, the impact that the automobile would have on the quality of the residential neighborhood. It was their desire to reduce its effect on the residents. Benton MacKaye, one of the Regional Planning Association's founders, remarked, "Radburn was the first town to be planned on the assumption that through motor traffic must be completely separated from the communal aspects of the environment." Maintaining this goal was important to both the safety as well as the beauty of the community.[17]

A critical difference between Radburn and other later new communities was that Radburn was not constrained by the more restrictive zoning ordinances developed during the 1930s and 1940s. These ordinances would have set minimums on lot sizes, densities, street widths, and setbacks, all which would have challenged the innovative aspects of the plan for Radburn. Even with all of its creativity, it still took considerable effort to convince the county assessor of the village's merits.

These planning elements—the superblock, the innovative street system, the common lands, the separation of pedestrians and vehicular traffic, and the dual home frontage—all constituted to the orientation of the village away from the street and toward the common parklands and walkways. This concept was adopted by later-twentieth-century planners as a fundamental element of their new towns.

Unfortunately, Radburn was never completed, and it did not become a Garden City. The first families moved into Radburn just five months before the Oc-

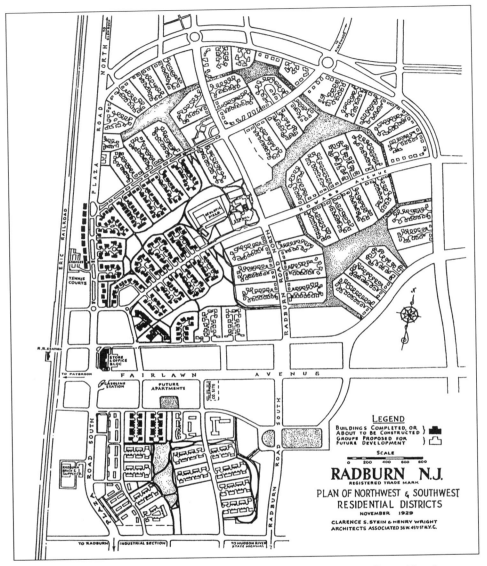

Fig. 11. Plan of the Northwest and Southwest Residential Districts, Radburn, New Jersey. The dark buildings were those completed before the stock market crash of 1929. *Source: C. S. Stein, Toward New Towns for America.*

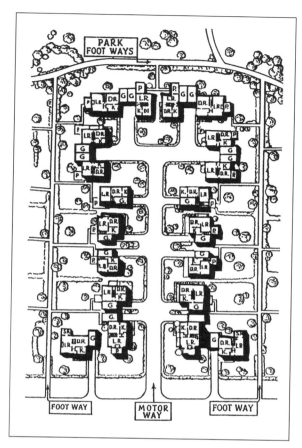

Fig. 12. Plan of a typical "lane" at Radburn. The park in the center of the superblock is shown at the top; the motorways to the houses are at right angles to the park. *Source:* redrawn from C. S. Stein, *Toward New Towns for America.*

tober 1929 economic collapse of Wall Street. The City Housing Corporation, through no fault of its own, was forced into bankruptcy. Only a small portion of the overall plan was completed, and when the residential market finally came back, after World War II, it was too late for the plan to be resurrected. The dream for a complete new town, a Garden City for thirty thousand people, was destroyed by the Depression. The events of that time demonstrate how difficult it is to bring a new town to fruition. There are so many unknowns: changes in the national economy, vagaries in the residential market, and the high costs of building and maintaining the infrastructure. Yet even the limited success of the Radburn neighborhood plan provided a significant advance in community planning.

Clarence Stein recalled later that the keys to successful housing developments for those of limited incomes had been defined by Sunnyside Gardens and Radburn:

1. Low cost land, adequate in size and easy of development.
2. Transportation to take people easily to working places in relatively short time.
3. Continuous large scale building of complete sections with installations of utilities and streets paralleling construction of buildings, the building to be followed immediately by marketing and use.
4. Rapid development so as to minimize carrying charges [of land and costs].
5. Simple standardized units.
6. Grouping [of structures] for unity and variety of appearance as well as to add to the feeling of spaciousness given by the open areas.
7. Limited interest rate on capital invested.[18]

These seven fundamentals are no different today then they were seventy years ago. Low-cost land, or the financial basis for the community, establishes the starting point for all later cost determinations. Costs may increase depending on what the market may bear, but the starting point has always been the initial investment in the cost of the land.

Transportation, specifically the railroad, in the 1920s, and later the automobile, establishes the marketability of the property, along with its affordability. Ease of access and nearness to job centers fix in the minds of the buyer the relationship of the community to the region. Remote and inaccessible locations had a difficult time becoming successful, regardless of the price.

Continuous and rapid building of complete neighborhoods almost goes hand in hand with the success of a community. The economies of scale in a continuous construction schedule allow the builder to buy greater quantities of materials at better prices and to employ workers in an assembly-line fashion. This helps to meet the real demand for affordable public housing in a timely manner. The competition is also forced to meet the same goals and demands of buyers. High production counts and high sales and occupancies also reduce the carrying costs for the builder. These savings are passed immediately on to the buyer. In a competitive market this can significantly reduce the cost of a house.

Standardization is not always received in a favorable light, and there is a perception that it leads to monotony and lower quality. The reverse is often the case. Standardization reduces the cost of architectural design fees and engineering costs and is directly related to the final cost of the building. The architect's fee can result in one structure, a custom design, or a thousand buildings, all of which share the same initial fee. The economies of scale will win out. It is the talent of the architect which determines the final design of the structure, and there is seldom a direct connection between the fee and the quality of the design.

The overall plan of the community is the most critical component affecting the quality of the residential village or new town. Placement of the roads and structures is paramount to the spaciousness, ease of access, and circulation into and out of the community. It is this interaction of the physical elements of the plan with the amenities which adds to the improved livability that new residents demand from the builder.

Finally, the cost of money, or the interest paid on borrowed money throughout the process, is critical to insure success. It is not only the buyer of the house who pays interest on a home loan, but every subcontractor pays some form of interest on the costs of goods, materials, and services. If interest rates are high, the cost is magnified throughout the construction process and results in the home price rising. Rising rates also cast a pall on the future cost of the home and can reduce buyer demand. A lower interest rate allows the home price to remain stable which permits the builder to see farther into the future to develop a long-term marketing strategy.

The Radburn plan, according to Stein, accomplished the important objectives of being safer, more orderly, and convenient. The community was spacious and peaceful, and it brought people physically closer to nature. What is more important, it cost less per unit than other types of developments with an equivalent amount of open space. Stein suggested, as a final point, that conveniently placed and varied industry is an essential requirement of a New Town. The timing of industrial development must be synchronized with that of the building of homes and community development.[19] It was also about this time that the English phrase *Garden City* began to be Americanized to *New Town*; unfortunately, more than the name was lost in the translation.

In the spring of 1933, four years after the development of Radburn was stopped, Franklin D. Roosevelt was inaugurated. As he held up his hand to swear to the American people his fealty as their new president, more than ten million American workers were unemployed, great numbers were homeless, and many were on the verge of losing their homes. That same year, in Germany, Adolf Hitler was appointed chancellor by President von Hindenburg.

One element of Roosevelt's New Deal, the legacy of which extends even into the 1990s, attempted to create jobs through massive and extensive public works projects. Roosevelt succeeded in creating jobs that were, for the most part, temporary and transitory. These jobs only existed during the life of the government program and ended when the need or the program disappeared. Two notable exceptions created jobs that were both permanent and continuing. The greatest and biggest was the Tennessee Valley Authority (TVA), and the second and smaller program was called the "Greenbelt Towns."

The TVA, an extensive system of dams, lakes, and electric power production plants along the Tennessee River, required new communities be built to house construction workers and administrative staffs for these facilities. The "satellite town," as it would come to be known, is best seen in the village of Norris, Tennessee. Designed as a community for the TVA personnel working on the Norris Dam near Knoxville, it would never achieve its independence as a fully planned and self-sustaining town. Planned by Tracy Augur, it follows many of the Howard-Wright concepts and principles and is an excellent example of structure and organizational innovation. Unfortunately, even though these TVA new towns contributed to the early planning efforts of American Garden Cities, they were remote and had little impact on existing regional conditions.

The basic ideas of circulation, land use, density, and social justice which evolved during the planning of Sunnyside Gardens and Radburn became public policy within the concepts of the Greenbelt communities. All government projects of that time needed justification, and therefore the purposes for the Greenbelt communities were officially stated:

1. To give useful work to men on unemployment relief.
2. To demonstrate in practice the soundness of planning and operating towns according to certain Garden City principles.
3. To provide low-rent housing in healthful surroundings, both physical and social, for families that are in the low-income bracket.[20]

Unfortunately, these guiding principles were short-lived, flawed in concept, and overly costly for the benefits they produced.

Four Greenbelt communities were authorized in 1935 under legislation passed as the Emergency Relief Appropriation Act and National Industrial Recovery Act. The functions of the Greenbelt towns—which included Greenbelt, Maryland; Greenhills, Ohio; Greendale, Wisconsin; and Greenbrook, New Jersey—were prescribed through an executive order by the president. The last of the four, Greenbrook, was dropped due to legal issues and local objections that arose during the planning. Henry S. Churchill, a leading architect and planner of the time, noted that it was "stopped by injunction proceedings brought by the Liberty League at the behest of an irate local magnate" who wanted "no wops or polacks" near his prerevolutionary manor. The notion of the Not-In-My-Back-Yard (NIMBY) movement, took shape under many guises, long before the heady environmental days of the 1980s.[21]

Roosevelt placed Rexford Guy Tugwell, a member of his inner circle, or "brain trust," and a true believer in the Garden City idea, in charge of the Resettlement Administration. Tugwell taught economics at Columbia University when he was selected by Roosevelt as an assistant secretary of agriculture and would coauthor the Agricultural Adjustment Act. It was under his authority the Greenbelt communities would be designed and built. Their creation, due to the usual federal reorganizations, later found a home within another agency formed within the Resettlement Administration, the Suburban Resettlement Division.

Tugwell had been very interested in the concept of the satellite city regardless of its social impacts. "My idea," he wrote in 1935, "is to just outside centers of population, pick up cheap land, build a whole community and entice people into it. Then go back into the cities and tear down whole slums and make parks of them." The Suburban Resettlement Bureau was set up in a mansion on Massachusetts Avenue in Washington, D.C.[22]

Tugwell rejected the concept of individualism and believed that Americans shared a "cooperative mentality." He proposed a collectivist economic policy, which he believed could be achieved through planning and public control of the economy. It was his belief that the idea of the Greenbelt community was closer to the habits and aspirations of the American people. He was blunt and, at times, tactless in the presentation of his gospel and soon became a target of the press and a political liability for Roosevelt. He left the administration after one year but steadfastly remained a loyal supporter of the president. Tugwell's important legacy focused on the strength of suburban resettlement areas, which he thought were most consistent with the current trends in American growth. Tugwell initially proposed that twenty-five Greenbelt towns be built close to existing urban employment, yet only three were built. It was in this decade and during the worst economic time the country has ever known that some of the best and most creative talents in community and residential planning were hired and brought to Washington to design and develop these communities.[23]

Henry Churchill wrote an article for the *New Republic* in June 1936 announcing the concept of the Greenbelt town to the general public. In it he presented the New Deal's utopian idea on a level that was foreign to most Americans:

> It is a social experiment of the first magnitude, and may well set new patterns not only for housing but for city government, for these towns are to be self-governing, starting free of bonded debt, and without the possibility of speculating in land or over expanding. No land or houses can be sold; the ultimate sizes of the communities are definitely set . . . these towns must not be allowed to be defeated by real-estate foxery, double crossing and indifference—the indifference of those most vitally concerned, the people who will benefit by them, the landless and dispossessed, the constant victims of peculative greed, all of us, that is.[24]

Ten years later in his book *The City Is the People* Churchill would continue to espouse his strongly held belief in the benevolence of government and the

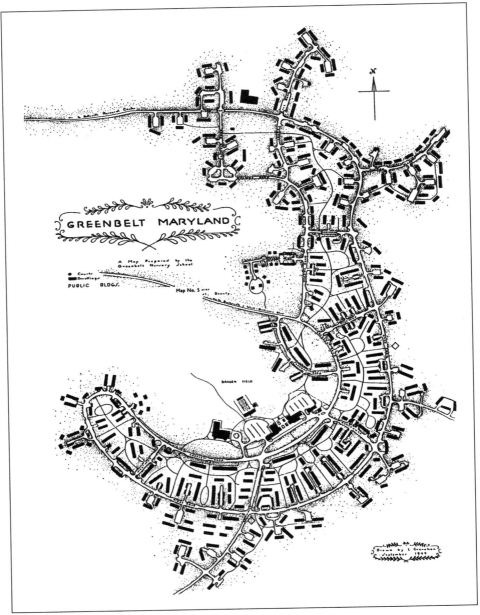

Fig. 13. The plan for Greenbelt, Maryland, near Washington, D.C. The streets curve to follow the shape of the hill, and walkways interconnect the superblock neighborhoods. *Source:* redrawn from C. S. Stein, *Toward New Towns for America.*

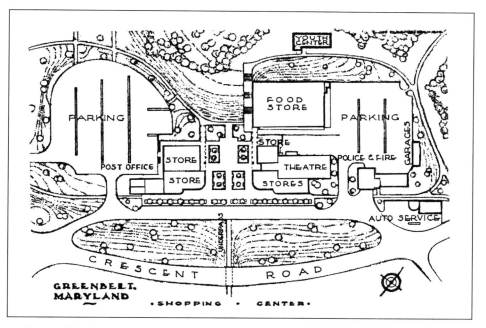

Fig. 14. The shopping center for Greenbelt is centrally located for the residents of the community. *Source:* redrawn from C. S. Stein, *Toward New Towns for America.*

continued ownership of land by government: "With municipal ownership of land . . . Possession [is] under long term lease, 'due process' could apply as well to the value of the lease and to the structure as to land held in fee, broker's could still could still make money buying and selling and leasing; the city's fiscal problem could be much simplified, and the problem of 'unearned increment' [speculation] could be much more readily adjusted."

With the land owned by the municipality, long-term planning could be more easily accomplished because one body had complete control of density, use distribution, and eventually the disposition of the structures on the land. Churchill blatantly placed the belief before the American public that "urban redevelopment purchase and subsidy *should* be a first step towards municipal ownership of *all* the land."[25]

Greenbelt, Maryland, is located approximately thirteen miles northeast of the nation's Capital. Now, sixty years later, the community is engulfed within the growth that has occurred in and around Washington, D.C., but in 1935 it was in a sparsely settled area of Prince George's County, Maryland. Purchased at the time by the federal government for an average of ninety dollars per acre, the thirty-three hundred acres were poor, overly farmed land with little agricultural value. Even today much of the land purchased remains a buffer against the pressing growth in the area.

The design team, headed by town planner Hale Walker and chief architects Douglas D. Ellington and R. J. Wadsworth, divided the site into five residential "superblocks" that followed the hilly topography. The community was served by two parallel crescent-shaped loop roads that wrap the dominant hill and provide good access to all areas of the community. Each of the internal residential superblocks take their conceptual lead from Sunnyside and Radburn. The clusters of buildings do not align with or front these main loop roads but face inward toward the open-space areas. The residential clusters are separated by extensive greenways and open areas that are interconnected by walkways and lineal parks. Overall, the plan is shaped like a crescent moon that embraces the hill.

The majority of the buildings are four- to eight-unit row houses. Two-family houses (duplexes) and a few apartment units were also built. The open areas are not as well defined as they were at Radburn, and, even though the park areas are extensive, they do not create an intimate and enclosed feeling; much of the open space just bleeds away. The primary focus of the town is the community center, which is cradled in the inside arc of the moon. Here are located the administrative offices, swimming center, athletic fields, marketplace, schools, library, and entertainment center.

The first residents of Greenbelt moved into the homes as they became available between October 1937 and the summer of 1938. These residents were selected because of their incomes and existing housing situations. They were also selected for their ability to pay the rents established for these first units. The result of this selection process was a very young population: fathers and mothers were typically under the age of thirty, and most had small children who were under school age.

Greenbelt went through two growth phases. The first was the initial settlement by the Resettlement Administration, and the second, about two years later, was during the "Defense" period, when the country began to gear up for the possibility of war. The second growth spurt was hastily built and detracts from the original construction. Greenbelt, by the end of the 1940s, would house almost seventy-five hundred people.

Greenbelt, like Radburn, also failed to meet the goals of Howard's Garden City. There was no industry, no job center. This was intentional on the part of the government planners, but it is unfortunate that, even with the almost unlimited funding of the federal government, a sincere effort at creating a total community was not attempted. Today, almost sixty years later, most of the residents still commute into Washington.

The second of the Greenbelt communities, Greenhills, was located eleven miles north of Cincinnati, Ohio, on a hilly and wooded 5,930-acre property. The community's plan placed the 676 residential units around the community center and school complex. These facilities were interconnected to the rest of the community by trails and greenways. Like Greenbelt, the residential units were predominantly apartments and row houses. Only twenty-four detached homes were built. Unlike Greenbelt, where most of the units were oriented inward and surrounded by roads, Greenhills faced many of its residential units outward toward the open lands of the property. Considering the exposure of the property and the ridges, many of these homes have direct views into open space. Again, the community harkens back to the Garden City, with its surrounding and separating greenbelt, but fails to live up to the dream of an integrated industrial, commercial, and residential village. The community had a severe lack of good regional access, especially a railroad, and no employment or industrial center. In some respects it is nothing more than a well-designed subdivision.

The Resettlement Administration, in 1936, purchased 3,510 acres eight miles southwest of Milwaukee, Wisconsin, for the construction of the third Greenbelt community, Greendale. It was designed to provide low-rent homes for families with modest incomes. The Milwaukee area was considered for one of these communities because it had, since the early 1920s, a deep involvement in public housing programs that provided single-family dwellings. In 1934 the city played host to an international tour of housing experts, including Americans Henry Wright and Ernest J. Bohn and the English Garden City planner Sir Raymond Unwin. Unwin expressed his opinion, during the course of the conference, that "this tendency to move out [of the city] is very healthy and I think there is infinite more danger in trying to bolster up a desire to live in the city center than doing a little too much to live on the [city's] outside . . . To me, the desirable life is to live in a one family house with a garden." It is surprising to hear the "American Dream," even in the 1930s, being voiced by an Englishman.[26]

It was here, at Greendale, that planners Jacob Crane and the noted landscape architect Elbert Peets, created the smallest yet, considered by many, the best of the Greenbelt communities. Initially, only about 385 acres were used to develop 750 potential residential units. The plan included 370 group- or twin-type units and 380 single-family designs. Its size and large greenbelt buffer allowed the community to grow within itself and create a living village.

To assure the planners of the market for the homes, residents in and around Milwaukee were surveyed extensively about their incomes and housing requirements. Social amenities they would like see built were listed and even the extent of commercial facilities they would patronize were tabulated. Unfortunately, the surveys overlooked attitudes about living in an isolated housing project. Elbert

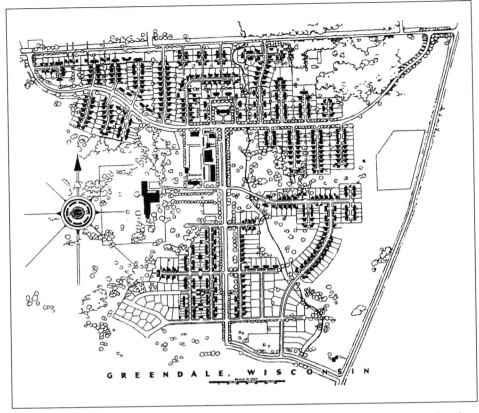

Fig. 15. The Greendale Plan, by Elbert Peets and Jacob Crane, shows the neighborhood concept that is now accepted as the basic unit for new community planning. *Source:* redrawn from C. S. Stein, *Toward New Towns for America.*

Peets later noted that, even with all the survey data available to the planners, they usually relied on federal guidelines and their own professional experience and not on the survey of potential future residents.[27]

Greendale was initially subdivided into five neighborhoods that surrounded the elementary school and town center. The residential size and scale was smaller than the other Greenbelt towns. There were only a few row houses. Most homes were singles and duplexes, which reflected the preferences gathered in the surveys. Some neighborhoods were also subdivided into conventional lots, with fewer interior properties held in common ownership. Most streets and cul-de-sacs had less than twenty-four units facing the street. These subneighborhoods were oriented to have direct access to the open-space buffers and greenways. The

Fig. 16. Elbert Peets, planner of Park Forest, Illinois. *Source:* courtesy of Park Forest Public Library.

streets were designed to direct through-traffic away from the residential areas; only those autos having business on a residential street or cul-de-sac should be within that quarter. Pedestrian paths were also separated from the roadways and led to the school and town administration building. Peets and Crane also included a recommendation for a collective farm on the surrounding greenbelt, with all the farmers employed on a salary basis with a share of the profit.[28]

There was a fundamental flaw in the execution of all the Greenbelt plans: the land was federally owned, and the entire marketing strategy was toward renters. It was not until 1949, after extensive lobbying by the residents and twelve years after the start of Greendale, that Congress voted to sell it and the other Greenbelt communities to private enterprise, with preferential purchase rights for nonprofit or limited-dividend groups of either veterans or tenants. Even these meager efforts at "property ownership" failed to maintain the communities. Eventually Greenbelt, Maryland, was sold to private developers, sliced into pieces by freeways, and its physical integrity erased.

Greendale was able to maintain the integrity of the original plan because a group of Milwaukee businessmen formed a public spirited investment group to purchase most of the town. Later, in 1953, the Milwaukee Community Development Corporation acquired an additional twenty-three hundred acres of vacant land, the shopping center, and administration building. The Public Housing Administration, the 1950s newest name for the Roosevelt administration's Federal Public Housing Authority, then sold Greendale's homes directly to their occupants. Greenhills, Ohio, went through similar machinations, and eventually the remaining open lands were converted to county parks or Army Corps of Engineers "flood control" districts, or they were sold for development.[29] The dreams of Tugwell, Churchill, and others for the government control of land and property disappeared with the sale of these developments.

Many reasons have been sited for the failure of these Greenbelt communities, but the one that few point to as the best reason was their cost. When Greendale was stopped in the summer of 1937, almost 10.5 million dollars had been spent by the government. If allocated to the real number of units built, 572, the cost per residential unit was $18,350. This was more than five times the current price of a home in that market. Although the village's roads were paved with good intentions, the product fell far short of its goal: affordable housing.

Greendale owed much of its planning concept to Radburn. The pedestrian scale of the village, the central grouping of its public buildings, and, most directly, its street plan all reflect the planning of Radburn. The concept and execution of the short cul-de-sac, or court, is similar in scope and length. Peets admitted that, in designing the village, he drew from the layouts of midwestern county seats, European Renaissance marketplaces, and the reconstruction of Williamsburg, Virginia.[30]

One other element of planning sets Greendale apart from Greenhills and Greenbelt: the form of housing proposed and built. Most planners of the time agreed that attached housing, the row house, was the only affordable type of housing for moderate incomes. Experts referred to a detached house as "sentimental without much to recommend it." At Greendale, Elbert Peets disagreed. He felt that the detached house was far superior to the traditional eastern style of the row house. He thought each house should stand apart, with its own fenced yard around it. It was his merging of the concept of the detached house with the defined cul-de-sac which set Greendale apart from the other Greenbelt towns.[31]

All three—Greenbelt, Maryland; Greendale, Wisconsin; and Greenhills, Ohio—were under the watchful guardianship of the federal government. They were incomplete, and, eventually, adjacent development precluded their expansion. Although the three communities had basic health and safety services, some commercial facilities, and more parks than most comparable communities, they lacked one fundamental element common to most other small towns: they were not operated and managed by the residents. Eventually, there was a natural tendency by the residents not to care as much as they would if they were in charge.

Fifteen years later Tugwell wrote, "We were doomed to failure from the start." He couldn't accept the facts that these new towns were failures due to conception or planning techniques; they were failures of "character." He continued to believe that the participants had neither the commitment nor the self-discipline to make these communities work. He blamed the press and what he called the "pulpit." These New Deal towns should have set the standard by which postwar communities were to be built, but they resulted in a collection of squandered opportunities, indifferent bureaucrats, exorbitant costs, and confusing goals. There was also a strange atmosphere about the agency doing the planning. Resettlement, wrote Marquis W. Childs of the *St. Louis Post-Dispatch*, was "a cozy conspiracy of good will to remake America on a cleaner, truer, more secure pattern." But Childs also noted that the effort failed to take the American people into their confidence. It was an attitude of "Trust me, we know what we're doing." But those who were resettled by the process did not trust the government. The basic concerns of Americans were self-interest and a desire to prove themselves. The needs and desires of individuals and their families could not find a satisfying outlet in these self-contained communities.

The government and its planners failed to consider the essential reason that contributed to the failure of these new Greenbelt towns: the residents were transients and renters who lacked private ownership, responsibility, and the power to control their own properties. The social engineering beliefs of the New Deal planners neglected to give the residents the control they needed in their daily lives. As such, these communities floundered, and it would not be until the early 1950s that the residents could buy the homes they lived in. It was only then that these communities acquired a significant life and purpose of their own.

The communities were somewhat isolated and, as the government proceeded, hardly anything was done to fold these new towns into the fabric of the region. There was little if any involvement by local governments and counties. These new communities were forced into the local culture and were intended to house what many were to consider outsiders. The need for a regional consciousness, as voiced by Howard in his Garden Cities and Mumford and others in Radburn, was never seen as a priority and may have been seen by Washington as a nuisance or hindrance. As Clarence Stein, the architect and patriarch of American new towns, later said: "You can't plan a new town by itself. It's part of a regional problem. We have no administrative way to develop regions."[32]

It is safe to assume that Philip Klutznick was aware of the problems that these Greenbelt towns had faced. They had been, after numerous reorganizations, under the control of the Federal Public Housing Authority, an agency he directed, since February 1942. With his knowledge of the Greenbelt towns and their problems, it is understandable why Klutznick took such a strong position on the two issues of community incorporation and property management. In these two issues he was to prove himself prescient. In a memorandum written in July 1946, soon after joining the team that was to build Park Forest, he voiced his concerns about managing property acquisitions:

> In our original concept of an integrated city, we always envision the ownership and control of a band of surrounding land. It seems foolhardy to add the value that our program will add to the surrounding territory without participating therein. In our recent planning, we seem to have lost site of this objective. It is, of course, desirable to project a complete utilization of the land which we presently have under control. However, some thought should be given to methods and means to protect ourselves against a huge enrichment of abutting owners without participation on our part in the benefit.[33]

Klutznick also would require that the new community be incorporated and form its own government as soon as possible. The town must have legal standing in the region and obligate the residents to be responsible for the future of the village; they would not be tenants on a government-sponsored resettlement project.

In the United States between 1900 and 1939, concurrently with the English Garden Cities, many new communities were being planned and built. The Country Club District in Kansas City, with its seminal shopping district, began modestly in 1907. Forest Hills Gardens on Long Island, child of the philanthropic Russell Sage Foundation, started in 1909. By October 1910 Shaker Heights, just east of downtown Cleveland, had extended itself across some six and a half miles of rolling land and had incorporated.

Many of the new towns were subsidized by industrial growth and the need for employee housing. The Kohler Company moved its factory into the countryside near Sheboygan, Wisconsin, and developed Kohler Village. The Goodyear Company in Akron, Ohio, and the Norton Company in Worcester, Massachusetts, also undertook suburban residential communities for their workers. These new towns were similar to the mill towns of almost one hundred years earlier, but there was a difference. Most privately built communities were land ventures built to create housing not only for their workers but for others in the community as well.

Lewis Mumford would define, in 1938, almost exactly what would be required to meet the needs of new towns. Writing in *The Culture of Cities* he said that the garden city can take form, in other words, only when our political and economic institutions are directed toward regional rehabilitation. What is important to recognize is that these new principles of urban development, as demonstrated by Sir Ebenezer Howard and his associates, are universal ones: they point toward balanced urban communities within balanced regions: on one hand, a wider diffusion of the instruments and processes of a high human culture, and on the other the infusion into the city of the life-sustaining environment and life-directed interests of the countryside.[34]

The experience that was gained in community design in the United States prior to World War II formed the foundation for the Park Forest village plan. Park Forest was the first real opportunity to pull together the three basic ideas of modern postwar community planning. As noted by Clarence Stein in his book, *Toward New Towns for America*, the three fundamental concepts were the Garden City, the Radburn Idea, and a new term presented by Stein, the Neighborhood Unit. Each of these elements created a new vernacular of design and planning which, when combined, formed the ideal of the New Town.

Peets expanded this list to include the "multicellular city" as the model for his planning. It created "a new texture for the dispersion of the urban population, a texture that preserves much of the countryside, conforms to the best principles of regional traffic circulation, keeps land open for the gradual movement of industry, and groups the people into neighborhoods having a stimulating autonomy in many social ways without giving up the sound foundation of participation in the industrial and economic life of the urban region."[35] Park Forest was the child of these planning concepts and a direct blood relative of these communities and the grandchild of Chicago's own Riverside. It is also possibly the only child of this parentage to mature and grow old.

The most obvious difference between the Greenbelt communities and Park Forest was that Park Forest was built by private developers with the intention to sell the housing to the residents. The most important change from the planning of the prewar era was that Park Forest would become an entity unto itself. It would be incorporated, and the residents would control their fortunes, something the government did not grant to the residents of the Greenbelt towns. Its conception and birth would be special.

CHAPTER THREE

Acquiring the Site and Other Players

Son, there is only one thing they're not making any more of
. . . and that's land.

—Anonymous

PHILLIP KLUTZNICK had not yet committed to their venture by early spring 1946, but his encouragement prompted Nate Manilow to begin looking for suitable sites for a new town in the Chicago area. Two possible candidates were found, the first on the west side of Chicago and the other on the far south side straddling the Cook and Will county line. Manilow asked Klutznick whether he was coming through Chicago in the near future and would he look at these parcels of land. He agreed, and on his next trip to Omaha he stopped off in Chicago to look at the prospective sites.

The two sites had been found by J. Alton Lauren, a broker hired by Manilow. Lauren was a distinguished-looking gentleman and quite efficient in his work. Manilow and Sweet had met with Lauren and outlined the type of property they were looking for. The site needed to be large enough for ten thousand homes and would probably require at least 3,000 acres. Since the market they were looking at would consist of people employed in downtown Chicago, it would be important that the site be near a commuting rail line and not more than 30 miles from the Loop, Chicago's central business district. It was also important that the property not be within an existing city, since property values and taxes would be higher than in the more outlying unincorporated areas.

Klutznick met with the Manilow and Sweet in Chicago in the spring of 1946, and the first site they took him to was on the far south side of Chicago, about twenty-eight miles from downtown. It had a golf course, a peat bog, and marginal farmlands. Manilow had purchase options on some of the parcels and believed that he could secure options on the others. The property prices were fairly inexpensive, at about five hundred dollars an acre, and would remain so if a low profile could be maintained. Secrecy was paramount. Of equal importance was the location of the Illinois Central rail line that passed along the westerly side of the properties. This line would give access to all the cities along its route to down-

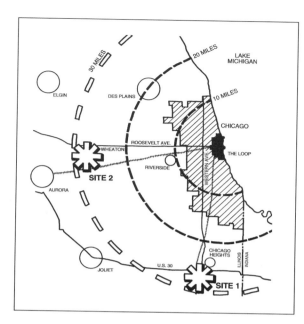

Fig. 17. Nate Manilow chose two sites to show Philip M. Klutznick, one on the South Side and one on the West Side of Chicago. *Source:* author's drawing.

town Chicago; direct connections to Harvey, Riverdale, Calumet Park, Evergreen Park, University of Chicago, and all the downtown entertainment, government, and business centers of the Loop.

The second site was on the west side of Chicago, near Wheaton. Located along the Chicago and Aurora railroad line, it included a privately owned daily fee golf course, farmlands, and a higher price per acre. This additional cost per acre would raise the initial investment, cautioned Klutznick. Additional investigation also found that the golf course owner would not sell, since the course was his only source of income. The idea of a golf course within the community was tempting, but it would also leave two hundred acres of land not in their control and which might someday compete with them. Both west and south side properties were controlled by the First National Bank of Chicago.

Klutznick's preference was for the south side parcel. Known as the Batcheldor property, it contained a golf course (an eighteen-year-old championship course called Indian Wood Country Club), some beautiful stands of trees, farmhouses and outbuildings, and a boggy swamp. The initial property contained about eleven hundred acres.

"Phil, if I were to buy enough of this land," Manilow asked Klutznick, "would you serve as president of a company that would organize and manage the construction of a GI town on it?" Klutznick demurred. Manilow also offered to provide the seed money, and Klutznick would be offered half the common stock and an annual salary of $25,000, a figure well below what Klutznick had been offered elsewhere. Klutznick told Manilow that he was interested, but he had made a commitment to President Truman to stay at his post for a while longer. When he was free to return to private life he would give Manilow a definite answer.

Congress, in May 1946, appropriated more than $250 million to convert barracks, wartime housing, and trailers into temporary homes for veterans and their families. These conversions only provided marginal and temporary housing for a small number of the needy. Truman wanted to stimulate the construction of 1.2 million new homes, but Congress frustrated these goals by refusing to provide larger subsidies to lower the cost of building materials. Congress also responded by refusing to remove price controls that would have led to an immediate upsurge in materials costs and by shelving the Wagner-Taft-Ellender Housing Act being considered.

Philip Klutznick and his family left Washington, D.C., and the troubled presidency of Truman in early July 1946, for the opportunities Manilow offered in Chicago. He was concerned about whether he was doing the "right thing" leaving his friend, the president, and returning to private life. He hoped there would someday be a way he could render some small service to Truman. Truman told Klutznick at his departure that "perhaps the most lasting contribution you have made has been your clear, sound enunciation of the role of public housing as an essential part of a healthy private enterprise system and a well-housed nation. Your principles have won the respect and support of responsible leadership throughout the country and have broadened public understanding of the importance of good housing in the national welfare." In many ways Klutznick would never really leave Washington, and its pull would greatly affect his later life (he would become secretary of commerce under Carter).[1]

Klutznick, with his wife, Ethel, and their four children, moved into a rented apartment at 199 East Lake Shore Drive, and he immediately began to pull the final parts of the development team together. It was obvious before Klutznick's arrival in Chicago that some of the best people in and out of government had been contacted and hired to put this development together. Setting up an office on the second floor of the Harris Trust building, Klutznick and Manilow formed American Community Builders (ACB), the team that would build Park Forest.

For the architects of the community Klutznick suggested that they contact Chicago-based Jerry Loebl, whom he knew from the Federal Public Housing Authority, and his partner, Norman Schlossman. During the war Klutznick had worked closely with Loebl, who was a member of the architects' advisory board to Klutznick's housing commission. He also had known the architects from his short stay in Chicago in the early 1940s. Chicago-born Jerrold Loebl and Norman Schlossman had been educated at the Armour Institute of Technology (now the

Illinois Institute of Technology), and they formed their architectural firm in 1925. Located in downtown Chicago, they concentrated on public housing projects before shifting to defense and military housing during the war.

Loebl and Schlossman's connections to Park Forest came about by their association with Klutznick. Their firm had completed the initial designs for a high-rise public housing project in Chicago, Dearborn Homes, and they had to go to Washington, D.C., to receive approval. Approval was to be made by the Federal Public Housing Authority, Klutznick's department. According the Schlossman, after the presentation, which went well, Klutznick asked them to dinner and told them of the idea for a new town south of Chicago. Klutznick then recommended Lobel and Schlossman to Manilow. The commission, it seems, was a fringe benefit of their public housing work.

The third member of the architecture team, Richard Bennett, was hired after an impromptu interview on a train by Jerry Loebl. Bennett had written extensive articles about the subject of new communities for many of the popular magazines of the time, and during the final days of the war he strongly believed that there would be a great need for new towns to house returning veterans. Bennett was tenured at Yale University, Carroll Sweet Sr.'s alma mater, and was the architecture department's youngest full professor. At Yale he was involved in the theories of what was to happen after the war, especially in housing for GI's. When asked to present his views to the American Institute of Architects at their annual convention in Atlantic City, he gladly accepted. It was on the train trip to that meeting that he met Loebl. Bennett made such an impression on the older Loebl that a few months later, in the spring of 1946, he was asked to "come and do a town, like the ones you were talking about." He was hesitant to leave and join one of Chicago's largest and most prestigious architectural firms but tentatively joined it in August 1946, a "trial run" as it were, but stayed for thirty years. He was "Mr. Design" of the group. Since the community was operating on a tight budget funded by Manilow, the architects took a 10 percent interest in American Community Builders, 5 percent from Klutznick and 5 percent from Manilow, in lieu of some of their fee.

In the words of Richard Bennett, Elbert Peets was "a quiet, lovely genius, because he loved the land and he didn't think people should destroy it." Peets was born in Cleveland, Ohio, in 1886 and educated at Western Reserve University and the Harvard School of Landscape Architecture. He was an academician and scholar as well as a landscape architect and planner. He had coauthored a book on civic art along with Werner Hegemann in the early 1920s, *The American Vitruvius: An Architect's Handbook of Civic Art*, and later wrote extensive articles and essays on the design and growth of Washington, D.C. During the 1930s, when the Roosevelt Administration embarked on an ambitious program to create "Greenbelt towns" across the United States, Elbert Peets was assigned to the Wisconsin community, Greendale. After the development of Greendale was cut short, Peets continued to practice planning throughout the United States. During the war he was chief of the Site Planning Section in the Federal Public Housing Authority, Klutznick's agency. It was during a visit by Klutznick to Omaha to examine a project site of the Omaha Housing Authority that they first met.[2]

Peets brought to Park Forest an extensive knowledge of planning and how to conform these communities to the shape and feel of the land. He believed that a texture evolved from the planning of the community and that there was a relationship between the house and the lot, the lot and the street, and the street and the community. He also had an understanding of the impact that zoning had on the livability of a community and how many of the problems of the past, such as overly wide streets and rigid street patterns, continued into the present. He believed that it was these and other older, antiquated planning styles that pushed the costs for new development higher. Peets understood that within the concept of the Greenbelt towns two fundamental objectives were sought: first, to spend as little as possible on streets and utilities and, second, to hold down the municipal operating cost—a high tax rate being the town's great competitive handicap.[3]

It was Peets' thinking, as well as that of others within the Greenbelt movement, that the principle of a low gross density justified a relatively high net neighborhood density—a concept that became the fundamental basis for future planned communities. This "density transfer" allowed for wide variations among the neighborhoods of the new community. Each neighborhood could have different housing types, densities, and lifestyles. The higher densities of the apartments offset the relatively low densities of the single-family homes. This concept also allowed for the appropriate placement of the commercial and public facilities without affecting the overall residential densities needed to support them.

Among the planners of the team Peets was the most detached. He worked with the team through 1950 from his Washington, D.C., office. He was, as Philip Klutznick called him, a "fount of wise counsel." He knew the property intimately. He had walked its entirety and was often called upon to remind the others of the shape and contour of the land. He suggested ways to save many of the trees within the village, and his ideas were not necessarily based on aesthetic grounds but founded on sound economic facts. Proper planning reduced the costs of grading and utility placement, and, as early design studies for Park Forest show, there was even an attempt to reduce significantly the amount of streets servicing the single-family homes.

Three men brought their construction talents to the table at the request of Manilow and Klutznick: Charles Waldmann, for his engineering expertise, and Hart Perry and Carroll Sweet Jr. (Carroll's son and a navy veteran), for their management skills. Waldmann, Hungarian by birth and graduate of the Royal Academy in Budapest, held three degrees in electrical, mechanical, and civil engineering. He was brought to the United States by General Electric and eventually had his own consulting firm in New York. He worked as senior chief engineer on the Greenbelt towns, with his primary focus on Greenhills, Ohio. Klutznick had known Waldmann while he was section head responsible for electrical and mechanical utility systems with the Housing Authority. He was also involved with the Detroit defense and aircraft plant at Willow Run, Michigan. Klutznick brought him to Park Forest as the director of utilities for ACB.

Hart Perry was a graduate of the University of Chicago with degrees in political science and public administration. He was special assistant to Klutznick in the Division of Defense Housing until he was called up for military service. He was with the Office of Strategic Services (OSS) during the war and returned to the FPHA as general expediter in the veterans' temporary housing program when the war ended. Perry came to ACB at Klutznick's request after resigning from the agency, in September 1946.

The inspiration for Park Forest was a young naval officer and namesake son of Sweet. Carroll Sweet Jr., through his wartime letters to his father, professed a concern over housing for the returning GI. Carroll Sr. shared these thoughts and helped to shape the profile and set the tone of the community. Carroll Jr. was born in Grand Rapids, Michigan, in December 1912, and now, thirty-four years later, the end of the war meant the end of his military career. He was released to inactive duty in February 1946. Carroll Sweet Jr. had five years of sea duty, including two years on an aircraft carrier in the Atlantic and three years commanding escort ships in most of the major western Pacific campaigns. Commanding a ship is more an exercise in managing personnel than fighting, and his skills at managing in high-stress situations served him well. He was brought on board as an assistant to Klutznick.

Rounding out the initial group were two others whom Klutznick brought with him from Washington. Israel Rafkind was another midwesterner, from Menomonee, Wisconsin, who came on board as comptroller. Rafkind, an expert financial analyst and accountant, had worked with Klutznick in Washington as comptroller for the FPHA covering the mid-Atlantic states. He held numerous positions in the Federal Housing program during his almost ten-year tenure with the government. The other was Allan Harrison, a New Yorker, who was assigned the position of chief constructor. Harrison had extensive experience in large-scale construction in Turkey, Northern Ireland, and Scotland. He was with the New York City Housing Authority before coming to Park Forest. Unfortunately, for health reasons Harrison had to leave before construction began. Later that fall one more man, Dick Senior, with extensive experience in large-scale construction, would be hired by Harrison. Harrison had worked with Senior in Northern Ireland.

Assembly of the land continued through the summer of 1946, with closings on the parcels extending into October and November. To help expedite the acquisitions and closings, Manilow's men operated a resettlement office to assist farmers and landowners in acquiring new land if they would sell. Finally, eighteen parcels were purchased for the initial construction of the village. The community would start with 2,376 acres for a total price of $986,884.02, about $415 per acre. Eventually, the final plan for the village would contain 3,151 acres.

CHAPTER FOUR

The Planning

Make no little plans; they have no magic to stir men's blood, and probably themselves will not be realized. Make big plans: aim high in work and hope, remembering that a noble, logical diagram once recorded will never die, but long after we are gone will be a living thing, asserting itself with growing insistency.

> —Daniel Hudson Burnham (1846–1912),
> Chicago architect and planner of the 1893,
> Columbian Exposition in Chicago

PARK FOREST lies atop a broad, sloping, and swelling bulge of Paleozoic bedrock called the Kankakee Arch. This region of bedrock connects the Wisconsin Arch to the northwest and the Cincinnati Arch to the southeast. Two depressions, the Illinois basin to the southwest and the Michigan basin to the northeast, flank these arches, or ridges. The formation lies 150 to 200 feet below the surface of both the land and Lake Michigan. The closest exposed bedrock to Park Forest which penetrates to the surface can be found in and near the quarries in Thornton, Illinois.

Four hundred and forty million years ago this bedrock, a hundred feet or more under Park Forest, formed the bottom of a shallow inland ocean. This great sea spread across what is now Indiana, Illinois, and Wisconsin. Reefs formed, made from the marine animals and plants that lived along the shores of that Silurian Sea, in conditions similar to those found in today's oceans. As the waters receded and then refilled the marginal areas, microscopic sea life died and left their calcium shells and skeletons mixed with the fine grains of sand. This material, compressed with time and the weight of the thickening overburden, became Silurian dolomite, an almost pure limestone that underlies thousands of square miles of the Chicago region north into Wisconsin and south to the western edge of Indiana.

For hundreds of million years this region was subjected to significant physical changes that saw new oceans and lakes form only to be covered, pushed up, and eroded. Antediluvian changes left deep canyons filled with vegetation debris that changed to coal and other bituminous materials. High ground saw the dinosaurs and the evolution of life.

The last two million years, a blink in geologic time, saw successive glaciers cover the North American continent. They pushed as far south as the Ohio and Missouri Rivers. Park Forest was covered by most of these glacial onslaughts, and the last, the Wisconsin era, saw a succession of glaciers that began sixty thousand years ago. After a short withdrawal of about six thousand years, these glaciers returned again twenty-four thousand years ago. This last period, called the Woodfordian glaciation, lasted twelve thousand years, pulsing back and forth across the northern part of Illinois and extending south of Urbana, Illinois. Park Forest, at the maximum time of coverage, sat under three to five thousand feet of ice.

The debris plowed up and accumulated by these advancing glaciers dropped out as they melted, leaving piled formations of soil called moraine and till. The material ranged from cobblestone and bouldery gravels to fine clays and silts that would segregate themselves into layers depending on whether it was outwash from the glacier or was subjected to high or low flows of icewater melt. The clays accumulated in thick layers by settling out of the slowest moving flows.

Park Forest sits on a portion of the Valparaiso Groundmoraine. This formation of moraine, which represents a series of minor pulses of the glacial ice front during its retreat, deposited considerable amounts of extremely fine clay materials. During a late surge the glacier plowed forward again to the southwest and formed a series of lakes that were trapped between the previously left moraine and the ice wall of the glacier. Lakes Orland, Tinley, and Steger were formed. It is possible that the region from Crete to north of Tinley Park may have been a large lake at one time. Lake Michigan's southern edge was very close to the northern border of Homewood. These lakes no longer exist, but some areas designated as Cook County Forest Preserve contain the remains of many of these lakes as boggy lowlands.

Between these glacial advances and retreats the area would return to climatic conditions similar to what might be found today. Grasslands and woodlands would retake the land, and in the low spots and pockets small lakes and ponds would appear. In time these riparian habitats would fill with dead vegetation and eventually create peat bogs. The central park area of Park Forest is a classic example of these extinct lakes and bogs.

The Silurian limestone bedrock, the glacial clay, and the peat were all to have immediate and expensive consequences for Park Forest.

The land that was to become Park Forest was an extensive and varied tract enclosing over three thousand acres. The properties were bounded on the west by the Illinois Central Railroad and the villages of Matteson and unincorporated Richton Park. To the north, running east and west, was Route 30, America's road

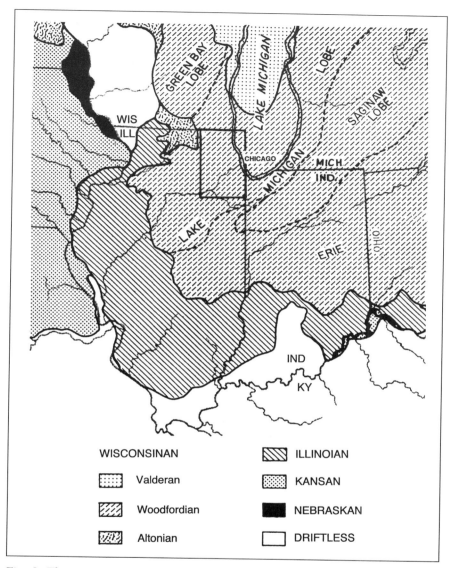

Fig. 18. The extent of historic glaciation across Illinois and Indiana. *Source:* Illinois State Geological Survey.

through its heartland, also named the Lincoln Highway. To the east and extending to the south were Sauk Trail and Thorn Creek Forest Preserves. Two rail lines crossed the northerly portion of the property, one owned by the Michigan Central Railroad and the other by the Elgin, Joliet & Eastern Railroad. Bisecting the

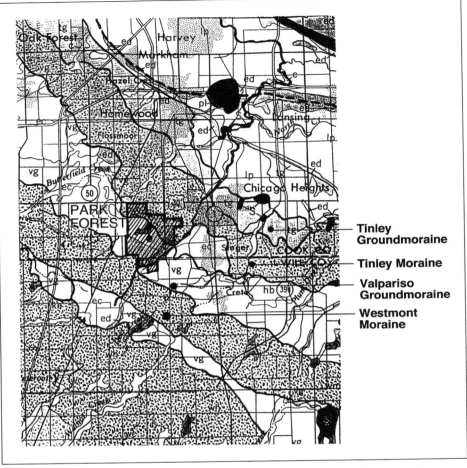

Fig. 19. South Side of Chicago moraine deposits, with Park Forest in the center. *Source:* Illinois State Geological Survey.

property from north to south was Western Avenue, a road that led directly to downtown Chicago. Cutting through the property from east to west was the oldest of mid-America's prehistoric roads, Sauk Trail.

The land, especially in the northwestern corner did not drain well. The heavy clay soil prevented much of the water from soaking away. The result was a boggy wetland that, in rainy years, formed a shallow lake. The southern portion of the property was somewhat rolling in its terrain as it drained and sloped toward Thorn Creek. An eighteen-hole golf course formed the central open space of the property, with open farmland, hedge rows, and minor tree copses spread through the rest. For the most part the property was an excellent choice for development. Ebenezer Howard, Clarence Stein, and Henry Wright could not have selected a better site for a "Garden City."

As Philip Klutznick prepared his family in Washington for their move to Chicago, the architects Loebl and Schlossman entered into a contract with Elbert Peets on May 14, 1946, for the planning, as it is written on the first drawings, of a "City in Rich and Bloom Townships." Peets was to cooperate with the architects in preparing tentative schedules for the housing and other construction. He was also to do all the necessary drafting to present a preliminary plan in accordance with the general program prepared by the architects. Loebl and Schlossman would supply additional drafting assistance as might be necessary, as well as a working space, secretarial service, supplies, and printing while Peets was in Chicago. Peets was contracted to spend not less than twenty working days in the execution of his work. It was also understood that the twenty days would be during the month of June 1946. For his work Peets would be paid the sum of $1,050 within thirty days after the completion of his work.[1]

The team, by June 11, had produced the first of a series of site plans that turned the Batcheldor property from a swampy lowland into a community of homes. The first plan, simply called "Study #1," left the existing four main roads—Monee, Sauk Trail, Western Avenue, and Twenty-sixth Street—in their historic locations. The primary retail center was placed directly on the western side of Western Avenue. Surrounding the retail center were over twenty-five hundred high-density row houses and apartments. The single-family lot areas were placed throughout the remainder of the property where the soil was high and dry enough to support the structures. Extensive open-space areas were left to contain the boggy ground.

The street circulation was simple. The primary residential collector street was a circular road that crossed Sauk Trail in two locations. This loop road fronted on the retail center and serviced a substantial number of the residential units, both for sale and rental. Short spurs extended out from this loop road to Monee, Twenty-sixth Street, US 30, and Western Avenue. Contained within this loop street was a large central park and lake that connected north toward the rail lines and southeast to the forest preserve.

This initial plan proposed six thousand residential units on 1,140 acres of residential development for a net density of 5.3 dwellings per acre. The plan included large custom lots, sixty-, fifty-, and forty-foot-wide lots, row houses of three types, and apartments. The plan was ambitious. It was redesigned and adjusted, throughout the month of June, to meet the conditions of the site. Trips were made to the property to check the plans against the site conditions. And, most important, the intent of the owners became better understood. The plan, by June 21,

TABLE 4.1
Town Plan Land-Use

Classification	No. dwelling units per acre	Acres	Density
Large Lots	200	260	0.8
60' Lots	1573	390	4.0
50' Lots	1372	273	5.1
40' Lots	325	45	7.2
Type A Rows	246	36	6.3
Type B Rows	252	23	10.9
Type C Rows	1032	74	13.5
Apartments	1000	40	25.0
Totals	6000	1140	5.3

Note: The first land-use estimates are based on the first plan, dated June 11, 1946.

depicted a surprising and very interesting proposal: having a train station on Western Avenue within the retail center. This station, serviced by a spur from the Illinois Central Railroad, would create a strong and positive center to the village, not unlike other towns along the Illinois Central rail line. The plan also began to show industrial development between the Elgin, Joliet & Eastern rail line and the Michigan Central tracks.

The plan also showed Western Avenue realigned and passing under the rail lines, reducing crossing conflicts. Western became a divided highway along its right-of-way within the village. Higher-residential densities still surrounded the shopping center and train station. Lower densities extended west and south from the loop road. An extensive system of greenways and lineal open-space areas connected to the forest preserve and the lowland areas. Many of these contained the drainage ways for the community. The June 21 plan also calculated the land uses into fairly accurate acreage amounts and percentages for the first time. These relative percentages represent the expected land uses within a total developed property of 2,560 acres (see tables 4.1 and 4.2).

TABLE 4.2
Schedule of Dwelling Types

Classification	No.	Acres	Average Density
Lots over 60'	200	260	0.8
60', 50', 40' Lots	3270	708	4.7
Row Units	1530	132	11.5
Apartments	1000	405	25.0
Totals	6000	1140	5.3

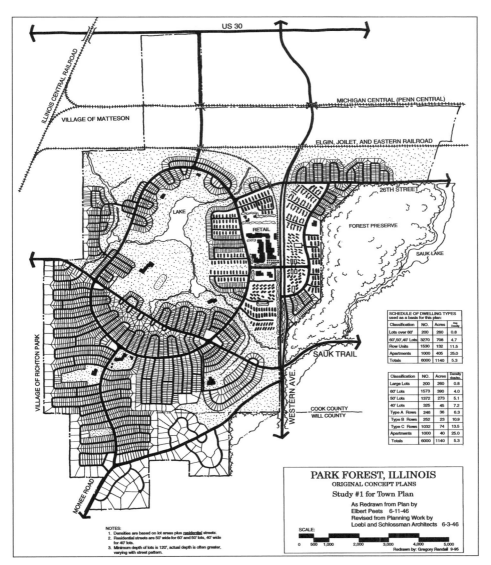

Fig. 20. The original study plan drawn by Elbert Peets on June 11, 1946, for the new town of Park Forest. This is the revised plan based on work by Loebl and Schlossman, architects, on June 3, 1946.

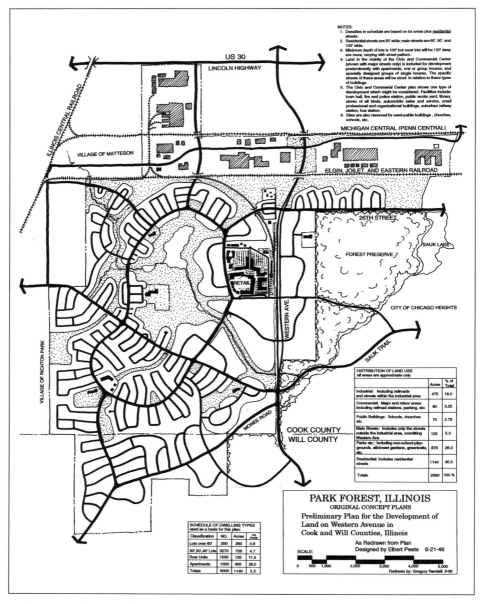

Fig. 21. Preliminary plan for the development of land on Western Avenue in Cook and Will Counties, Illinois. Redrawn from a plan designed by Elbert Peets on June 21, 1946.

The first two official meetings of American Community Builders (ACB) were held in July 1946. They were convened almost immediately upon Philip Klutznick's arrival from Washington. Klutznick believed in a strong organization; maintained schedules and weekly staff meetings were characteristic of his management style. As summer moved toward fall, the weekly meetings held at the architect's offices took on a fevered pace.

These midsummer meetings were concerned with the corporation's organization and the fundamental elements of the new community. A detailed business plan and prospectus were written defining the responsibilities of each corporate position. This was obviously the result of Klutznick's experiences with the government, and, true to his style, he would manage ACB based on this prospectus.[2] Some of the issues discussed were the town's name (which wouldn't be determined until the following spring), protective agreements for the transfer of properties, implementation of zoning and building codes, architectural review commissions, and maintenance agreements for the proper management of the property. The numbers of anticipated schools and churches were brought to the table for the first time. They also discussed the significant engineering problems they would encounter. Earlier spring visits to the property found large areas of the lowlands under water; these would have to be drained. Other construction problems also needed to be resolved, such as standardizing street widths and anticipating the costs of utilities. No final decisions were made, but these issues were placed on the long-term agenda for the first time.

It can be assumed that extensive and detailed discussions between the principals also occurred outside these formal meetings, because shortly after the July 25 meeting a written prospectus was presented describing the new community in detail. This document would prove to be quite accurate. In the prologue to the prospectus the objective of the community was simply stated: "The goal is to provide a fully integrated and livable community. The aim is to capture all the advantages of country living in an urban atmosphere within the economic reach of those who will live in the town. In its full realization a harmonious variety of homes will be blended into a simple but artistic abundantly green landscape."[3] This first prospectus called for five thousand or more dwelling units of all types. Twenty to 24 percent would be row houses or garden apartments, and the remaining buildings would be free-standing two- and three-bedroom homes. The home prices would be between seven thousand and ten thousand dollars, and the rents for the apartments would be equivalent to a seven thousand–dollar purchase price.

This conceptual description, based on both the early schematic plans and Klutznick's and Peets's beliefs, envisioned a totally new town. It anticipated the physical center of the community to be a large park providing for the community's "outdoor life." Public education facilities were projected to include three elementary schools and one high school. In keeping with the Garden City concept, distinct residential neighborhoods would revolve around these schools, providing additional open space and recreation facilities. Municipal services, including police, fire, and a town hall, were planned as a part of a retail center. Land was to be set aside for churches at little or no cost to the denomination, but ACB would maintain architectural approval of the church buildings.

The key to this community—what set it apart from most others being built at the time—was the inclusion of a centrally located shopping plaza. Projected purchasing power for the region was placed at thirteen to eighteen million dollars at 1945 incomes, and the shopping center, along with a smaller convenience center, would be designed to serve this market. From an in-house analysis that looked at existing retail conditions in other towns of the same size, ACB projected quantities of food, gasoline, and other services required. In all cases the builders felt their new community would not require as many facilities. They were sure they could manage the market better than an unlimited number of uncontrolled entrepreneurial businesses could. This planning resulted in the strict management of the type and number of stores needed to meet the community's needs. All stores would lease their space from ACB.

Lastly, the town plan provided a logical location for clean industrial development between the railroad tracks. The principals thought that the inclusion of an industrial zone would be essential for the development of a sound tax base for the town while also providing jobs for the residents. The team believed that time and market conditions would determine whether these commercial and industrial projections were sound.

The construction and operation of the utility systems became an important economic consideration during this early stage of the planning. ACB knew, from the beginning, that the revenues generated by these services would be essential to the financial success of the town. They outlined the establishment of a broad and inclusive utility system that would provide financial returns. Electric power would either be generated by a new ACB-owned plant or purchased wholesale and resold to the residents. Domestic water would be from their own wells, pumped and sold. The sewage treatment plant would also be operated by ACB. Steam production was even considered for distribution to industrial users. (The use of coal to heat residential units would be prohibited for health and cleanliness reasons.)

On August 1, at the third planning meeting held at Loebl and Schlossman's office, Charles Waldmann, director of utilities, conveyed Klutznick's instructions that the staff prepare a performance schedule that had construction starting in the spring of 1947. All plans and construction documents would need to be completed for bidding by February 15, 1947. The men also discussed possible use of the proposed expansion of Chicago Heights' sewer system but decided to avoid contacting Chicago Heights until a final plan for ACB's facilities was complete. Only the concept for the new ACB system would be discussed with regional authorities. The urgency of test borings for a confirmed source of water was also emphasized. Waldmann stressed water supply and sewage treatment as the most important elements of the planning. Without exception they agreed that the time schedule would be met.

Elbert Peets continued working on the community plans at the architect's offices and in his Washington office throughout the summer. Richard Bennett, who had just joined Loebl and Schlossman, was assigned to work closely with Peets during this stage of the planning. Bennett and Peets often visited the property together to understand the site and its particular conditions. The centrally located low area, they thought, if excavated, would make a great lake. Bennett recalled years later that: "[Peets] thought that water would be great, he could make it into a little lake or beautiful pond, but it couldn't be done. It would have cost a hell of a lot of money. Peets couldn't wait for the survey to see how deep it was; so he said if I would excuse him, he took his clothes off and went wading all over the thing with a tall stick to check the depth." The lake would never be built due to costs.[4]

While the planning of the site continued, detailed studies of the building types and construction methods were started by the architects. The September meetings also discussed the temporary facilities that were needed: warehousing, shop space, housing for personnel, on-site offices, and power and water. Analyses were performed for drainage, grading needs, utilities, and circulation. Construction techniques were investigated for the buildings including foundations, wall construction, exterior and interior finishes, and standardization of kitchens and bathrooms.

By the September 24 meeting surveyors were working on the site, identifying property lines and topographic features. Their work was proceeding under conceptual plans agreed to by ACB. A final plan would be approved in early October, after the surveyors had finished gathering their information. The architects had begun conceptual sketches for the shopping center and would present these in early November; plans for the first phase of residential units would also be presented then. Waldmann was preparing his utility plans and presentations for the mid-November meeting. Time was becoming critical to meet the February deadlines imposed by Klutznick.

One Sunday, in late fall, after the golf course had finally been closed, a group of the new owners and staff, including Carroll Sweet Jr., had one last picnic and round of golf. The fairways and greens had not been mowed for some time, so play was severely hampered. Sweet remembers that putting was almost impossible. This was the last round played at Indian Wood Country Club. Klutznick encouraged Sweet to sell anything from the property they couldn't use, and soon Sweet learned of a market for the sod from the golf course greens. Subsequently, the sod was sold, and American Community Builders picked up a few thousand dollars.[5]

Even with the continued financial support of the Manilow Company it was necessary to add two silent partners to the venture, each with $250,000 (in exchange for ACB preferred callable stock). One was the Chicago Title and Trust Company, which would receive the community's trust and title business, and the other was Henry Crown, whose firm, Material Services Corporation, would be the source for all the concrete needed for the job.[6]

Concurrent with the completion of final designs, Klutznick was in contact with potential store tenants for the shopping center. Their concerns had a significant effect on the planning. They wanted improved and assured access to the Matteson market to the west and Chicago Heights to the east and suggested that this could be done by extending a new street to connect to Main Street in Matteson and by expanding Twenty-sixth Street to four lanes and directly connecting this street to the retail center. Revised and alternative plans during the next four years would continue to show this connection as a four-lane limited access highway paralleling the tracks. These potential tenants also strongly emphasized that the shopping center be near the railroad terminal to take advantage of the higher traffic counts.

Peets, by early fall, had developed two detailed plans for the community. They were simply called plans A and B, each of which located the commercial center in a different area of the property. Plan A located the commercial center on the northerly side of the property, very close to the Elgin, Joliet & Eastern Railroad. This location would also have a commuter train station. The center would be adjacent to this station and sit directly on an extension of Twenty-sixth Street. This location also provided a convenient connection to Matteson to the west. Western Avenue was also relocated westward, passing under the two rail lines and extending south along a new route that eventually rejoined the existing right-of-way just north of Saulk Trail. Arguments for plan A held that this location would attract more customers from outside the community without increasing interior residential traffic. The location also had higher existing traffic counts and the possibility of lower utility costs due to its proximity to the industrial area and rail lines.

Plan B placed the commercial center nearer to the geographical center of the community and away from the earlier location directly on Western Avenue. Plan B's advantages were simple: it would be closer to the residents and, as a re-

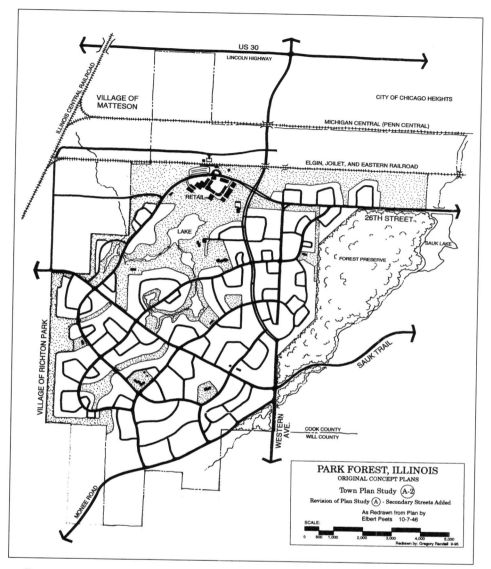

Fig. 22. Town Plan Study, A-2, Revision of Plan Study A, secondary streets added. Redrawn from a plan designed by Elbert Peets on October 7, 1946.

sult, decrease interior traffic. The internal site also would allow the planners more freedom to include additional stores. This new plan would be better than the earlier Western Avenue site and would not be as severely restricted in its eastward growth due to the highway. An unfortunate loss was the train station.

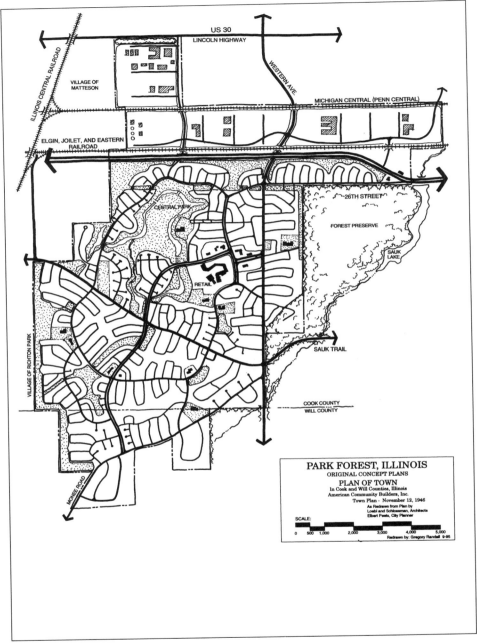

Fig. 23. Plan of town, in Cook and Will Counties, Illinois, drawn for American Community Builders, Inc. Redrawn from a plan by Peets and Loebl and Schlossman, November 12, 1946.

At the October 1 meeting, after extensive discussion, plan A was tentatively selected as the preferred plan. The builders and planners also agreed to a self-imposed condition that would later change the group's support for this plan: plan A would need the approval of Illinois Central Railroad. It became clear, after ACB held discussions with the Illinois Central Railroad, that the railroad would be involved in more of the planning of the community than just allowing the shopping center's location to be near the tracks. The railroad was found, as negotiations proceeded, to be intractably antagonistic toward the new community. Plan A would require an improved commuter station to handle the greater number of riders as well as impact the passenger flows downstream toward Chicago, but the railroad did not support the expansion. ACB also wanted to discuss extending a spur line from the existing Illinois Central Line into the town, but even on this the railroad was unsupportive. It became apparent that the Illinois Central would strongly resist even the expansion of the overall commuting business itself. The railroad saw this new community as a liability. Their answer was direct: "The State Commerce Commission regulations, under which we operate, require us to provide transportation for any person who presents himself to us for transportation. We are not required to do anything further to accommodate travelers or solicit new business." Their attitude was simple, "Freight makes money, passengers make trouble." There was nothing the development could do to dissuade the railroad from this attitude.[7]

In 1946 there was only a small parking area at the existing US 30 (Lincoln Highway) train station, but adjacent to this parking was a larger area that would hold over one hundred cars. Unfortunately, on the assessor's maps this area was noted as a cemetery. When members of the team visited the spot, it was obviously not a cemetery, only a large empty field. They found out that land speculators had buried a pauper on the property some forty years earlier; it had then been recorded as a cemetery and, as such, was not taxable. Since then the property had been owned without taxes having been paid on the land's real value. A few years later, after the community was well under way, the increased commuter volume forced the railroad to address the needs of the passengers. The parking area was expanded and a bus stop built. Due to the lack of support from the railroad, a great opportunity was lost which would have integrated regional transportation with the community's center. This integration would become one of the strongest tenets in modern community planning.[8]

The project had become public knowledge by mid-fall and Klutznick knew it was important that the an announcement be made to quiet speculative rumors. On October 28, at the Palmer House in downtown Chicago, Philip Klutznick announced the intention of American Community Builders to build a new housing community south of Chicago. The plan, as presented to the members of the press and other officials, would provide 2,800 single-family units, 650 twin houses for 1,300 families, 200 "town and country four-plex" homes for 700 families, and apartment buildings for 600 families. It would be divided into five contiguous residential neighborhoods. It would feature a central park, a major retail and commercial plaza, and supplementary neighborhood shopping centers. A town hall was proposed to house all municipal functions. Jerry Loebl added that the regimented and unimaginative appearance often criticized in large-scale, middle-income housing developments would be avoided by varying the sizes of dwelling units and differing site conditions. He also described the underlying architectural concept of the residential section as a "Park Block," a poorly coined term that tried to describe the parklike atmosphere. Klutznick estimated that the prices for the homes would start at about seven thousand dollars. The community received national press and was announced in the *New York Times* the next day.[9]

Concurrent with the Palmer House announcement, a small paragraph describing the village appeared in the October 26, 1946, *Collier's Magazine* article about the poor housing conditions that existed in Chicago. The paragraph was meant to show the reader how some efforts at improving the housing numbers in the Chicago region were under way; the article in which it appeared predated the public announcement by two days. For the next few years *Collier's* would be an excellent source of positive articles about the new town.

The results of the intransigence on the part of the Illinois Central quickly changed ACB's support to plan B, with its more centrally located commercial center. Peets's revised town plan, dated November 12, 1946, borrows heavily from his experiences with Greendale, Wisconsin. There is a definitive hierarchy of streets that reduce in size as the demands of traffic lessen. The plan uses the existing north-south alignment of Western Avenue as its spine. A gateway boulevard leads directly to the shopping center from the spine and then tees to a loop street that services all the neighborhoods. Interwoven within the plan are greenways and parks that help to separate the neighborhoods. The residential loop streets of the June plans were still evident. Extending east to west and paralleling the Elgin, Joliet & Eastern line was a divided Twenty-sixth Street that would directly connect Chicago Heights and Matteson.

The plan differs from the Greendale and Radburn plans in the basic residential street layout. Greendale's residential lots were laid out along dead-end courts that had a mixture of attached and detached rental units; Peets's town plan did not. The early November plan showed looped streets reinforcing the neighborhood concept with the traffic flow controlled by the street hierarchy. Through traffic stayed on the major avenues, local neighborhood traffic flowed to narrowing "residents only" streets. According to Peets: "Looped streets are preferable to dead-end streets. One reason is that they can be longer. The use of short cul-de-

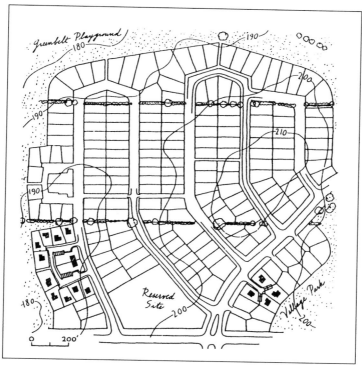

Fig. 24. Peets's concept for a loop street pattern that returns to primary road. *Source:* P. D. Spreiregen, *On the Art of Designing Cities.*

sacs so increases the expenditure for collector streets as to make it a heavy construction and maintenance burden—and the increase in the number of collector streets tends to cancel the safety and convenience that are the justification of the special residential street."[10]

Throughout his planning career, both with the government and as a private consultant, Peets was a fervent supporter of the "neighborhood" concept of planning. His writings before, during, and after World War II bear this out. In articles for the *American City* he described how military and defense housing sites with barracks-type facilities can be recreated as tight neighborhoods of resident-owned single homes with recreational facilities.[11]

In 1948 Peets responded to a charge that neighborhood planning was restrictive and possibly racist and as such the neighborhood concept itself was wrong. "It is incomprehensible to me," said Peets, "that any planner should wholly reject so plastic a planning motif as the neighborhood since that is equivalent to saying that no amount of imaginative adjustment in plan, composition, scope, or size

Fig. 25. Peets also developed a
questionable single-family
cluster concept, sharing a dead-
end cul-de-sac, with no driveway
access to the lot. *Source: P. D.
Spreiregen, On the Art of Designing Cities.*

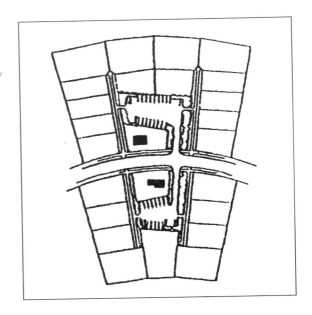

can make it a useful approach to the design of residential areas. Though well
aware that it is not often possible to assemble the elements of an ideally appointed
neighborhood, I find that the concept has value even when imperfectly realized
. . . I would say that the best 'substitute' for the neighborhood concept is newly
and more intelligently designed neighborhoods." He also challenged the thinking of civic leaders who drafted subdivision codes and zoning laws to thwart "ex-
ploiters" who chopped up farms into thirty-foot lots improved with only corner
stakes and cinder sidewalks. To these civic leaders, who demanded wider and
wider streets, larger lots, and substantial improvements, Peets answered, "These
measures quite successfully keep out the predacious subdivider, but unfortunately they also keep out everything except the American street."

Postwar suburbs did not have the charm of Radburn's courts and parks or the
Greenbelt's shady superblock. Radburn's and Greenbelt's plans contained two
practical objectives that Peets employed in his studies for Greendale, Wisconsin.
These objectives were applied to ACB's plan as well: first, to spend as little as possible on streets and utilities and, second, to hold down the municipal operating
costs. For Greendale it was the high tax rate that forced this concern. For ACB it
was the simple fact that they, the builders, would be paying for the management
and operations for the first few years (until incorporation), and these costs reduced the meager profits (if any) that the first years would produce.

During the term of his work in Park Forest, Peets would also be rehired as a
consultant by the U.S. Public Housing Administration to plan for the enlarge-

ment of the community at Greendale, Wisconsin. The revised Greendale plan covered almost five square miles and reflected many of the elements of ACB's conceptual community plan of November 1947. It is noteworthy that both plans, in Peets's words, "stress a union of a simple basic structure with emphatic modulation and variety in its component (i.e., neighborhood) parts."

The planning for the ACB community also showed Peets's affinity for the "solar" house—not the current idea of a solar house, with heating and sun orientation. Peets called the planning solar because the "center of interest is the lot rather than the house. The lot is considered to be one of a series of lots, so that a group of families may cooperatively enjoy the full advantage of sunlight orientation." The results of his thinking are evident in the November 12, 1946, plan. A considerable number of lots and streets are arranged north-south, where they can benefit from the "superior" light effects of this orientation.[12] The November 12, 1946, Town Plan shows a community of almost all single-family homes. Significant changes were to occur within two months, however, which would forever change the community and its future.

Carroll Sweet Jr., in one of his earliest assignments, investigated the zoning for the property. This complicated search was required so that the planners would be able to process the plats (plans) in accordance with the existing county zoning or understand what changes would be required so as to proceed. The central and largest portion of the property was in unincorporated Cook County, the southern portion was in Will County, and an easterly piece between the railroads was in the city of Chicago Heights. Sweet found that the Chicago Heights portion—which was out of the initial planning area—was zoned "industrial." That existing zoning and the fact that the Will County portion was too remote for the early phases of the community's development only left the Cook County parcels available for the initial development. Unfortunately, these parcels were zoned for "rural residential" of at least one-acre lots or larger. This rural zoning required individual water wells and septic sewer systems. The proposed plan showed at least 3.5 lots per acre, a normal city density, and would have municipal water and sewer service to each home. The existing Cook County zoning would not permit the new town to be built according to the plan. Sweet found only one provision within the ordinance which might allow some flexibility, and that was for multifamily dwellings.

The community, as planned, would require variances or amendments to the existing zoning to be built. Maintaining a low profile was still an important part of the planning process, and to start requesting zoning changes (with the resultant publicity) might increase land prices as well as spur speculation. The greatest impact would be on the schedule. To change the zoning or file for variances would take months, time that ACB felt they did not have.

The following Monday—three days after Sweet told Klutznick of his findings about the properties' zoning—Klutznick arrived at American Community Builder's office, smiling and a bit jaunty. According to Sweet, Klutznick had been thinking about the problem all weekend, when suddenly he had the solution. The project would become a rental community in its first phase, solving two problems. First, it would allow them to qualify for the FHA section 608 loan guarantee program, and, more important, it would meet the current demands of the real market: rental housing.[13]

The Federal Housing Administration (FHA) had been created by the National Housing Act of 1934 to improve and modernize housing and businesses. It was also intended to stimulate owner-occupied small-home construction as well as rental home construction built by corporations. In addition it was to promote sound private financing, through federal guarantees, to help stabilize the mortgage market and to reduce the chaos in financial institutions. Financial and building institutions had been in disastrous condition after the 1929 financial collapse and resulting depression. It had been the Roosevelt Administration's goal, through one sweep of a political sword, to help all of these institutions.

The most important role of the FHA was to guarantee the loans granted by private institutions for housing developments. These developments must meet the criteria not only of the lending institution but the standards of the FHA as well. This elaborate appraisal procedure measured the borrower's income, the physical condition of the property, neighborhood characteristics, and the property's location in the metropolis; urban planning and land-use controls, deed restrictions, and market demand all entered into the evaluation. In this regard, then, the federal government was able to exert a tremendous degree of control over residential growth across the country.

Community builders welcomed the role and influence provided by the FHA. They felt that they would be better served by this agency than they were currently being served by local planning commissions, for two reasons: first, this form of government help would significantly widen the ongoing weak market for property development and sales; and, second, the FHA was largely run by members of the real estate and banking industries.[14]

Klutznick, by proposing rental units in the first phases of the community, was acknowledging the problems the group would soon face in acquiring financing for the town. With federal guarantees, financing would be easier to get. In addition, Klutznick was well aware of the impact and assistance that the FHA could have for a multifamily community. Through the use of a regulation called the "conditional commitment" Klutznick would be able to secure, after his community met FHA underwriting standards, guarantees from the government which protected the investment of his various lenders. These guarantees applied to any qualified builder whether they built one dwelling or thousands and whether these were for sale or rent. The greatest impact came from FHA commitments to large-scale builders of new residential subdivisions.

Soon after its formation the FHA published four sets of standards and guidelines—*Subdivision Development* (1935), *Planning Neighborhoods for Small Houses* (1936), *Planning Profitable Neighborhoods* (1938), and *Successful Subdivisions* (1940)[15]—which were to have profound impacts on community planning for fifty years. In his book *The Rise of Community Builders* Marc A. Weiss explains the primary reason for the FHA's success.

> The genius of the FHA system and its popularity with lenders, borrowers, builders, and subdivision developers is that mortgage insurance fit the American image of voluntarism. Unlike direct government police power regulations, FHA always appeared to be noncoercive to the private sector . . . Property owners and real estate entrepreneurs viewed FHA rules and regulations as similar to deed restrictions—private contracts which were freely entered into by willing parties—rather than as similar to zoning laws, which were sometimes seen as infringing on constitutional liberties.[16]

Weiss also quotes landscape architect S. Herbert Hare, who designed the Country Club District in Kansas City for J. C. Nichols and summarized in 1938 the effectiveness of FHA's approach to guiding subdivision development and urban land use:

> While this method of control is indirect, it has probably been more effective in many cases than the strictest regulations of local governmental units because it has established an advantage or a disadvantage in relation to other properties for conformance or nonconformance with the requirements, and at the same time has had no element of compulsion . . . The greatest value of the Federal Housing Administration regulations has been in raising the standards of design in districts for less expensive houses.[17]

Five years earlier, just prior to the start of the war, an exciting apartment community admired greatly by Klutznick had been completed, Baldwin Hills Village. The village was located on an eighty-acre tract of flat land on what was the southern end of Los Angeles in 1938. Planned and built as an apartment complex according to many of the tenets and concepts of Radburn and Greenbelt, Baldwin Hills may be the best of the prewar planned communities. Clarence Stein acted as consulting architect and planner to the builders.

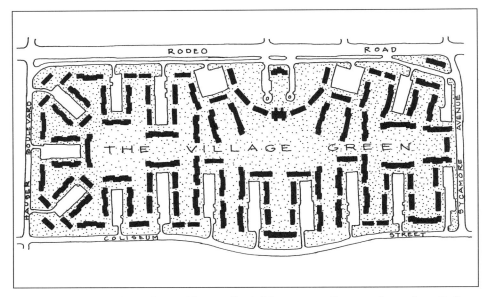

Fig. 26. Simplified site plan, Baldwin Hills, California, 1941. *Source:* redrawn from C. S. Stein, *Toward New Towns for America.*

After a difficult three-year planning process and with the help of the FHA and the Reconstruction Finance Corporation to obtain financing, Baldwin Hills Village project began construction in 1941. Pearl Harbor closely followed the arrival of the first of the 627 tenants. The apartment units were built within a large superblock complex subdivided into three areas that focused on their own spacious garden courtyard. The apartments were contained within low multiple-unit structures that enclosed a parking court on one side and narrow pedestrian greenway on the other.

Baldwin Hills' garden courts are a notable improvement on Radburn's narrow pathways that led to a central park. The pedestrian greenways insure privacy while interconnecting the community. No cross-streets cut the block apart. Heavily landscaped pedestrian walks interconnect the apartments within the village. The units themselves are simple stucco structures with flattish roofs in pastel colors typical of southern California. Most of the buildings are two stories varying from three to six apartments in length. A few have a one-story "bungalow" unit on the end, and there are nine short one-story buildings with three units each.[18]

The layout is symmetrical and balanced; on the ground the symmetry is not as noticeable as when viewed in the plan. The spaces tend to flow in and out while at the same time narrowing and expanding. There is not the sense of rigid-

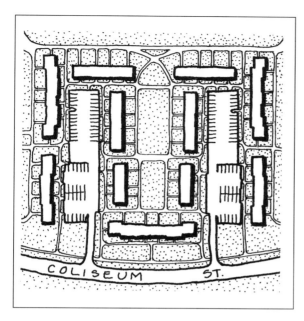

Fig. 27. Court detail plan,
Baldwin Hills, California, 1941.
Source: redrawn from C. S.
Stein, *Toward New Towns for
America.*

ity which might be expected when viewing the plan. The village is ordered without being pompous or repetitive. The planting scheme also supports the layout
out of the buildings and helps to define the spaces.

Two concepts separate Baldwin Hills from earlier planned communities.
The first is that it focused on the problem of the automobile and its relationship
to the residents and their homes. Second, it challenged the speculative builders
who had gridded out the Los Angeles basin in an effort to maximize lots and marketing of properties. Baldwin Hills successfully induced the planning board to accept the superblock concept, over the objections of the city engineers. The car
was tamed and managed within the parking court; the village does not suffer its
intrusion. Lewis Mumford said of Baldwin Hills Village: "Here every part of the
design speaks the same robust vernacular: simple, direct, intelligible. I know of
no other recent community that lends itself so fully to strict scrutiny, simply because every aspect of its physical development has been thought through."[19]

Klutznick understood the assistance that the FHA programs made in the success of Baldwin Hills. In the case of Park Forest, however, the housing programs
as defined by the FHA limited guarantees to five million dollars per mortgage.
ACB's first phase would exceed that amount by an estimated twenty-two million
dollars. Acquiring FHA guarantees would be impossible for this total amount.
The solution turned out to be rather simple. The planners divided the first phase

of the community, the rentals, into nine separately incorporated areas. Each area would have its own mortgage, and each would be guaranteed within the financial limits imposed by the FHA.

Klutznick was pleased with the decision to change the project's direction; this would resolve a number of his concerns. "Study of such projects as Radburn and the Greentowns," he would later say, "indicated that if we wanted to create a town, we had to bring a sufficient population into the area right away or else we might never achieve our objective. The only way we could visualize this was with rental housing." Klutznick's belief in Baldwin Hills and the type of housing which it championed and the Greenbelt communities and their open spaces would be melded together in this new town.

His concern about inflation was also an important factor in deciding for rental housing. "We were afraid of the sales market," he said. "As a matter of fact, this was no time to build rental housing either. But we think we fall into a different category. To profit on rental housing is secondary to our central concept of building an integrated (i.e., housing and commercial) town with commercial and industrial advantages and increased values abutting land for residential uses." Klutznick was simply stating that the rental units would help to support the commercial areas and their future sales and profits while also creating a stable and attractive community. A successful community would then encourage future sales of the single-family homes, and the renters would become potential buyers.

Loebl and Schlossman's office and Peets and Bennett quickly began redesigning the November plan for rental units. Two issues were important: the plan's layout and the ability to mass-produce affordable buildings. The core area of the plan, straddling Western Avenue, was selected for the rental properties. This area, without having to build new roads, already had good access from Western Avenue, and the units would support the central location of the shopping center. In addition, the utility runs (especially sewage) would be shorter.

The revised plan arranged the apartment buildings around a parking court. These individual courts were then grouped into superblocks. The final design had 3,010 rental units, arranged in 600 buildings that were divided into 204 one-bedroom, 2,104 two-bedroom, and 702 three-bedroom apartments. All the buildings were two-story frame structures over a basement that contained additional storage space and a gas heater. Exterior treatments varied from brick facing to wood siding. The buildings ranged in size from two-unit duplexes to eight-unit "row house" configurations. The builder called them townhomes to distance themselves from that other, "inner-city" term. There were also four- and six-unit layouts. The three-bedroom apartments were paired as duplexes and were also used as end units. There were single-story one-bedroom end units that were "stacked" over an identical ground floor plan.

Some of the original study plans for the apartments considered three-story walkups requiring common stairways, janitorial services, and other extraneous expenses. Since the project's goal was to achieve a comparatively low rental rate, this "urban" form was abandoned due to the extra maintenance costs it created. According to Richard Bennett, FHA funding would be difficult for anything other than the tried and true, the row house. Row houses were being built all over the Chicago area after the war, but in Bennett's opinion they looked cheap and like subsidized housing. Why did they look that way? According to Bennett, it was "because the ends always look cut off. They're sliced like a sausage. We got the idea that if we styled the ends it wouldn't look like row houses. We designed a whole lot of end units and sometimes there'd be bay windows and sometimes it would be a door on that side. If you go to Park Forest, really it doesn't look too much like row houses because when you see the ends it looks like one house." The majority of the units were arranged in this courtyard configuration, but about two hundred duplexes were arranged along secondary streets and cul-de-sacs. This configuration would allow these duplex units, at a later date, to be platted and sold separately.

The courtyards were laid out with the kitchen side of the units facing the parking court. The front doors, which entered directly into the living rooms, faced landscaped "malls," or open-space areas between the courtyards or the street. Bennett was not happy with this solution as it was being built; there was almost no connection from the parking court to the front door of the unit, and everyone was directed to the kitchen door. He made such a fuss that Klutznick took a survey of the current residents, who thought everything was fine, and, after Klutznick's wife said she liked it, the designs remained as designed and built. The interior courtyard contained the parking for the apartment—about one space per unit—and a fenced play area for the children. The plans were similar to Baldwin Hills but were far less symmetrical and ordered. There was a looseness about the layout. All apartment structures were planned to be set back a minimum of 120 feet from the primary streets, creating well-landscaped corridors throughout the village.[20]

Peets worked under the assumption that the financial conditions would make the completion of the construction difficult. To this end he tried to keep costs down. A good example of this is the connection of many of the courtyards directly to Western Avenue, thus reducing road construction costs. He also reduced street widths wherever he could. He also tried, unsuccessfully, to build a median into Western Avenue. This was not done due to its cost and because it was not owned by ACB but the county.

It was at this time that the shopping center was formally pushed west away from Western Avenue, as shown in plan B. This placed the plaza more toward the

Fig. 28. Apartment plan as redesigned by Loebl, Schlossman, and Bennett, with Peets—a reflection of the "superblock" concept of Sunnyside. *Source:* Cornell University Archives.

center of the community, but it also freed up more land directly on Western Avenue for the rental units. This helped to keep costs down by the reduction of infrastructure costs, especially the cost of roads.

A plan, dated November 4, 1947, clearly shows the final plan of the apartments. This plan also shows an extensive central park and wetland to the west. Twenty-sixth Street is shown extending west from its existing right-of-way in Chicago Heights and curving south to meet up with Sauk Trail.

Fig. 29. By the fall of 1947 the first plans integrating the detached single-family homes with the apartments were begun. *Source:* detail from a redrawing of a plan by Loebl, Schlossman, and Bennett, November 4, 1947.

The country's economic picture by late fall of 1946 had brightened considerably, but there was still a cloud on the horizon, especially the political horizon. In November, only a few days after the Palmer House announcement of the Town Plan, the Republicans swept both houses for the first time since the Depression. Chicago's Democratic "machine" was defeated. The *Chicago Tribune* said that it was the greatest victory for the country since Appomattox. The New

Deal, Klutznick's Democratic home, had been put to rout. Housing issues within the new Congress had a friend, however, in Republican Robert A. Taft, son of President William Howard Taft. Taft was selected to share the power of the head of the Senate with Arthur Vandenburg. Robert Taft was extremely conservative, incorruptible, and independent, yet his stands on some social issues, especially education, health, and housing, were at odds with the old guard of his party.[21]

For three years an ongoing battle had raged in Congress on the merits of the Wagner-Taft-Ellender Housing Bill. Having been resubmitted to the Senate in March 1947—for the third time in less than three years—the general housing bill was designed to establish a permanent housing program that was directed to provide "a decent home and a suitable living environment for every American family." Influential members of both the Congress and the Senate could not support such an omnibus bill, which would return significant funds to the cities for public housing and slum clearance with minimal government oversight. Other members were trying to load the bill with every social program they could think of. It included protection from loss of property due to unemployment, private financing aids to low- and middle-income families, and special considerations for the callow prefabrication industry. Much of the debate focused on public housing. The United States Savings and Loan League, at its annual convention, adopted the following resolution: "Socialized housing has no place in a society where private ownership of real estate is expected to flourish . . . because the Wagner-Ellender-Taft Bill was largely directed toward expanding the socialized housing program, we recommend continued opposition to this measure." Klutznick had gone on record as supporting the bill and publicly spoke on its behalf. It would be two more years before an adequate housing bill would be passed.[22]

The country was beginning to prosper. Food production was at its highest ever. Incomes were high, and unemployment was low. Truman sang the praises of the country in his January 1947 State of the Union message and asked for programs for mental health, child care, and hospital construction. Most important, he asked for an "aggressive" program of home construction.[23]

By January 1947 the eight-month-old federal housing program of Wilson W. Wyatt's was a disappointment, if not a disaster. The idea to construct housing as a wartime type of program failed in two simple respects: the United States was not at war, and the people would not behave anymore as if it were. The home building industry had jumped in and started new home construction at a frantic rate. Housing was under way in quantities only dreamed of two years earlier, and the supply of some building materials jumped to highs that met or exceeded levels of 1929. Unfortunately, the proverbial "for the want of a nail the war was lost" would almost break the back of the resurrection. Some materials were plentiful, but, more important, others were scarce or unavailable. Throughout the country rows of houses stood unfinished due to the lack of electrical boxes, pipe fittings, plumbing fixtures, and even water pipes. The darling of Wyatt, the prefabricated housing industry, was accused of hoarding materials with government support. Escalating costs increased rents well beyond the promised forty to fifty dollar a month level.

Wyatt's plans called for specific numbers of housing units to be built. In almost all cases these numbers were never met. As an example, Detroit's need was determined to be fifty thousand new homes, and yet only three thousand completions were anticipated by the end of 1946. This was a pattern found across the country, where less then 10 percent of the need was being met in most of the largest urban areas. It would be many months before the impact of the dropping of price controls on November 10, 1946, would bear fruit.[24]

Home builders in 1947 would try to comply with Truman's request. The government assisted by consolidating the numerous federal housing agencies into the Housing and Home Finance Agency. Under the impetus supplied by this agency and the increasing availability of building materials, home production increased but not to levels that would meet the demand. Special housing surveys were conducted by the Bureau of the Census in 108 selected localities which discovered that more than six million low-income urban families were living in slums and other types of housing that were unsafe, hazardous, and in poor quality. In addition, the number of couples who were living "doubled up" was almost a million more than in 1940. The survey also found that most people still could not afford to own a home of their own, and, what is more important, they could not find quality rental apartments for themselves and their young families.

After American Community Builders decided to transform the community's direction, the first approval steps would be through the FHA. This process required numerous forms to be completed and lengthy approval times. And at the top of the first forms was a line that required a name for the community. The public relations firm of Bozell and Jacobs could only come up with names that were vaguely funeral, and with such names the village sounded more like a cemetery than a thriving community of young families. In fact, a fairly lengthy discussion was held during the meeting of October 8, 1946, in which the name "Cando," a phrase well-known to the veteran community, was discussed. It was decided that unless the public opinion samples showed otherwise that name would be discarded. Since the community was the brainchild of Carroll Sweet Jr.'s father, it was all the more important to him that the name be just right.

The problem of the name was put on the back burner for a while to deal with more pressing issues. One day, as Carroll Sweet Jr. relates it, Klutznick called Hart Perry, Israel Rafkind, and Sweet into his office. "We're going to make our FHA application tomorrow morning and we have to have a name for our project before that," Klutznick said. "Will you three please study this matter this afternoon and come up with an answer by 5 o'clock?" The three decided to go to the Chicago Public Library, undertake individual research, and then get back together about 4:15 to compare notes. When they rejoined, nothing seemed to fit, they had hundreds of names, but none seemed to work. Walking back to the office, they continued their discussion. A remark made Sweet comment, "You know, just because there's already a Forest Park doesn't mean there can't be a Park Forest." Hart hesitated a moment and said, "Park Forest, Park Forest, that doesn't sound too bad." Rafkind said, "No, in fact that sounds pretty good."

"Any luck?" Klutznick asked when they returned. The name was repeated. Phil rolled the name about and then asked Nate Manilow to come in. Nate liked the name and the sound of it. From that moment on the project would be called "Park Forest." It was also decided that, when the community was incorporated by the new residents, they would have a chance to pick a name they liked. But for now and for the government forms Park Forest was it. Based on the available record this decision was made between February 25 and 27, 1947.[25]

Collier's Magazine, in an article printed in February 1948, reaffirms that the name Park Forest was temporary, yet no other alternative was mentioned. Even eighteen months after the name had been selected there was still a lack of conviction by ACB concerning the name. The residents' decision on the name would not be made until November 28, 1948.[26]

Years later Norman Schlossman recalled that Al Chase, the real estate writer for the *Tribune*, wanted to know what the name of the village was to be. He said: "Well, I hope one thing. I hope they don't call it a park. They've got all these forests and all these parks that you hear, like Highland Park and I hope they don't call it a forest, like Lake Forest, and all this." In June 1950 Elbert Peets, in a letter to Walter H. Blucher, the executive director of the American Society of Planning Officials, simply stated, "I hate the name—they chose it while I was in Puerto Rico and insisted that it was just—temporary."[27]

Several of the main village streets were identified with existing features: Indianwood Boulevard passed through where the old golf course was, Lakewood Boulevard passed the peat bog that was hoped to someday become a lake, and Orchard Drive bisected an orchard. Victory Boulevard was named for the final event of the war that led to the creation of the community.

The primary streets were identified for the areas of the FHA guarantee program, A through J. The major street's for each area corresponded to that letter: Area A had Ash Street, Area E had Elm Street, and Area H had a Hemlock Street, and so on. The streets within the areas themselves were named for Illinois residents who had received the Congressional Medal of Honor during the war. After obtaining a list of these heroes, the men found more names then they could use and unfortunately had to reduce the number of possibilities. Carroll Sweet Jr. compiled the list and then asked for permission from the recipients or their next of kin to use their names throughout the village. This honor role of war heroes extended throughout the apartment complex.[28]

The team contacted the top official in Chicago for the U.S. Post Office to get "expert" advice on the numbering of the houses within the village. Showing him a map of the planned village and asking him which side of the curving streets should be odd or even numbers and from what end should the numbers start, the man answered in all seriousness, "Very simple, just straighten out those streets, make 'em all go east and west or north and south, as they do in Chicago." Sweet thanked him for his advice and left, realizing that a solution would not come from the post office. The numbering was resolved with minimal difficulty. ACB numbered the houses as it saw fit.[29]

The plans for apartment portion of Park Forest were finally completed and submitted to the FHA for their review and approval in mid-March 1947. Carroll Sweet Jr. and Hart Perry were appointed titular president and secretary, respectively, for each of the nine corporations that the initial construction phase was divided into. These appointments saved the time and writing hands of Klutznick and Manilow but not those of the Sweet and Perry. Every page and document submitted to the FHA had to be initialed or signed by these "interim" officers. There were an uncountable number of documents. It took two days of signing to complete the task. Sweet said to his wife, LaNe, after returning from this autograph session, "I have just (personally) signed for $27.5 million in mortgages, I have no idea how we'd ever pay them off if the project flopped."

TABLE 4.3
Loan Commitment Schedule

Area	No. of Rental Units	Mortgage ($)	Insurance Co.	Monthly Mortgage Payments ($)
A	290	2,634,600	N.Y. Life	12,075.25
B	370	3,444,200	N.Y. Life	15,785.92
C	260	2,247,300	N.Y. Life	10,300.12
D	384	3,616,300	Sun Life	16,574.71
E	404	3,756,300	N.W. Mutual	17,216.37
F	220	1,810,900	Sun Life	8,299.96
G	190	1,653,000	N.W. Mutual	7,576.25
H	502	4,498,500	N.Y. Life	20,618.12
J	390	3,551,200	N.W. Mutual	16,276.33
	3,010	27,212,300		124,723.03

A significant and costly problem occurred in midsummer: an FHA official got "cold feet." The community was by far the largest to ever receive FHA commitments, and someone, somewhere within the FHA bureaucracy, was concerned. They were worried about the size of the guarantees, the complexity of the multiple corporations, and the friendships that Klutznick had with many of the officials within the government. The appearance that a "special favor" might be involved was a possible factor. As a result, the FHA ordered a complete review of all the documents. This review delayed the approval by two months and cost ACB the construction season of 1947.[30]

The loss of the 1947 building season was a great setback to ACB, but finally, in September 1947, after countless revisions, the FHA approved the housing scheme. According to E. J. Kelly, director of the Chicago office, this was the largest FHA commitment to a single project in the history of the agency. The nine corporations that were formed to build the apartments totaled almost twenty-eight million dollars in guarantees. The nine 4 percent mortgages, after negotiations with ACB, were assumed by the New York Life Insurance Co., Northwestern Mutual, and the Sun Life Assurance Co. of Canada. (Table 4.3 shows the various commitments and their loan values.)[31]

On a gray morning, October 28, 1947, exactly one year after the announcement at the Palmer House, a yellow bulldozer pushed and cut the first dark clay of the Batcheldor property. The new village of Park Forest had begun.

CHAPTER FIVE

The Construction

A decent standard of housing for all is one of the irreducible obligations of modern civilization. The people of the United States, so far ahead in wealth and production capacity, deserve to be the best housed in the world. We must begin to meet that challenge at once.
    —Harry S. Truman, *Message to Congress*, September 6, 1945

IN 1946 there were significant and paralyzing shortages in many building materials such as lumber, bricks, structural clay tiles, clay sewer pipes, concrete blocks, gypsum board, the wood used for lath and cast-iron soil pipe and drain lines. Almost all of these shortages were a result of a lack of manpower and facilities. Men were still in the armed forces and were untrained for these manufacturing jobs, and many plants had not been converted to the demands of peacetime production. Workers were not going back to their family homes and neighborhoods, and this translated into a temporary yet critical lack of workers in the older traditional manufacturing regions. An additional factor was the low wages that these unskilled jobs paid. Many vets, better educated and in school under the GI Bill, would not accept a low-paying brick or lath making job. Fortuntely, by 1948 the country was beginning to meet the demand for building materials. Materials were becoming available, albeit at higher prices, and were less of a problem than in 1947. It was this increasing availability of construction materials that permitted Park Forest to move ahead.

The planning and design of the Park Forest utility systems continued throughout the summer of 1947. By early December the first water well had been drilled about a quarter-mile to the west of the future water treatment site. Good, but very hard, water was tapped exactly at the aquifer elevation Charles Waldmann had expected. Waldmann commented to Carroll Sweet Jr. one day, while they watched the water flow from the well, "that's worth more to us than gold. Without it we have no project."[1]

It was determined from the beginning that Park Forest would have its own sanitary system. The treatment facility was initially to be located at the south end of the property on the east side of Western Avenue. The treated effluent would then flow into Thorn Creek. ACB would then meet all state water quality levels, obligations, and requirements—unfortunately, the State of Illinois had different ideas about their plans.

Northeast of Park Forest was the Bloom Township Sanitary District, which had a facility on the north side of Chicago Heights, also on Thorn Creek, which served the city and a few other areas. The state, to no avail, had been trying for years to upgrade the quality of the plant's management. The plant had often been cited for polluting the creek, and the state blamed this on the qualifications of the plant staff; the district claimed that they could not afford to hire a truly professional superintendent. The state saw this as an opportunity to push Park Forest into the role of savior. Park Forest, if included, would almost double the income of the sanitary district. The state told Park Forest to see if it was possible to re-design the collector system to use the existing Bloom facility and to then annex themselves to the district. This would avoid the potential problem of two marginal facilities and would improve the overall quality of the existing Bloom treatment plant.

ACB and Waldmann determined they could build a thirty-six-inch sewage interceptor pipe from the north end of the property east, between the railroad lines, to Thorn Creek. It would then parallel the creek to the treatment facility. Since the district had no uncommitted funds, ACB would pay for the installation then deed it to the district. American Community Builders, from the beginning, assumed that most of the assets it would build for the community would eventually be sold back to the village. It was from this sale that they would get their money back. To Klutznick and the other directors' credit, they believed that what was good for the community would ultimately be good for them. They followed the state's recommendations, and after a local referendum on January 13, 1947, they joined the Bloom Township Sanitary District. ACB then allocated the estimated quarter-million dollars that the interceptor would cost and then built it.[2]

Goals for the community's utility planning were safety, cleanliness, and cost-effectiveness. Up until this time almost all electrical service to homes and commercial users was supplied from poles and above-ground wires. ACB planned that all service lines would be buried underground in order to eliminate the unsightly overhead lines and the hazard and unreliability they caused. Unfortunately, later, when most of the single-family homes were built, ACB's home construction firm, Park Forest Homes, Inc., reverted to poles at the rear of the lots to save money. Cleanliness would be promoted by the elimination of the delivery, storage, and use of oil or coal fuel throughout the community. Luckily, a major natural gas line crossed the property and was tapped to be the primary fuel used for heating, cooking, water heating, and refrigeration.[3]

The engineering designs for Park Forest, subdivision plats, grading, streets, and utilities were being done by Consoer, Townsend and Associates, a large engineering company located on the near North Side of Chicago. The project engineer, Joe Schudt, was put in charge. Later, as the magnitude of the work required extensive on-site engineering, Schudt set up his own engineering firm in an old farmhouse on the property and worked almost exclusively for ACB.[4]

The wells that Charles Waldmann bored into the earth were drilled into the Silurian dolomite formation that underlaid the village. Cracked and fissured, this underlying bedrock had stored its water for millions of years, and, as Chicago Heights and Matteson found in their wells, though it is a reliable source, it contains extremely high levels of dissolved minerals and iron. If it were not "softened," this untreated water would result in significant problems with pipes and appliances; a simple chemical reaction brought about by processing the water with a lime-soda ash mixture removed these minerals, leaving relatively pure water. The treatment facility was built west of Western Avenue along the Elgin, Joliet & Eastern rail line.

For American Community Builders and the new residents it was the overburden of clays which was to provide annoyances, ordeals, and expenses far beyond what they could have imagined. The first hint of potential trouble came as ACB began to remove the upper soil layers. These layers, a gray-black clay with a high content of organic material, needed to be stripped to provide a more stable base for the parking areas, streets, and walks. Bulldozers were used to excavate apartment basements. Successive layers were peeled and sliced away by heavy equipment and then pushed into large, ever-increasing piles of lighter colored gray-brown clay. Later the excavated material would be respread before replacing the blacker topsoil in the landscaped areas. The successive stripping, moving, and replacing compressed the already dense clay material and eventually sealed the ground. If adequate gradients and surface drainage catchments were not constructed, the rainwater could not quickly move out of the area. The rainwater would only be able to drain into the lowest spots, typically the apartments' basements. These basements were cut into the ancient subsurface layers of gravels and soils, exposing them, and this cutting allowed water to migrate through these porous layers into the excavations. Even during this early stage of the site work the accumulation of water began to be a serious problem.

The first rental buildings—built on the east side of Western Avenue, south of Twenty-sixth Street—were begun very soon after the October 28, 1947, groundbreaking. Units directly north across Twenty-sixth Street were started soon after. ACB's cash flow calculations were totally dependent on the prompt completion of the rental units, their occupancy, and the payment of rents. Coordinated scheduling was an absolute necessity. The construction site was subdivided into eleven superblocks, within which there were smaller residential groups, or courts.

Fig. 30. The"superblock" concept of apartment development is obvious in this view of the community under construction in the early 1950s. *Source:* courtesy of Park Forest Public Library.

The phases of the construction within those superblocks were then grouped into major job assemblages. First came the installation of underground utilities, then foundations, followed by framing and exterior finish. The goal was to weatherproof the structure as soon as possible to allow the interior crews to begin their work. The building operation moved like an assembly line and, with the exception of wartime military housing, may have been the first time that such a system was employed to build that much housing.

The earliest construction schedules were established to allow ACB to draw against the FHA-insured mortgages and hopefully stay ahead of the looming specter of inflation. Twenty to twenty-four foundations were begun each working day. Every operation throughout the construction process was scheduled, and every subsequent building operation, including occupancy, was based on the completion of the basement.

The foundations were built with a combination of poured concrete floors and precast interlocking wall panels to reduce crews and field demands. The concrete plant, located near the railroad and water treatment plant, used the rail

Fig. 31. By August 1948 the first apartments were ready for occupancy, even before land-scaping was completed. *Source:* courtesy of Park Forest Public Library.

line for cement, sand, and gravel deliveries. This location also had ready access to Western Avenue. The concrete was batched at the plant for either on-site placement or use in precast concrete panels. Porches, door stoops, and foundation walls were cast in large molds and then stockpiled. The finished pieces were then transported to the apartment sites.

After bulldozing out the basement, each apartment had its floor poured with a built-up beam or curb surrounding the slab. This edge was designed with a slot to permit the placement of the precast wall panels, which were cemented in place. Window locations had been cast into the panels. These "window wells," with their steel casement windows, were below the finished elevations of the ground outside the basement. Outside, in front of the window, a half round steel bulkhead was secured to the building to allow light to reach the window. Drain rock was placed in the bottom of the well.

The winter of 1947-48 accomplished little in raising the apartment structures because concrete could not be poured during the cold midwestern winter, but ACB was able to precut and stockpile lumber for the spring. A 20,000 square foot sawmill was assembled on the site near to the concrete plant, and, when it was warm enough, lumber was cut. The trusses for the roofs were cut and assembled along with the prefabrication of the door and window frames. The size of the construction project required that the lumber supplier be reliable and local, and the only one that could meet that requirement was the Edward Hines Lumber Company. It was, by some reports, the largest lumber job ever let at one time in Chicago. The community would eventually consume over thirty million board feet of common lumber and six million board feet of trim lumber. The project demanded as many as thirty-five truck loads of common lumber a day from Hines.

The structural lumber was cut to size, and, as the trusses were completed, they were banded together, labeled, and stored in the sawmill area. The bundles were then trucked or forklifted to the individual apartment sites as each building required its lumber. Often the trusses were hoisted by crane directly from the truck onto the frame of the building. Each job area also had its own gasoline power saw and electric generator. The saw was used for cutting the floor joists, and the electricity was used for operating the smaller hand tools.

The framing for almost all the rental buildings was a conventional "platform" system in which one floor, wall studs, and ceiling joists were completed before the second floor was begun. "Balloon" framing, in which the wall studs extend from the foundation to the roof, was tried but abandoned, possibly due to the quality of the lumber and the propensity of the lumber to twist, causing significant structural problems.

After the war most wood was newly harvested and very green. This lumber needed to be dried to stabilize it and reduce warping, but it was not always practical or possible to do so. Rough structure framing for the apartments often used this greener lumber, and later, just before lath and plaster, any twisted studs were cut out and replaced.

The water treatment plant was finished in late spring of 1948, along with its own railroad siding. The thirty-six-inch diameter interceptor sewer line was completed, opening the door for the annexation to the Bloom Township Sanitary District. Park Forest now had water and a sewer connection.

Underground wiring was in, and all storm and sanitary sewers were installed as well as the water mains. Ten percent of the roads had been paved, and six hundred yards of precast and structural concrete products were being turned out daily. Slabs for the basements of 320 units had been poured, and production was up to over 20 units a day. Tight scheduling provided for the digging of a like number of basements per day. This kept excavation crews two days ahead of the building construction gang.

By May 1948 significant work had been completed throughout the rental

Fig. 32. View toward the east to the corner of Western Avenue and Victory Boulevard. The Plaza site is to the lower left, and the Cook County Forest Preserve is beyond the units and power lines. *Source:* courtesy of Park Forest Public Library.

complex, and by June 1, 635 men were reporting daily to the job site. Union contracts had been well thrashed out prior to the start of construction. There was no single master agreement, but separate agreements were reached with the carpenters, lathers, bricklayers, and plasterers. These were the trades with the least number of workers, and any shutdown by them would cause significant delays. Considering the market for their skills, premium pay for these trades was expected. ACB managed to keep the wage scale lower by offering longer and steadier periods of work. By late summer of 1948 the work force had expanded to over a thousand workers on the job site, and, according to Klutznick, the company "could still use 300 to 400 more men right now."

After the buildings were framed to the second-floor ceiling, the prefabricated trusses were lifted into place and the roof sheathed. With the roof in place and waterproofed, the masons, plumbers, and electricians moved in to place bricks and utilities. Steel sash windows were inserted next, then interior partitions, then the door frames were set. A weather-tight seal to the structure permitted the lath-

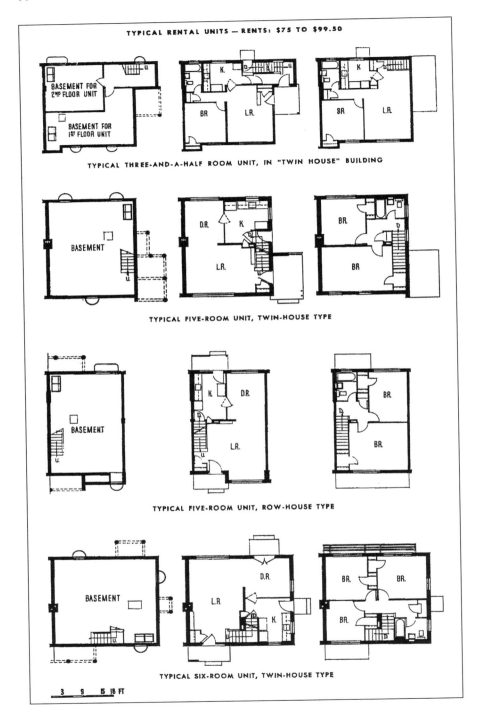

TYPICAL RENTAL UNITS — RENTS: $75 TO $99.50

TYPICAL THREE-AND-A-HALF ROOM UNIT, IN "TWIN HOUSE" BUILDING

TYPICAL FIVE-ROOM UNIT, TWIN-HOUSE TYPE

TYPICAL FIVE-ROOM UNIT, ROW-HOUSE TYPE

TYPICAL SIX-ROOM UNIT, TWIN-HOUSE TYPE

ers to plaster and finish the walls. A tile man then set the tiles in the bathroom. Interior trim began when the stairs and oak flooring were completed. Then hardware, doors, and kitchen cabinets went in. Finally, after getting paint, asphalt floor tiles, plumbing fixtures, and a coat of wax for the floors, the unit was ready for the tenant.

At the peak of construction the armies of workmen were completing twenty-one units a day. The parking courts contained the children's play area, surrounded with a Davey Crockett stockade-type fence. The mud was disappearing under green grass, and the temporary wooden walks had long ceased to exist. The apartments had consumed 13 million bricks and 200,000 gallons of paint. Fifty-seven miles of sidewalks interconnected the village. Prefabricated porches had been poured at the rate of seventy a day. A skyscraper could have been built from the steel that went into the buildings. The rentals, nearing completion, now formed the clusters and shapes that the architects and planners had anticipated.

Within this turmoil of construction, if a community were ever to have an antagonist in its midst, it would be someone like Sam Beber, brother-in-law of Philip Klutznick, who joined ACB in the spring of 1947. Beber had been Klutznick's law partner in Omaha before Klutznick's tenure in Washington and now was asked to come on board American Community Builders as vice president and one of the directors. Beber's responsibilities centered on costs and the management of expenses. To Beber deals were never two-way, and he would make sure that any edge went in his direction. He would try to ferret out waste where he could find it, and his own team was not immune to his attacks. He was a Dr. Jekyll and Mr. Hyde. In the office and while dealing with ACB business, he was strict, uncompromising, and frugal. He would act as though each dollar saved was his own and, in so doing, challenged many of his own associates. Those who bent were placed in one category, and those who stood their ground often became his friends. On the other hand, in social situations outside the office he could be extremely charming and delightful. As Carroll Sweet Jr. recalled, "Pity so many were exposed only to the business side of him."

On Friday night, October 6, 1949, almost two years to the day after the start of construction and one year after the first residents had moved in, Dick Senior, project manager, nailed a small tree to the roof of the three thousand and tenth house. This tree was the traditional symbol of the completion of the framing, or last truss, on a construction job. It would be the following spring when the last family moved in, but the tree signified a major change in the growth of the community. The apartments were complete.

Fig. 33 (opposite). The apartments were typically two-floor town homes with a basement. End units were flats. One-, two-, and three-bedroom floor plans were offered. *Source: Architectural Record*, May 1951.

CHAPTER SIX

The First Residents

We have realized two things from the start, one is that no matter how much planning goes into a project like this, it will only be judged by results. The other is that no matter how much work and time we have spent, the people who live there can form the spirit and character we have sought for it. We all feel that unless the town-hall spirit in which Park Forest was created is captured and held by the people we will have failed. This is our gamble. We're betting on the people.

—Philip Klutznick, President ACB

FOR thousands of years before Philip Klutznick's words of anticipation the central woodlands of America from the Mississippi River and Ohio River to Canada were the hunting and gathering grounds of the great Algonquian family of the Sauk, Fox, Potawatomi, Chippewa, and Ottawa. Intertribal warfare, by the early 1700s, forced significant alterations to boundaries of these homelands. Some of the change in the delicate political balance that existed in the region was due to the French and English wars, but in many cases the readjustments were a result of the forceful expansion of the more militant and organized eastern Indian tribes.

During the seventeenth century the confederacy known as the Five Nations—made up of the Mohawk, Onondaga, Cayuga, Oneida, and Seneca—was formed. It was from one small tribe, the Iroquois, which joined the confederacy around 1720, that these nations acquired their feared reputation. This confederacy violently and aggressively expanded westward and northward, subduing all the tribes of the Algonquian linguistic family in a vast region from the Atlantic Ocean to the Mississippi River. One of the Canadian Algonquian tribes, the Ottawa, was pushed south out of its Lake Huron homeland westward into Michigan.

Within fifty years the power of the Iroquois had receded as a result of their inopportune alliances with the British in the colonial wars. The Ottawa and the remaining tribes in the Algonquian confederacies would eventually regain control of lower Michigan, parts of Ohio, Indiana, and Illinois as well as some areas along the Canadian side of Lake Huron. The Ottawa fought on the side of the French against the British, but later, during the American Revolution and the War of 1812, they fought on the side of the British.

In 1804, for an annual annuity of one thousand dollars, two Algonquian tribes, the Sauk and the Fox, agreed to cede their lands east of the Mississippi River to the aggressively expanding United States. Ma-Ka-Tae-Mish-Kia-Kiak, one of the chiefs of the Sauk and better known by the English name Black Hawk, repudiated the treaty and fought on the side of the British against the expanding United States.

After the War of 1812 and three treaties that continually pushed the Sauk and the Fox further west and eventually across the Mississippi River, white settlers began to move into the vacated Indian lands. In April 1832 to stem growing hunger and attacks by aggressive Sioux from the West, Black Hawk and many of the Sauk and the Fox tried to return to Illinois and their more fertile homeland to plant crops. This action resulted in panic by the white settlers and the inexperienced soldiers, and settlers reacted by shooting the peaceful emissaries sent by Black Hawk. To the Sauk this was a breaking of a sacred trust. The Black Hawk War had begun.

Black Hawk quickly routed the unorganized soldiers and local militia, but this was to be his only victory. Unsupported by other tribes, Black Hawk continued the fight with small and ineffective skirmishes. He was forced, throughout the campaign, to move with the women and children of his tribe, which slowed and hampered his actions. On August 2 part of his tribe was caught, defeated, and ruthlessly slaughtered near the Wisconsin and Bad Axe Rivers. Three weeks later Black Hawk surrendered. His surviving tribesmen were moved to a reservation near Fort Des Moines, and Black Hawk was imprisoned at Fort Monroe in Virginia. Upon his release he became somewhat of a celebrity and traveled throughout the East presenting his autobiography. After tiring of the notoriety, he returned to his tribe in Iowa, where he died in 1838.

Interconnecting the Midwest region from the Detroit area in Michigan to the Mississippi River near Rock Island was the historic Sauk Trail. The high ground, south of Lake Michigan and well away from the swampy regions of the Calumet and Chicago Rivers to the north, had always been an important crossroads. Sauk Trail connected the Ottawa and Potawatomi Nations and was used to move trade goods east and west. The trail was also used by the Iroquois nations to wage war on the Algonquian. White men would later use the trail to move furs eastward to market and have supplies return as payment.

Sauk Trail did not go to Chicago, at the time an unimportant village, but kept to the south and west of it by almost thirty miles. With use the trail deepened in places to almost two feet below the surrounding ground and would eventually be widened to allow for wagons. The trail was later used by the "49er's" going after California gold and by homesteaders heading to Kansas and Nebraska. The expansion of the railroads lessened the trail's regional importance, but it was still heavily used by local farmers to move their produce to market and to the train station at Matteson. Hubbard's Trail was the region's most important north-south route and would later become Chicago Road (Dixie Highway), which linked Chicago south to Danville.

The State of Illinois was twenty years old at the time of Black Hawk's death. White settlers had moved continually into the southern and western areas of the state since the early 1700s, primarily due to the easier access up the Mississippi from New Orleans. Many also arrived from the east by way of the Ohio River and then northward up the Mississippi. The defeat of Black Hawk and changes in federal land laws brought a significant increase in the numbers of settlers into the northeastern area of the state.

In 1833 Adam Brown became the future Park Forest area's first white resident when he settled along the old Sauk Trail where it crossed Hubbard's Trail. Chicago, that same year, had a population of 550 and had incorporated as a town; within five years it would grow to more than 4,200 residents. One of the earliest settlers in the region was Scotsman John McCoy and his wife, Sabra. Their farm, homesteaded in 1834, was located along Sauk Trail on high ground above Thorn Creek. It provided a gathering place and campground for pioneers and Indians alike for many years. The McCoy's kindness was not forgotten, and, when the last of Potawatomi were forced out of the state in 1835, they stopped to say good-bye especially to the "good white woman" Sabra McCoy.[1] In 1835 the J. H. Batcheldor family settled the area around Western Avenue and Sauk Trail, along with the John Bell family. The Bells stayed until about 1860; when they left, the Batcheldors bought the Bell farm and added it to their own. This property would later form the largest portion of Park Forest.

The Batcheldor's and McCoy's were devout Methodists and members of the church in Crete. They were also abolitionists and offered their homes as stations on the "underground railroad." Runaway slaves from Missouri were hidden during the day in their basements while they waited for the best time to continue their nighttime trek to the next stop in Dyer, Indiana, and eventual freedom in Canada.

In 1836 Henry Merker, a German immigrant, purchased forty acres from a "friendly Indian" for five pounds of tobacco. This event was one of the first recorded mentions of the price of land in the region. Within a few years, after the federal Pre-Emption Act of 1838, settlers from the East and immigrants from Europe began to buy land in the region from the government for $1.25 an acre. This low price was the standard for many years. Eventually, Merker would buy several hundred acres of land that later straddled the boundary of Park Forest and Richton Park.

Rich Township was organized in 1850 and, until the creation of Park Forest, contained only two towns, Richton Park and Matteson. Families who moved into the region during this period would still be there a hundred years later. Names such as Blattner, Weishaar, Scheidt, Stuenkel, Mahler, Mueller, Stelter, and Klein would remain within the area and give strong testimony to the German immigrants who settled there.[2]

By 1850 Chicago had a population of thirty thousand, and Cook County had over forty-three hundred residents spread over the region. In 1860 Bloom, Rich, and Thornton townships contained more than eleven hundred people. Chicago was a classic example of a village grown into a city in too short a time. The first trains reached Chicago in 1848, only a few years after the settlement of the Sauk Trail and Chicago Road area. By 1855 over seven hundred miles of track had been laid in Illinois, with the major north-and-south line being the Illinois Central. Soon rail links were established which made Chicago the greatest rail and commercial center in the United States. Scores of businesses were formed which used rail to ship their goods throughout the country, and, because of the regions strong agricultural base, food was transported as well. Growth built upon growth, and it was inevitable, as shown by the development of Riverside on the West Side, that suburban expansion was about to begin.

Southern Cook County land was rich and fertile, and, within a few years, numerous small villages formed. Bloom, Crete, Matteson, and Richton Park were four of these newly settled towns. The most important, due to its location on the Illinois Central rail line, was Matteson. Named after then governor Joel Matteson, the village was surveyed and platted in 1855 and by 1880 contained over five hundred people. The village and the surrounding farms supported the growth of a town complete with stores, churches, schools, hotels, and other businesses.

In comparison to other areas of the region, the south side of Chicago's most expansive growth began soon after the Columbian Exposition of 1893. Harvey, a city six miles to the north, was established by evangelist Turlington Harvey and temperance leader Dwight Moody. It was an industrial town that was to be "an earthly paradise which had never been defiled by painted windows and the music of gurgling bottles." It was advertised to manufacturers as a town with a sober and orderly workforce.[3]

In 1890, directly east of Matteson along Lincoln Highway, the new community of Chicago Heights was formed. Developed out of land purchased by the Chicago Heights Land Association, this new manufacturing and industrial center would become, by the turn of the century, one of the Midwest's most important industrial and steel-producing cities. Chicago Heights was incorporated in 1901.

Chicago's expansive growth following the 1893 World's Columbian Exposition would continue throughout Cook County and the region. By 1900 the population of Chicago was 1.7 million and would grow to over 3 million by the start of World War II. The quality of the South Side's residential growth continued upward. A few miles to the north of the Batcheldor property the Flossmoor Country Club (formed as the Homewood Club) was built in 1899, and Olympia Fields Country Club, home to a U.S. Open in 1925, was built in 1923. The heady days of 1920s, with their seemingly unending speculative growth, saw the expansion of the residential areas of Olympia Fields and a proposal for a complete city, called Indian Wood, on the old Batcheldor farm. The builder, Victor C. Carlson, was from Evanston. He envisioned city dwellers moving out to the country from Chicago and building new homes along his recently finished eighteen-hole private golf course. He failed to attract the attention of the buyers, however, who went elsewhere. The course became a public golf course in 1929, and for that one summer was quite successful; the collapse of the market in October cost Carlson most of what he had. The golf course and adjacent lands were taken over by a syndicate of individual investors and, later, by Chicago's First National Bank.

In 1933, during the "Century of Progress" World's Fair in Chicago, Carlson made one last attempt to make his village a reality. He built a small camplike resort with small cabins and other recreational buildings and called it Beacon City. His attempts to attract visitors and tourists out of Chicago after a day of activities to this countryside resort were moderately successful but could not be sustained, and the venture eventually failed. In the end the bank took all the property.

The Lincolnshire area, due east along Sauk Trail, was a new and favorite residential haunt during prohibition days. It gained a reputation as a community that catered to bootleggers and Chicago gangsters. It straddled the southern end of the same State Street that ended directly in the Chicago Loop. The area also included one of Chicago's better racetracks, Balmoral Park.

Shortly before the purchase of the lands for Park Forest by American Community Builders (ACB) in 1946, there was one last attempt to build a residential community. It was reported in the Chicago newspapers that a financial group called Village Developers would build a black housing development and country club with over a thousand homes around the Indian Wood golf course. The plans were never realized.

Marketing of any development was almost as critical as the plans and designs. Whereas others failed in the area due to economic conditions and possibly poor management, the initial success of Park Forest can be almost directly attributed to a February 14, 1948, *Collier's Magazine* article. *Collier's* was the first to announce the idea of the community, in October 1946, and eighteen months later it was still a national voice for the community. The February 1948 article, written by Harry Henderson and Sam Shaw, announced to the whole country America's first "planned" postwar city designed for safety, cleanliness, GIs, and "a better life."[4]

The long and detailed article described the three "godfathers" of the community—Klutznick, Manilow, and Sweet Sr.—in such radiant postwar terms that if you met them on the street you would feel as though they were old friends. The article exactly located the property on the South Side of Chicago and described the surrounding forests and parks. It noted who the lenders were and the size of the federal guarantees. Nothing about the planning, the team, and the expected residential units was left to the imagination. Even the number of churches and the various denominations were described.

The descriptions of the construction site in the article softened the potential blow to prospective tenants by describing the conditions of the new village with incomplete roads and unavailable shopping. The promise for the future was made in glowing terms and expectations. A finer bit of preselling has never been done on such a great scale for such little money. The article prompted hundreds of calls to the ACB offices seeking more information on how to sign up for an apartment. The article presented to the whole country the idea of suburban living supporting an urban job.

Many of the first applications were a direct result of the *Collier's* article, which mentioned rental rates, invited families with children, and talked about greenbelts, parks, and farmland; the safety of the streets was emphasized. The article described the village's building organization around residential clusters and noted the simple fact that one resident would not be able to look out a window into the home of a neighbor. It also described the main shopping center and how the shops and theater were all connected under a canopied walkway. Schools, it said, would be not only for children but for adults as well. (The article hints strongly that this element, schools, would "depend almost entirely on the new citizens"; the lack of schools would be a rallying point for the new residents within a year.) Social distinctions between the rich and the poor would not exist within this new community, and, as Jerry Loebl said, "We do not want anyone—especially any kid—to feel that he comes from the wrong side of the tracks."[5]

This article was a master stroke of public relations and can be attributed to Philip Klutznick and his understanding of the use of the media for distributing information. The article cost ACB very little, if anything, to produce, yet there was little else that could have generated the national interest that it did. There was some natural skepticism regarding the veracity of the article, but, unlike other advertisements for similar communities, this one was going to live up to its billing. Within a few months after the first residents had moved in, some were complaining that all the things "promised" in the article weren't available when the residents arrived, especially schools and parks. The impatience of the residents and the paternal yet financially stretched benevolence of the builder made for very loud and intense meetings between them. The final sentence in the article foretold the future of Park Forest: "There is little question that this is one of the most important experiments in housing and in living to be attempted in many years."[6]

Throughout the summer of 1948, before the first tenants had moved into their units, ads were placed daily in the *Chicago Tribune*. These ads firmly established the paper as the primary source of information about the village for the public. Over the next three years significant ad coverage encouraged people to come out to Park Forest. Themes about the various organizations, clubs, holidays, and activities enticed people to visit and become a part of the life that had been created. ACB hired Mayer and O'Brien as the public relations firm to handle most of the advertising and promotion.

An intense screening program of applications and interviews was set up by ACB to insure the quality of the tenants. This screening focused not only on income but education, status as a veteran, and need. In addition to the application, there was also a personal interview. As the pressure for filling the units increased, many of the prospective tenants did not have to be personally interviewed, but there were other methods used to screen potential residents. Tom McDade, who was in charge of the rentals in 1952, later confided that he had arranged monthly parties for personnel directors of large downtown companies. After a short informational presentation, he would explain the benefits of Park Forest to the companies' employees. ACB also actively sought out tenants from specific employers in the area. Argonne National Laboratory, Swift Meats, Standard Oil, and the University of Chicago were just a few of the businesses and institutions to which they presented the village. The village also attracted many of the military personnel who were stationed at the Fifth Army Headquarters at the Chicago Beach Hotel on South Lake Shore Drive at Fifty-fifth Street. A very active social group in the village centered around the wives of these soldiers.

Tenant selection also forbid renting units to single people, especially women. This policy was to continue until about 1956, when the village hired the first librarian, who was single. The village had to get a special dispensation to allow her to rent a unit. When Reverend Luther Beckemeyer, pastor for Hope Lutheran Church, who was also single, arrived in the village, ACB would not rent to him.

Years later it was suggested, without foundation, that there had been an attempt by ACB to socially engineer the courts. Even if there were an unofficial "policy," the small staff of ACB could not have dedicated the personnel necessary to manage such an intrusive program. American Community Builders needed to fill 3,010 rental units and, considering the transient habits of the residents, also needed to continually refill the hundreds of apartments that turned over every year. There has never been any evidence, other than conjecture and rumor, of such a policy. Considering some of the antagonism toward ACB, much of this innuendo was wishful thinking.

If there were an area in which there may have been discrimination, it was in the leasing of rentals to Negro families. Even though the public record does not confirm an overt policy of discrimination, the facts do speak for themselves. It was not until 1959 that a black family moved into Park Forest. The high rental costs and income requirements eliminated significant numbers of people, including black families, who could not afford to live in the community. If there was discrimination, it was tacit and indirect. Considering the social and liberal credentials of Philip Klutznick, he certainly would not have directly condoned such a practice, but he may not have actively sought racial minorities as tenants. With the housing situation as bad as it was in the Chicago region at that time, there were thousands of applicants to pick from, and selectively picked they were.

On May 30, 1948, Edward and Rose Waterman signed the first lease for an apartment in Park Forest. The Watermans had read about the new town in *Collier's* and the *Chicago Tribune* and had contacted the offices of American Community Builders regarding availability of units. They knew about Klutznick and Beber and their activities with Jewish organizations such as B'nai B'rith and felt that this "lent a character of repute to the project." They completed the application and were contacted by Hart Perry for an interview. After the interview they were asked if they would participate in a promotion for the village: the signing of the first lease. The Watermans agreed. To get an apartment in those days you would do anything the prospective landlord would ask you to do. Waterman also believes that one of the reasons that Perry wanted them to sign a lease was so that he could get their basement apartment in Chicago. Perry's housekeeper needed a place to live nearer to the Perry home, and the Waterman apartment, as small as it was, would be perfect.[7] Within a few years after moving into Park Forest, Ed Waterman went to work for ACB in the accounting department and later managed the rental apartments. He would eventually become president of the new real estate company, Park Forest Homes, Inc., formed after ACB sold most of its assets in the late 1950s.

Robert and Mary Dinerstein first heard about the new village at a party in late spring of 1947. Mary met Hart Perry at the party and, after some correspondence between them, was sent a preliminary application for rental housing. Robert was working at Standard Oil Research Laboratory in Whiting, Indiana, and thought that the village would be an excellent place for new employees of the

Fig. 34. The regional interest for Park Forest was so great that ACB was able to promote the village by having the *Chicago Tribune* publish a photo of the first lease signing by Edward and Rose Waterman. *Source:* courtesy of Park Forest Public Library.

rapidly expanding company. Employees were coming from across the country and were facing the same problem—a lack of housing. The Dinersteins's formal application came the following spring, in 1948.[8]

In a letter to the Dinersteins, Perry told them that the homes would be rented in order of initial inquiries, with preference going to World War II veterans, especially those who were disabled. A few years later one such wounded veteran, Bud Tozer, applied for an apartment but was delayed due to the number of applicants. Ed Waterman, who was now with ACB and in charge of the rental units, heard about Tozer's difficulties and sped up the process for moving his family in. Local merchants gave the Tozers gifts, a luncheon was put on for them, and there was some publicity in the *Park Forest Reporter*. Even though the need was great, there were no complaints about the treatment extended to the Tozers. The new residents respected the veterans and what they had accomplished.[9]

Hundreds and eventually thousands of families would apply, be interviewed and notified of their acceptance, have their deposits taken, and move into Park Forest. They were remarkably similar economically and socially. The veterans were young, most under thirty and newly married. They had at least one preschool child. These new tenants were children of middle-class parents, well educated (over half had graduated from college), and professionally employed. They had been disciplined by the war and the frugality of the 1930s and were used to hardships and fear; they also had an abundance of hope for the future. They were vibrant and interested in the growth of the village. It was these people who made Park Forest a community.

The power American Community Builders held as landlord allowed it to affect the governing of the village in many ways. An example of this power would be exercised by ACB in an incident with a school board member, John Kelly. Kelly, an outspoken critic of ACB, felt that the developer was not doing its job in providing funds and facilities for the school district. He was hard-nosed over the issues, and, when his lease came up for renewal, ACB would not renew. Everyone was shocked. There were marches in support of Kelly and signs placed around the village. ACB never explained why they did not renew Kelly's lease, and soon Kelly left the village. Today lawsuits would be filed, and it would be months before Kelly might be forced, if ever, to leave. In 1950 the landlord had the power and exercised it.[10] As time passed, other leases came up for renewal. Each resident had to go back for an interview, even the village president, Henry X. Dietch. There was seldom a problem, but the element of approval and the process of renewal were unnerving and insulting to many.

The first move-ins were scheduled to begin on Monday, August 30, 1948, and, if there is one enduring aspect to this event, it was who was first. All those first 3,010 families who moved into the new village from August 1948 to August 1950 could rightfully be called pioneers, but, as with any such human event, who was first among equals would be argued for years. The first completed court, short of grass, sidewalks, and pavement, was B-1. Into this court moved three families that day, Manuel and Madeline Kanter, William and Jane Heckman, and Ross and Leona DeLue. The Kanters and the Heckmans stayed in their units that night despite the confusion caused by construction and workmen. The DeLues returned to Chicago and stayed in a hotel. According to Carroll Sweet Jr., who was in charge, all did not go well. That Monday when he arrived at the on-site ACB offices Sweet was met by one of the security guards. He was told that a family had arrived on Sunday ready to move in. The guard let them in because they had nowhere else to go. He asked Sweet what unit the Manuel Kanter's were supposed to be in. "2695 Western," replied Sweet. "I think I put them in the wrong unit," answered the guard.

Fig. 35a–b. The advertising for the village stressed the quality of schools and organizations and that veterans were welcome. ACB used the *Tribune* almost exclusively for its advertising. *Source*: courtesy of Park Forest Public Library.

HOMES for RENT *in Park Forest*
CHICAGOLAND'S PREMIER SUBURBAN DEVELOPMENT

This Unit of Park Forest's "Get Acquainted" Series Brings You Facts About Our Veterans' Groups.

Photo by Bernard Klein

Pictured above are Robert Schwartz and Porter Russell of the American Veterans' Committee, with O. E. Collins and Henry Marshall of the American Legion. John Lange, Resident Director for American Community Builders, explains the master site plan of Park Forest which will soon house 30,000 people. These veterans' organizations are but two of numerous social and professional groups that have arisen within the rapidly growing population of this already famous new city.

★ Many of you reading this story come from smaller cities in the Midwest. Recall for a moment the friendly, heartwarming, social life that was so much a part of your everyday experience. If life in a big city has denied this enjoyment of human companionship to you and your family, here is an opportunity to regain these privileges.

★ Early in the history of Park Forest spontaneous movements among our first residents led to the creation of many social groups. Among them are: The League of Women Voters, Holy Name Society, Park Forest Drama Club, the Park Forest Bridge Club, and many others. You can participate in as much, or as little, of this activity as you wish. Every new resident of Park Forest finds a cheerful reception and friendly invitation from the "old settlers" of 1948.

PARK FOREST RENTAL BUILDING IS NOW VIRTUALLY COMPLETE

Completion of this tremendous rental project involving an expenditure of some $35,000,000 has astounded professional observers everywhere. Final construction details are being finished as weather permits and our crews of interior finishers and decorators are releasing homes for occupancy every day. As originally planned, there will be no further rental building. These units represent your final opportunity to rent a home.

ACT TODAY! Secure the Many Benefits of Park Forest for Your Family

Sweet hurried over to the apartment and found Madeline Kanter sitting on a bar stool looking "haggard and forlorn." Household furnishings were piled all about. Sweet introduced himself, and she said, "Mr. Sweet, please don't tell me we are in the wrong apartment."

"I am afraid that's true," he replied. "You should be in the one next door and you will have to move as soon as possible. The rightful tenant for this apartment may appear any time."

Manuel Kanter had already gone to work, and it was obvious that Madeline could not move without help. Sweet gathered up a couple of the laborers and helped her move her belongings into the correct apartment next door. Within a month all the tenants had moved into the first court units at the southeast corner of Western Avenue and Twenty-sixth Street.[11]

The "official" designation of who was first is not debated. Phil Klutznick (whose family may have really been the first) designated the Heckmans on July 5, 1951, as the first family to take up residence. The Kanters were so anointed by an article in the local paper and are supported by Carroll Sweet's memory. The DeLues continued to believe they were the first to arrive. But, without a doubt, these were the first three families of Park Forest. Fifty years later, after almost all the other original residents had moved on, the DeLues were still living in and contributing to the village.

Philip Klutznick was determined to be a part of this new community, and he showed it by moving his family into the first duplex. In fact, his wife, Ethel, and their newborn fourth son, Sam, came straight from the maternity hospital to their new home. He modified the building to incorporate both units into one dwelling. It would remain the largest home in the village for many years.

Henry X. Dietch saw himself as a pioneer. When he arrived as one of the first residents most of the village was still farm land; he recalled later that, across the road from their new apartment, a big silo and old barn were being dismantled. Dietch, like the other new settlers, had to go into Chicago Heights for their shopping and banking; food and clothing stores had not yet opened in the shopping center, so even a loaf of bread required a trip to Chicago Heights. Only the catering truck that served the construction crews had some sandwiches and other foodstuffs. Very quickly the caterer realized he had a new market and began to supply some of the basic household foodstuffs for the housewives. To cash a check residents had to go to Chicago Heights. There wasn't a bank in the village yet, and the local grocery stores wouldn't cash a Park Forest resident's check—cash only. For many of the residents without cars this required hiring a taxi, going to Chicago Heights to cash a check, then on to the store, and then catching a cab back to the village. There was a true sense of isolation for many of the residents.

One unfortunate aspect of the hurried occupancy program was the unacceptability of the village's water for drinking. The contractor had requested approval of the drinking water by the Cook County health department, but, after testing, it was found that the coliform bacteria count was too high. The water was safe for bathing, cooking, and cleaning but not for drinking. The momentum of the move-ins required a quick-fix solution, so ACB provided all tenants a free five-gallon bottle of drinking water, which was replaced when empty. Mothers had to wrestle with the jug whenever a child needed a drink, so it was only natural that the innovative residents would find other ways to solve the problem. Dinerstein remembers that one could tell the engineers from the lawyers quite easily. There were a number of residents who worked at Argonne Laboratories, and others who worked in legal firms in the Loop. The engineers and scientists invented ways to siphon the water from the bottles. They brought tubing and clamps that allowed them to build a setup that worked like a faucet. The poor lawyers continued to struggle with pouring directly from the bottle

The one food item that was not in short supply was milk; in those days milk was delivered directly to the home. There was also a tremendous rivalry between milk companies. The milkmen were paid by the number of customers they had, so it was not unusual to have a milkman meet you to sign you up as you were emptying your moving truck. It was also not surprising to have one company's samples dumped by a rival and replaced with its own bottles. Milkmen almost came to blows a few times. Eventually, as more tenants arrived, the competition worked itself out.

There was no direct mail service either. All the mail for Park Forest had to go through Chicago Heights. The U.S. Post Office would not permit its carriers to make house deliveries without sidewalks, and there were still hundreds of apartments without walks. ACB, as an interim solution, would send a security guard to the Chicago Heights Post Office, collect the mail, return to Park Forest, sort the mail, and then deliver it. There was no set schedule, and mail was delivered at all hours of the day and night. The timely delivery of the mail was also confused by the similarity of the new community's name with those of Forest Park and Oak Park.

Around-the-clock private security patrols paid for by American Community Builders provided police protection. The first firemen were the daytime employees of ACB, one of whom was a former Chicago fireman. Nighttime crews were volunteers recruited from the first tenants. A loud siren was mounted on the construction office barn, to summon the volunteers in case of emergencies. The barn also held the first fire truck, a converted army jeep, and soon an old LaFrance fire truck, which ACB had bought.

When the first residents arrived, the only phone available was mounted on a

Fig. 36. At the first meeting of the residents in a large army tent, banners proclaimed the "Birth of a City, Park Forest." *Source:* courtesy of Park Forest Public Library.

pole at the corner of their court. Residents could be found gathered there at all times of the night talking on the phone. The first private phones were on party lines. It was not unusual to have seven or eight homes per line. The residents were from all over the country and were a talkative group. It was tough to get a line out, and they often found themselves unintentionally listening in on bits of their neighbors' lives. Instead of pushing the new residents apart, it brought them closer together. The many shortcomings were taken as one more part of the adventure of Park Forest.

In early November 1948 President Harry S. Truman was elected president. He wasn't supposed to win but did, and with his win the Congress was again Democratic. For three years after assuming the presidency, Truman battled the postwar changes that had overwhelmed the United States, a country with a rapidly expanding economy, incipient inflation, and the most difficult social element of all: a young population that had fought for its country and wanted the fruits of that fight. That fall, in keeping with the changes in Washington, significant changes were about to happen in Park Forest.

Fig. 37. It was a chilly late-November day in 1948 when the residents gathered for the first time at a barbecue hosted by ACB. *Source:* courtesy of Park Forest Public Library.

On a chilly Saturday, November 27, 1948, at 1:00 P.M., ACB tossed a barbecue lunch for the first 175 families that had moved into the rentals. In addition, hundreds of others who had signed leases and were waiting for their apartments to be finished were invited. They gathered under a huge tent set up by the developer near the construction site for the new Plaza Shopping Center. Inside, rows of folding chairs were organized according to residential courts. A rough wooden dais had been set up in one corner, a railing ran across the front, and an American flag was fastened to it. It was a festive day, with a town crier announcing proclamations throughout the crowd. Signs hung about the tent declaring "The Birth of a City, Park Forest."

After everyone had a chance at the grilled chicken and burgers, Philip Klutznick called the "meeting" to order and introduced himself and the other principal officers of American Community Builders: Nathan Manilow, Beber, and Jerry Loebl. Those ACB employees who lived in Park Forest sat among their respective courts. Klutznick and Manilow, after a few preliminary remarks, talked about their plans for the community, its incorporation, and its name. They pointed out the advantages of incorporation—election of trustees with authority to enact ordinances for health and safety and to levy taxes. Klutznick suggested to the residents that they set up a committee made up of two representatives from each court on a court-by-court basis to study this possibility. He offered the services of ACB's law office to advise and handle the incorporation.

The name, Park Forest, was also brought out for discussion, and a poll was taken which offered twelve new possibilities. Park Forest was the preferred name. Other names proposed by the residents included Indianwood, Willow Ridge, Westlyn, Thornwood, Brynhurst, Southwood, Sheraton, Sauk Park, Skyline, Ashford, and Saukton. The decision was thought to be final, but during the next two years an increasing number of residents wanted the name changed. Their opposition was based on the belief that the name was "confusing and trite in the Chicago area." In December 1950 a mail-in vote was held to resolve the name for one last time. Sixty-three percent of the ballots supported the name Park Forest, with Indianwood coming in second. There seemed to be more of a relief by the residents that the issue of the village's name was behind them than there was an overwhelming acceptance of the name. The name of the village, even if trite, would not hinder the growth of the community.

One result of the tent meeting was that residents were nominated and committees formed to discuss incorporation. Shortly thereafter the members of the Committee for Municipal Incorporation were elected from their respective courts. In addition, four representatives of the tenants-to-be and two representatives of American Community Builders were selected. Tom McKay, an attorney and resident, was named to head the committee.

Mrs. Dennis O'Harrow nominated her husband (who was out of town the day of the tent meeting) to be one of the court representatives. O'Harrow was at the time assistant director of the Association of State Planning and Development Agencies and later, after incorporation and elections, became the first village president of Park Forest. The committee's two goals were to circulate petitions among the residents calling for incorporation of the community as a village and to file the petitions with the Cook County court, all by the end of January 1949.

Most, if not all, of the meetings were held in the small prefab house that was the nursery school run by Elizabeth Waldmann, Charles Waldmann's wife. The school had limited furniture, and the few chairs it did have were for five-year-old children. Often these people, who were forming the new community, would sit in the small chairs and from that perspective discuss the events that would lead to the formation of Park Forest.

Why did American Community Builders want incorporation? Robert Dinerstein suggests that there may have been a number of reasons, including the need by ACB for tax revenues that would not have been available directly to them as developers but would be available if the streets and utilities were built as village-owned improvements, or perhaps it was a requirement of the FHA, which underwrote the loans. He was half- right: incorporation would, at a future date, shift the tax burden to property owners, but the FHA had no requirements for incorporation. Zoning may have been another motivation behind ACB's desire to incorporate. One element that shaped the initial plan of the village was county zoning, which resulted in the building of apartments. The development proceeded under existing county ordinances until they were redrawn by the newly incorporated village. The new zoning followed the specific requests of ACB and its development plan. In addition, all fees for the building inspections by the county would go to the county; after incorporation these fees would return to the village. These building inspections were done in addition to those by the FHA.

The reasons Phil Klutznick wanted incorporation were many, most were fiscal, but, what is more important, some were social. Incorporation would not help initially to reduce the financial burden of ACB. It was the sole owner of the rental complex, and, as such, it was the only taxpayer. Later, however, as single-family homes were sold and occupied, it would be important to shift most of the improvement and management costs to the homeowners and the village. It was this anticipation that drove part of the need for incorporation. In reality, the builder received little in direct financial benefits from incorporation, but there were some cost savings. Insurance rates for the apartments would be reduced if there were a standing fire department, and an incorporated community would have one. Motor fuel taxes returned to the village would assist greatly in operations of public facilities, and these, too, could only go to incorporated communities. During the next ten years special census counts were frequently taken to insure that the taxes returned to the village were equal to the ever-changing and increasing numbers of residents.

Klutznick had long been a believer in people working with other people for a common goal. He had spent much of his young career in voluntary service with a number of groups, both social and religious. It was through this personal experience that he believed in the intrinsic need for people to join for their common good. He believed that public service was a high goal and not the place for "arrogant little despots."[12] This basic ideology had been the cornerstone of his government service and was now being applied to the new residents of Park Forest, whether they knew it or not.

Klutznick had watched what had happened to the Greenbelt towns and had been directly involved with the Greenbelt residents' demands for home ownership and their attempts to wrestle control of the communities away from the government onto themselves. He believed that Park Forest's new residents must play a part in determining their own destiny, and incorporation was a major step along that path. This was a curious departure from Klutznick's public statements as a former FPHA commissioner. He strongly believed that local governments should provide the fundamental planning and operation of inner-urban redevelopment programs but that the federal government should provide the funding for such programs. Mr. Klutznick, president of one of the largest private suburban residential construction projects in the United States, was still a New Deal democrat. In March 1949 he was appointed by the governor of Illinois to a six-year term on the State Housing Board, whose primary responsibility was administering a thirty million dollar program of aid for urban development, low rent, and veterans' housing.[13]

Years later Klutznick would remark that he felt the tenants had not believed his stated motives when he called for incorporation. Most did not realize that it had been his plan since the first days of ACB. The residents were extremely skeptical and might have agreed with the group that did not favor incorporation, but Klutznick felt that it was good for the community so he emphatically pursued it and convinced the majority. Klutznick argued incorporation with many of America's biggest community builders, who had kept the management of their communities to themselves. Years later he talked about James W. Rouse, who built the new town Columbia, Maryland, in the 1960s:

> You take Columbia. What did Rouse do? He didn't incorporate the place. I argued with him about this. I think he made a mistake. He continued to control it for what?—fourteen years. And it is called a model village. I think the best democracy you have, the best demonstration you have is in the place where you live. That's where people grow up to be the right kind of people or they don't. They don't grow up that way because of government and I think they ought to be responsible for their acts to the degree that it's possible. I've always felt that way; I still feel that way.[14]

Probably not one resident at the tent meeting was aware of an interesting twist within the concept of incorporation: the timing. State requirements for incorporation allowed for two types, village or city. The village form applied to communities of less than five thousand people which were a maximum of two square miles in size (Park Forest would incorporate five acres short of that requirement). A larger community would have required a form of ward government and aldermen; Klutznick was insuring that, by insisting that incorporation immediately continue, Park Forest would have the village form. There would probably not have been significant organizing for incorporation, since every resident was a renter for at least two years. The sale of the first homes would probably have started the process, but Klutznick would not allow the residents to wait. By that time the population would have exceeded the five thousand maximum, and an entirely different form of government may have evolved. It should also be pointed out that, by keeping the number of acres to be incorporated to a minimum, ACB also reduced the number of acres rezoned at a higher tax rate. ACB would incrementally add parcels to the village only when it needed to so as not to pay the higher tax rate that residentially zoned land pays versus agricultural land.

According to Carroll Sweet Jr., the one aspect that shaped the initial plan of the village was the Cook County zoning, which resulted in the apartments being built. The property American Community Builders had purchased was not rezoned until the incorporation. The development continued under existing county ordinances until redrawn by the newly incorporated village. This new zoning followed specific requests from ACB and went according to its development program. It was only later, after discussions among themselves, that the elected members of the Committee for Municipal Incorporation understood the element of timing and its impact on the type of government they would select. Two forms were available: city or village.

The committee chose the village government form for two reasons. First, the legislative body of a village, the board of trustees, is elected at large, not by wards, as are city aldermen in Chicago. Such "at large" elections make it easier to keep municipal politics clean and make the dreaded ward politics impossible. Second, in Illinois the village form of government is more flexible. There are fewer prescribed officers and departments, and the village can organize itself according to the best and most efficient principles of municipal administration.

Robert Dinerstein would later call the barbecue and tent meeting one of the most important events in the history of the village. It was at this gathering that this new development would become an entity unto itself. Elsewhere, other large residential towns would be built—communities like Levittown in Long Island, New York—but they would be swallowed by existing municipalities. It was at this meeting, a carryover from the old tent revivalist days, that the residents took on the new religion of Park Forest with a confused yet excited understanding that they would be a part of a grand experiment.

On January 6, 1949, a petition signed by 117 residents was filed with the County Judge of Cook County. The petition "prayed" for the judge to order a special election of the voters in "Park Forest" so they may decide whether or not to vote for a municipal corporation. Three weeks later, on February 1, a special election was held, and by a vote of ninety to two the electorate chose to incorporate. The Village of Park Forest was born.

In the interim between the tent meeting and the first election the new residents were having their first Christmas in their new village. The volunteer fireman put on a party for the many children already in Park Forest, and Carroll

Sweet Jr. was drafted as the first Santa Claus—few mentioned that it was a natural choice because of his stature and disposition. Santa, sitting on the newly acquired LaFrance fire truck led a parade through the small village, ending at the temporary restaurant on Forest Boulevard. There, after Park Forest's first parade, Santa set up shop, questioned the children about what they wanted for Christmas, and passed out small gifts. It was a great party, but when it was over Santa was more than glad to rid himself of the itchy beard.

After the vote for incorporation, the presiding county judge ordered the election of the first village officers. A "meet the candidates" night to introduce the thirteen nominees for the Board of Trustees, the village clerk, and the village president, occurred in the basement of Jones Memorial Center in Chicago Heights.

Paralleling the Board of Trustees was the Community Council. This organization predated the board by a few months and provided the forum for the candidates to present their qualifications for the board. It would later be involved in many of the issues affecting the village. This group helped put together the various elections, operate community functions, and welcome new residents.

At the time of the meeting there were only about one hundred eligible voters in the village, yet over two hundred and fifty people showed up. All the candidates spoke. They all had similar backgrounds as former servicemen, and now most were business professionals and attorneys. None of them knew anything about being an elected official. There were two candidates for president, McKay and O'Harrow. When Henry X. Dietch stood to present his qualifications for the Board of Trustees, he proudly announced that he was a politician, since he had held a Chicago ward job. Dietch stood out from the others and was elected as a trustee because he was the only one with experience and because he had an X for a middle initial, which later some would remark was perfect for a politician. Beatrice Kane Patterson was one of the candidates for village clerk. When asked why she was running, she deferred to her English husband, Bryan, who humorously announced, "I regret that I have but one wife to give for my village."

The election took place on April 2, and inauguration of village officers was held on April 23, 1949. There were eight elected officials who took their place at the head of the growing community: a village president, six trustees, and a village clerk. Dennis O'Harrow was elected village president. The elected village trustees were Henry X. Dietch, Francis B. Norris, Frederick C. Roop, David Saxe, Marcus Wexman, and George W. Wright. Peter M. Bernays was elected village clerk. The first regular Board of Trustees meeting was held Tuesday, April 26, 1949.

Three important and critical issues faced the new board, and how it dealt with them would define the village for years to come. The first was pressure to inaugurate safety and health measures necessary to all urban areas; the first meeting would deal with fire and police protection. Second, the board faced an unusual financial situation. It had no money and no income. Because of delays in the way the state disbursed taxes back to municipalities, they would not see any tax monies until June 1950, over a year away. Until those first disbursements arrived the village had to be financed by American Community Builders. Later ACB and its home building company, Park Forest Homes, would prepay many of the permit fees for the single-family homes to help fund the financially strapped village.

Third, and most important, the village officers wished to lay the groundwork for efficient, enlightened municipal government. For this they chose to select the village manager form of government, which allowed them to find the best people to direct the day-to-day business of the village—a job that would require all the creativity, study, and best advice available. It also required the patient cooperation of the villagers themselves.

CHAPTER SEVEN

America Reborn

The powers not delegated to the United State by the Constitution,
nor prohibited by it to the States, are reserved to the States respectively,
or to the people.

— 10th Amendment to the Constitution of the United States

T HERE might be one overpowering aspect of Park Forest which separates
it from the hundreds of other new neighborhoods and subdivisions built
across the United States after World War II: it was the only one to form its
own government from scratch. There was no guidebook or instruction manual.
There wasn't a general pointing to a colonel to a lieutenant to a sergeant and a private to get something done. But there was a King George, a Jefferson, an Adams,
a Washington, and maybe even a Betsy Ross. The men and women who formed
up ranks that early spring of 1949 marched to a common drummer and piped a
tune that created something extraordinary where nothing had existed before.

In 1953 William H. Whyte Jr. published a series of articles about the American suburbs in *Fortune* magazine. These articles featured Park Forest and its residents. Three years later Park Forest was brought to the forefront of social exposure and national inspection when Whyte compiled and expanded these articles
into a book called *The Organization Man*. It focused on the temporal and transient nature of the young residents, their lives and families, and their social structures, friendships, and values. Never has a contemporary group been under such
a collective microscope by sociologists, psychologists, planners, and educators.
Young planning students wrote their theses about Park Forest and concentrated
on social relationships among the residents.

In some ways it was the phenomenon of the suburb which frightened and
confused many of America's social critics — rows of matched homes with a patch
of green lawn, endlessly aligned to the horizon, lived in by young couples, with
two children, all driving similar cars. To some, those living in the suburbs were
responsible for the economic problems that beset the cities because they took the
money earned in the city and spent it in the suburbs. They, the evil suburbanites,
extracted their living from mother city and gave nothing in return. *Collier's*, in an

Fig. 38. The "superblock" concept placed parking courts to the rear of the apartments and parkways to the front. Many of the parking courts had play areas in their centers. *Source:* courtesy of Park Forest Public Library.

article in 1952, called it a disease with the name "Suburbanitis."[1] Other articles called for widespread annexations to insure that the urban core would not loosen its grip on the citizen, the citizen's dollar, and, more often than not, his or her vote. In July 1952 the *Atlantic Monthly* a well-respected real estate developer of the time, William Zeckendorf, called these suburban developments "parasites."[2]

Unfortunately, the critic's didn't understand the fundamental changes that were occurring in America. The residents of Park Forest had no hidden agenda or social cause. They were not drawn by political slogans and promises of a better future. They had not moved there in protest. They simply wanted a decent place where they could raise their families. For the resident of Park Forest it was home and, for many, a hometown, and they made it the way they saw fit.

The shopping center was still almost a year away from opening in the late fall of 1949. To meet the day-to-day needs of the residents, ACB temporarily converted a six-family building on Forest Boulevard, just north of Victory Boulevard, into a commercial center. The company found tenants to open a makeshift restaurant, a grocery, and a few small shops. Two dentists, an optometrist, and several doctors also took over some of the space. With the number of small children in the village, pediatricians thought they had found heaven.

In the early days, after the Klutznick's moved into the first court, their two oldest boys took upon themselves the mantles of self-important people. Tom and Jimmy, eight and three, respectively, began to lord it over the newly arriving children with "My daddy run's ACB" and other, similar phrases. Ethel Klutznick felt this needed to be nipped in the bud, so Phil called the two boys together one night and said: "Look fellows, you know this company belongs to you as much as it does me. I'm going to make each of you vice presidents." He gave them each a badge like every other worker had and said, "Every time anyone moves in, if they have children, I want you to go over there and say to them that you would like to help them get adjusted to the community, get acquainted and so forth." A few days later Mrs. Klutznick was on the train going into Chicago, and a friend stopped her to say hello. Another woman passenger overheard the conversation and asked: "Are you Mrs. Klutznick? Are you by any chance the mother of Jimmy Klutznick?" She said yes. "You know, when we moved in, a little fellow knocked on the door. I asked who are you? And he answered 'My name is Jimmy Klutznick. I am the vice president of American Community Builders. You have children. I want to meet them.'" She told Ethel Klutznick that nothing nicer had happened to them in those early weeks than that visit.[3]

The new residents brought energy, education, and interest to the new village. More important, they brought a naïveté that allowed them to attempt things that other communities would never have tried. The village survived on voluntarism and community support. David Saxe, whose paying job was managing and compiling the budget for one region of the Atomic Energy Commission, volunteered as the chairman of the village finance committee and compiler of the village budget while also sitting on the Board of Trustees. Dean Swartzel, whose experience in planning was earned over a number of years in Iowa, Toledo, Chicago, and with the federal government, offered his services as the chairman of the Plan Commission. Charles Lohmeyer, whose real job was consultant to the Civil Services Assembly, acted as an unpaid consultant on village personnel administration.[4]

By the end of 1949 the village newspaper, the *Park Forest Reporter*, was being published on a mimeograph machine by a volunteer, nonprofit community group. The editor, Irwin "Pappy" Schechter, was a Neiman fellow and winner of the Chicago Page One Award for distinguished reporting. The paper had become an institution in less than a year, with five employees and an unpaid staff of over fifty. Four Ph.D.'s acted as contributing "newsboys."

One activity the residents seemed to enjoy more than any other was to form a group or club around their diverse interests and activities. Many of these groups were religious in nature, even though no churches had been built yet. The fraternal service orders were represented initially by the Lions.

Jack Rashkin, with ACB, recalled years later a clever idea he had had. He was concerned that during the holidays people would leave to visit family and friends and get killed on the highways. He thought that, if there were something exciting to do close to home, more residents would stay to take their holiday in Park Forest. Why not give a party, he suggested, and have ACB help them defray the expenses? He started small and began by giving a modest amount of money, about forty dollars, to the organized residents of each court. Eventually, there were over a hundred courts involved with this program. They could do anything they wanted with the money, but everyone in the court must be invited. The program ran for three or four years and was very successful.[5]

It was said during those early days that "people were clamoring" to get into Park Forest. One Chicago realtor had a different opinion: "All it proves is that your rents are too low." There may have been some merit in that statement because, if you are selling cheaper than the market, you are going to get higher demand. But in the case of Park Forest the rents were set based on FHA levels, and they were economically sound and competitive.[6]

Winter brought rains and mud. It was too cold to pour concrete, so many of the newly occupied courts did not have sidewalks or even grass to help cover the muddy ground. Duckboards, wooden lattices about six feet long and two feet wide, were used as temporary walkways. Made from two-by-fours and wood slats and looking like ladders, they were a poor excuse for a sidewalk but did get residents to and from their houses. One protester during this time ran for a village office and based his platform on the lack of sidewalks; he would often moan about the dangers and the perils of the duckboards. He quickly became a point of ridicule because, as someone pointed out, he wasn't running on a platform but a duckboard.[7]

Barney Cunningham, an early resident and later village president, fondly recalled a run-in with the duckboards. At the end of the day he and his family moved into their new apartment; he borrowed a car and went into Chicago Heights for a fifth of gin and a bottle of vermouth to celebrate. Trying to navigate the duckboards that led to his front door he stumbled and broke the bottle of gin. Instead of crying about the tragedy, he went next door to his new neighbor, introduced himself, and asked to borrow five dollars to buy a replacement bottle. What the neighbor thought of Barney was not reported, but he and his family did become close friends of the Cunninghams.

Problems with the drainage began almost immediately after the first residents had moved in. The buildings, set low to reduce their silhouettes, were ini-

Fig. 39. Mud was everywhere in Park Forest; those that seemed to mind it the least were the kids. *Source:* courtesy of Park Forest Public Library.

tially built with no underdrains below the basement slabs, and the foundations had no perimeter drains. The surface water, with no place to drain and facilitated by the low-set window wells, could only drain into the basements. And it did. In some instances the meager floor drain was located on the higher portion of the basement floor. The hydrostatic water pressure at times was so great that it would shoot out as small fountains from cracks in the walls and heave basement floors. During extremely wet periods this runoff would fill some units' basements to the rafters, and many of them would have four or five inches of water. This condition persisted for years and would cost ACB hundreds of thousands of dollars to correct.

One small court that had an eight-unit building was built over an area of unmapped peat. This peat quickly compressed with the weight of the building, and the structure began to settle into the mud. ACB was able to secure the building, jack up the structure, and pour a new reinforced pad under the apartments.

One solution to the drainage problem, however, proved disastrous. ACB felt that, by excavating the perimeter of the structure and adding a layer of drain rock, the water could then be bled off and away from the foundation. Prudent practice would have been to use crushed clean rock; instead, the company used local steel mill slag because it was cheaper. The wet slag released an incredibly obnoxious hydrogen sulfide gas that smelled like rotten eggs, and the resultant pollution made many of the units uninhabitable. ACB then had to go back and remove the slag, replace it with the cleaner material, add air vents that isolated the fumes from the apartments, and provide adequate sub-tile drains to insure proper positive drainage.

About this time an attempt was made to connect the storm drainage system to the sanitary system, but this only transferred the problem to the sewer system. Eventually, enough underdrains and tile fields were added to remove the water. About 1971 an additional interceptor, constructed by Bloom Township, seemed to help reduce the water problem. Unfortunately, even today there are still a few units prone to some water intrusion and flooding.

ACB claimed that some of the problems were due to the haste with which residents had been moved into the village. In some cases this may have been true, but more often than not it was the result of less than adequate engineering in the low areas. Tenants in the late summer and fall of 1949 even began discussing withholding rent money until these problems were fixed. Verbal and nonverbal protests would continue until the ground froze. A few residents protested by placing sarcastic signs in the muddy ground in front of the homes.

Park Forest, like other remote suburban developments, challenged the new residents. It was an environment that was foreign to most. Some psychiatrists have proffered the thought that what people really moved there for was to "mitigate sibling rivalries" and to "gain a father image," or the like. Actually, the cause was more mundane. Thanks to the shortage of moderate- cost housing for young couples with children, most of the people who moved to Park Forest did so because they had to. One of the most common sights, besides children, in Park Forest was the moving van.[8] William Whyte, in his 1968 book called *The Last Landscape*, addressed the transient nature of the new suburbia: "It is not a defect of new communities that they harbor transients; it is one of their great functions. No matter how 'balanced' the community, it is the college-educated, middle-income people who usually provide the leadership, whatever their numbers. When they leave a community they are not necessarily rejecting it. Many leave because they have to. Their organization may be transferring them to another post or they may be moving because they are switching to another company. It is the game."[9] Tenants were moving in at the rate of twenty to thirty families a week. In addition, the number of newborn babies also increased substantially and would continue for years. The common joke was: "It must be in the water!"

One elementary school teacher remembered, years later, that one fall during the early 1950s she had thirty-three students in her class. Nine months later she still had thirty-three students, but not one of those children had begun the year in her class. This turnover challenged everyone, but it was most dramatic and difficult within the schools.

A League of Women Voters survey in 1950 noted that the average adult male educational background for residents exceeded four years of college and that of adult females was not far behind. In addition, half the population was under fourteen years old. Over three thousand families lived in the village by this time, and the annual turnover rate was almost one-third. This resulted in a population dynamic that was continually infusing the village with new ideas and energies. The stratification that occurs in mature communities, where three or more generations develop social structures and protocols, was missing. There were some professionals who formed somewhat elitist social groups, but, as these individuals became more affluent, they tended to move out.

Whyte's book placed Park Forest in the forefront of the new era of planned communities. Depending on the villager who was asked, the book either characterized the village as a place peopled with social robots of conformity, or it was interpreted as presenting the village as a home of citizenship, friendships, and community. Many living there disregarded the book and its notoriety; others reveled in its fame. It is still obvious, forty years after its publication, that the book was a barometer of the village. Aspects of community life and the social interaction discussed within its pages have meaning to new communities even today.

Whyte found that the community forced people together—some willingly, others out of self-protection. By 1955 there were over sixty-six adult organizations and clubs, and, because of the high turnover of residents, there was an insatiable need for new members. As Whyte proclaimed, "Park Forest swallows up more civic energy per hundred people than any other community in the country." He tells the story of a young couple who were not joiners when they arrived but, as the wife explained, "it's gotten so now I practically have to make an appointment to see [my husband] on Saturdays. During the week we alternate; when I have my meetings, he baby-sits for me, and when he has his political meetings, I baby-sit for him."[10]

Without the established traditions of tenure and decorum found in older communities it was not unusual for some highly volatile civic meetings to generate into name-calling and rancorous debate. Considerable energy was expended in this regard, at the expense of Philip Klutznick and ACB, over many of the decisions that went before various committees, commissions, and boards on their way to a solution. More than once, at the peak of a debate, Klutznick would fall back to his simplistic position of allowing those with complaints to break their lease and move on if they did not like what he and ACB were proposing. This would even extend later to the for-sale homes, with offers to buy back a home if the owners were not satisfied. Nine out of ten times these were empty gestures, but in a few instances when leases were brought up for renewal the offending party, such as John Kelly, mentioned earlier, was not offered a renewal and was forced to move on. When this happened it was hard to determine if anyone was a winner. In a few instances the loser was the village, which had to do without individuals who strongly believed in the community and its future.

Where there are young couples, there are children. In the case of Park Forest, thousands. Within a few short years there were more children than any of the planners could have anticipated. Phil Klutznick was aware from the beginning that schools would be the focal points for the neighborhood plans. The 1946 midsummer prospectus called for three elementary schools and one high school. The intention was to revolve three distinct residential neighborhoods around the elementary schools. Each school site would also have park space for recreational use by the neighboring residents, and it was suggested that the stadium facilities of the high school be used for community-wide events and observances. These projections would fall far short of the eventual demand and would become one of the earliest rally points for the young village.

When the promotional *Collier's* article was published, in 1948, the school system had expanded into "a major element in the good life ACB hoped to provide." There would be schools for adults as well as children. Community education centers would be open day and night, and the social and political life of the village would focus on them. There would be classes in city government, foreign languages, cooking, literature, and hobbies. The schools would provide places for forums, dances, and sports. With characteristic ACB hyperbole, the schools would be whatever the new citizens wanted them to be.[11] Unfortunately, the demand created by the residents changed everything.

With the submittal of the FHA application in the late winter of 1947, the locations and costs of the school buildings became an important yet extremely difficult problem to resolve. The entire property of the village fell into six existing elementary school districts, two high school districts, and one non–high school district. The rental area, after the replanning for the apartments, was found to have units in three elementary school districts and one high school district. The FHA application required that schools be considered in the planning for the community. Through the assistance of paid education professionals, projections for student populations and classroom needs were undertaken. It was determined, after postwar veteran housing developments were surveyed, that the village could expect slightly more than one school-age child per family. Since the average age of the parents was under thirty, high school–age children would not be an immediate problem.

It was estimated that the rental community would provide 3,200 elementary age pupils. Since a significant number of students lived outside of the existing Chicago Heights district that covered the eastern portion of the village, American Community Builders would have to provide classrooms for over 2,225 students. ACB, to meet the immediate demand, proposed using rental units as classrooms until schools could be built. ACB hoped that the equipping and staffing of the temporary schools would be done by the new Park Forest school district with money received from the State Equalization Fund. It was quickly decided that, in view of the time lag in both tax and bonding powers, ACB would subsidize the school board of the Park Forest district. This wasn't necessarily a magnanimous decision on the company's part. It needed the classrooms for the children of its future tenants. Without schools they would be at a competitive disadvantage to other communities. ACB established a nonprofit corporation to build the first permanent schools, to which they loaned funds that were later paid back with interest.

In addition to the public schools, the Catholic Church was building a parochial school next door to new St. Irenaeus Church. This sixteen-room school would eventually have space for about eight hundred students, about fifty students per classroom. When the St. Irenaeus school opened in December 1951, parents formed a line through the night to insure a place for their children in the school. Parents rotated guard duty in order to keep their place. A Chicago radio station came down to the village to interview those waiting in line. The inclusion of the parochial school in the plans for the community was not necessarily an unappreciated gift; its construction saved ACB the costs of at least one public school and the funds to operate it.

When the first residents moved in, during the late summer and fall of 1948, glowing promises were made about the schools and the scheduling to open them. In Illinois schools have separate elected bodies of officials not connected to the management and operation of the village. Shortly after the November 1948 tent meeting, at what may have been the first meeting of the Committee for Municipal Incorporation, the subject of schools came up. Fred Roop, later one of the first village trustees, suggested that a committee be formed to establish a school board and policies for schools. The Municipal Incorporation Committee agreed, and, shortly after, the Committee for School Organizations was formed.

Robert Dinerstein recalled, from official meeting minutes and notes, that the first meeting of the school committee, on February 6, 1949, may have been the first meeting of the newly incorporated Village of Park Forest. Those attending that meeting were interested citizens; formal election of the school board would be held later. Dinerstein also suggested that ACB's method of solving the school problem was too simple. ACB wanted the whole village annexed into the

Chicago Heights school district, both elementary and high schools. This would quickly get the financial costs out of ACB's pocket while accelerating the time line of funding from the state. Since all the funding for the schools came from property taxes paid by ACB (it was the only property owner), belonging to the Chicago Heights school district would be a great advantage because of its industrial tax base. The district could afford to build the schools and pay the teachers. The advantages to Chicago Heights were minimal in the beginning, but, as the property values increased in Park Forest, the district would benefit greatly. The elementary school superintendent in Chicago Heights was all for the annexation. His district was mature, with a declining enrollment, and this would allow him to modernize and expand.

Chicago Heights was legally obligated to take the children east of Western Avenue. They were in the Chicago Heights district, and there was no question that this would happen. It was the remainder of Park Forest which was in question. A meeting was held to explore the point. Philip Klutznick was invited to present ACB's viewpoint, and, in a manner that was later described as typical, he responded to the committee in a direct and threatening tone. He challenged the committee and informed its members that, if any of them felt things had been misrepresented and if they were not happy in Park Forest, he would allow them to break their leases. The basic problem was that the village had a single property owner, American Community Builders. All the new students came from the rental properties, and, as such, tuition for the those students had to be paid by ACB. Klutznick felt they were doing more than they were legally required to, and, in many instances, they were. The school situation still needed to be addressed, for, without schools, the parents would soon be leaving for neighborhoods with schools.

In March 1949 Park Forest's first school board was elected and immediately started the process of building the first schools in the village. With a lack of funding and a significant delay in getting the funds, the district was restricted in what it could do. ACB proposed and then pushed through a bill by the state legislature allowing a school district to enter into a long-term lease for a school building, instead of having to build the structure. This lease arrangement would allow ACB to go to a bank and borrow the money needed to construct the building. Later, as the district was able to sell bonds, it would buy the school building. This would enable ACB to get the funds needed to build the schools as well as to be able to recover its costs, with interest, later.[12] So, in the fall of 1949 ACB was still in the education business.

Within a few years the east side of Western Avenue was de-annexed from the Chicago Heights district and annexed to Park Forest's district. A similar problem existed in the southern area of the village, the portion in Will County. That portion stayed in the Will County district, and, even though it caused some friction in the early days after nearby Blackhawk School was finished (students in Will county couldn't go there), the problem was solved after the Talala School was opened.

By October 26, 1951, Park Forest's School District had 1,106 elementary school students, and overcrowding was found at many grade levels. New enrollments grew to ten children per week with the opening of the for-sale home area. The problems of enrollment would continue for the next few years until most of the residential construction was complete and the schools were finished. Eventually, eleven elementary schools, one junior high school, and one high school would be built.

Anthony Scariano, one of Park Forest's more famous residents, was a young attorney who moved to Park Forest because of the article in *Collier's Magazine*. Scariano, who later became a well-respected Illinois state representative and an Illinois Appellate Court judge, recalled in 1969 a memory of those early days:

> Anyway—we were moved in, the town was new and starting to grow— one evening, a nice summer evening, my neighbor and I were standing out in front of my house. We were in one of the large courts, maybe 20 new houses in sort of a circle. It was a nice night, and the kids were all playing. You have got to realize what it was like then—all these young couples, all with children, I'll bet there were at least three children per house, almost all of them under five years old.
>
> It seemed that they were all outside that night—60 noisy, running, screaming children swirling around us—it was incredible. My neighbor and I just stood there, looking at all this activity, then he turned to me and said, "My God, Tony, they said we may have children here, they didn't say we must have children!"[13]

Two high school districts covered parts of the village. A large portion of Park Forest, west of Western Avenue, was not in any high school district, and it was this portion which would push Park Forest into the national limelight. The children in non–high school districts went to high schools in legitimate districts. The state allowed these non–high school districts to sell bonds and, with the proceeds, pay the tuitions of the non–high school district children. Children in Matteson and Flossmoor (a smaller and more affluent town to the north of Park Forest) went to Thornton or Bloom High Schools, and their tuition was paid by these bonds. Many of the students near the Illinois Central Railroad line went to Thornton, since it was close to the train station and easier to get to than Bloom.

This mechanism, as clever as it was, amassed a considerable debt. By the

Fig. 40. Children, most of them under the age of five, seemed to be a prerequisite for living in Park Forest. *Source:* courtesy of Park Forest Public Library.

early 1950s a movement was under way in the state legislature to eliminate the non–high school districts. Some of the people living in Rich Township, of which Park Forest was a part, were concerned that if this passed they may be saddled with the accumulated debt of the bonds. As other non–high school districts formed true high school districts, the remaining debt would escalate, it was thought, until the last part of the non–high school district would have the whole debt against them. In a defensive move people in the area around Park Forest, Matteson, and Flossmoor began to consider establishing a new high school district. Some were concerned about the need for the school, others with the accumulating debt of the bonds. A heated discussion about the matter of the high school was held in February 1949 at Flossmoor and attended by Hart Perry from ACB and Robert Dinerstein. Dinerstein was concerned about what he had heard and set up a village subcommittee concerning high schools. Jim Patterson was made chairman. Two years later the village voted and passed a bond issue to build a high school.

Considerable effort by the village and its citizens went into the formation and construction of Rich Township High School. Since 40 percent of the new village was in Bloom Township, a special "change in boundary" was required. Over fifty volunteers went house to house and collected signatures for a petition from over five thousand residents in the area. Signatures for the petition were collected in ten days, and by spring 1951 the boundaries were settled, and a referendum was scheduled for June 23.

One hundred and five citizens from Park Forest volunteered to get out the vote, and the result was the largest turnout in village history, with over 99 percent of the eligible voters in Park Forest favoring redistricting. At the same time this issue was being debated and voted on in Park Forest, the state legislature was rewriting the education code, and it eliminated the district in Park Forest because it was not operating a school. The villagers were very upset by this and secured an injunction in circuit court to stop the new law. The case was fought through the State Supreme Court in record time, and the court held for the village and the validity of the school district. This allowed bonds to be sold in the spring of 1952. Even more important was a follow-up to the referendum. If villagers wanted a school as ambitious as they had planned, they realized they would need an additional $350,000 in bonds. The bond issue carried throughout the village, and the new school was started in the fall of 1952 and opened for the fall term of 1953.

Park Forest was nominated for honors as an "All-America City" in 1954 because of the spirit of help and voluntarism shown by its citizens in the creation of the high school. It was one of eleven cities selected by *Look* magazine and the National Municipal League. Almost three hundred volunteers were honored by the article in the magazine.

Twenty-two years later, during America's Bi-Centennial year, Park Forest was again selected as an All-America City for its efforts in housing rehabilitation, fair housing, and racial integration. It was also recognized for its efforts to aid troubled youths and runaways through a counseling center staffed with trained volunteers and a new community center. Park Forest continued to be a community of volunteers and participants in its great experiment. Most of the similarities among the residents continued even after the for-sale homes expanded the village's social and economic boundaries. It is interesting to note that the original tenants developed the classic tenant/landlord, love/hate, relationship—not unlike those found in downtown high-rise apartments. The renters could be counted on to vote as a group against some of the more controversial ACB edicts and actions. They were a bit more socially liberal than many homeowners, long before tenants' rights had become a national topic. Yet, when these same tenants became homeowners, they began to vote with the landlord on taxes and other money issues. This change in the character of the village was noted by Al Engelhard, a local newspaper columnist of the time: "Of itself, harmony between tenant and landlord is a salutary thing, testifying to the tenant's intelligence and the landlord's good will. But the price has been high. Apathy has been the child of Peace,

Indifference the spawn of Concord . . . Since he is a man of many parts, I have hope that Phil Klutznick, alert to the disservice he has done to us by becoming a sweet and lovable old bug, is even now pondering some issue we can magnify into a monster, whisper about, conspire about, hang in effigy."[14]

There were two issues that brought to a head many of the problems the village encountered negotiating with ACB. Two papers had evolved in the area. The *Chicago Heights Star,* one of the oldest South Side papers, began to bring out a Park Forest edition. The other paper was the young and self-produced *Park Forest Reporter.* Both papers tended to support the villagers in many of the crises they confronted. Suddenly, in the early 1950s, a new paper called the *Park Forest News* appeared and presented a side that was very favorable to ACB and critical of the Board of Trustees. It even mocked the board and its actions. It was soon discovered that the paper was paid for by ACB and was published under its guidance. The lead columnist was found to be a member of the Board of Trustees who met regularly with the ACB and gave the company inside information about various village positions. The paper did not last very long.

The other, and more critical, issue was the need for a village hall. A small public safety building had been constructed to house police and fire, but there was no office space for the growing demands of the management staff of the village. The Board of Trustees decided to submit a bond issue to the voters for the construction of a village hall and a small maintenance building. ACB was able to get a new group of homeowners, calling themselves the Homesteaders' Association, to support ACB in opposing the bond issue. It is important to remember that at this time there were about equal numbers of renters and homeowners in the village, and the homeowners were now beginning to exert their power. Since bonds were to be paid for out of tax revenues, ACB and the homeowners had a lot more in common than the homeowners and the renters.

It was discovered, as the debate began, that it was a relatively small group of homeowners which sided with ACB. Manilow suggested a committee, unequally weighted with ACB and Homesteaders, be formed to formulate the building's program. Robert Dinerstein, chairman of the Public Works Committee and the one responsible for putting the village hall bond issue together, suggested instead that an advisory body be formed to work with the village during the final design process. He offered this to allow Manilow to save face and let the bond referendum proceed. The bond issue passed with over 90 percent approving the sale of the bonds.

It was this group, the Park Forest Homesteaders' Association, which was to play a significant role in the growth of the village as it shifted its balance from being a rental community to one of home ownership. It was reported that, at its peak, the association had over three thousand members and sixteen active com-

Fig. 41. Churches, such as Hope Lutheran, and community organizations provided the ethical and social backbone for the young village. *Source:* courtesy of Park Forest Public Library.

mittees that addressed such concerns as schools, public works and safety, utilities, streets, and recreation facilities. Its most important, respected work dealt with taxes and bonds. The group would continue to be a watchdog and conscience for the homeowners in the village.[15]

The pioneers who settled along the Sauk Trail were religious, and, when enough people could be gathered for a congregation, they built churches. The McCoys and Batcheldors were active members of the Methodist Church in Crete. In 1839 Sauk Trail saw Sunday carriages going to the St. James Catholic Church in Strasburg (later renamed Sauk Village) and four years later to a Presbyterian church in Thorn Grove (later renamed Chicago Heights). Later another Catholic Church, St. Anne's, was built on Sauk Trail near Westwood Drive. The old cemetery, which survived the pioneer days, still exists and is the oldest part of the village.

From the inception of the village Philip Klutznick, unlike many developers, set aside church sites throughout the village which would be free to any denomination that was organized and needed the land. In an effort to insure that an equitable and respectful direction be given the various denominations, Klutznick asked Hugo Leinberger to join the community and act as arbiter and coordinator of religious needs. His title was chaplain for the Cooperative Denominations.

Leinberger was a veteran and had served as a navy chaplain at sea; he would later refer to it as a great field experience for the "chaplaincy" of the village. He had no strong denominational bias, which enabled him to move from group to group with less of a perceived prejudice. He was there to help enlist people for various churches. He said very early on: "When you move into a formative community like this, you don't worry first what the educational philosophy is. You want to know if there is a good building, teachers, and things like that. You worry about the detailed philosophy only later."[16] Leinberger wanted a "useful" church, as William H. Whyte Jr. called it, not one that focused on theological points and differences. As he said in Whyte's *Organization Man:* "I think this is the basic need—the need to belong to a group. You find this fellowship in a church better than anywhere else. And it is contagious. In a community like Park Forest, when young people see how many other people are going to church regularly, they feel they ought to. Another need we fulfill is counseling. Young people want a place to take their problems and someone to talk to about them. Put all these things together and you get what we're after—a sense of community."[17]

The religious mix of residents of Park Forest in May 1950 was one-quarter Roman Catholic, two-thirds Protestant (with Methodist and Presbyterian denominations the largest), and about one-tenth Jewish. The residents, after a survey to determine their priorities of religious importance, listed the minister, the Sunday school, the location, the denomination, and the music.

The Catholics, through the Chicago diocese, elected to build a new church near the Plaza with Father Elmer Coogan as pastor and called it St. Irenaeus. It was opened on Christmas Day 1951. For about one year the Catholics had shared service space with the Protestants in the Holiday Theatre. A few Catholic residents would later remark that they often felt the need to genuflect when they got up for popcorn during the movie. The Jewish residents built Temple Beth Sholom, a Reform synagogue on Western Avenue, and may have also used the theater while their synagogue was under construction.[18] It was the Protestants who created something new and different. Leinberger, in response to the young residents' concern about a "community church," proposed that a United Protestant Church be formed, which joined the five largest denominations under one roof. The concerns were both practical and idealistic—practical because it would be less expensive than building five churches and idealistic because, by joining their resources, they would be able to do more for the community and themselves. One qualified pastor would be better than five and, amid the tenor of the time, more efficient.

The Faith United Protestant Church was built and opened by early spring of 1952. Dr. Gerson Englemann, of Cincinnati, Ohio, became permanent minister and an important part of the religious and social fabric of the village. Within a few years a second United Protestant Church was formed and built to take on the growing load of members, and eventually a third joined the other two. Initially, the leaders of the various denominations did not agree with the idea of a United Church, but their objections only steeled the residents to their efforts. And, in spite of controversial articles and comments in the *Christian Century* magazine, they eventually agreed to compromise. The Lutherans and Episcopalians, because of their significantly different liturgies and organization, went ahead with their own plans for facilities.

The United Church would have one basic service but, unlike community churches, encouraged its members to maintain their original religious affiliations. As other churches expanded, creative ways of financing the buildings were explored, such as floating bank loans with pledges of collateral. The parishioners bought their own bonds and sacrificed their time and energy. But they found little support from outside the village for their efforts. As one member said after the difficulties of trying to find a new minister, "I remember talking to one man we were considering. He kept telling me about having to wait for the 'Call of God.' Well, sir, I got the feeling that the 'Call of God' was going to have to come over the telephone—and was also going to have to say something about a pretty good salary. I tell you it's hard to get across to most clergymen the frontier we are offering."[19] Eventually, American Community Builders would offer land for buildings and churches to over twelve separate religious organizations.

Unlike the communities of the late twentieth century, safety was not an overly advertised and promoted issue in these new towns. Park Forest had essentially no crime. Crime was an urban problem, and people did not expect it in the new communities. Police attributed the lack of crime to the fact that most men were honorably discharged veterans and tenants, and homeowners had been subjected to economic screening. This would have eliminated the "riffraff" normally found in more diverse areas. It may have also been a result of the lack of overcrowded slums, poor neighborhoods, and sleazy bars and hangouts. Economic predation was a result of real poverty, and Park Forest had none. Other positive factors encouraged a law-abiding aspect to the village; strong family ties, the explosive growth of the churches and other social organizations, steady employment, and a responsive and supportive government structure.[20]

Very shortly after its incorporation the village of Park Forest found that, as much as it needed schools, it also needed to expand the police and fire departments. The residents showed ACB studies stating how many police and firemen were needed per thousand residents and said this should be the village's standard; ACB replied that the company couldn't afford them. ACB was then accused of not believing in maintaining standards, and the war of words would continue.

Initially, the fire department was manned by ACB employees during the day (this was along with their regular jobs) and with village volunteers at night. A private security company had been maintaining law enforcement. Now, as an incorporated village, the provision for police and fire protection was becoming the responsibility of the village. The initial village police force took over in November 1949, and by mid-1950 the police force had eight patrolmen and two radio-equipped squad cars for the eighty-five hundred residents.

Many of the same issues also affected the fire department. The village had grown, and the need for equipment and firefighters was grudgingly realized by ACB. Subsequently, the quality of the force was maintained by both infusions of money from ACB and by the promise of future revenues. A new $16,000 La France fire truck was delivered in the summer of 1951.

The first tax money for Park Forest did not arrive until July of 1950. The village by that time had a population of almost fifteen thousand people and was trying to operate on a budget of fifty thousand dollars.[21]

Schools, government, village growth, churches, and safety were paramount issues on the minds of the builders and villagers alike. Egos would clash. Robert Dinerstein called Philip Klutznick "a prophet without honor in his own country." The residents would continually demand more services. Time after time, because ACB was paying for all the villages' services, Klutznick would turn them down or try to reduce their demands to more modest levels. He was an internationally known and respected person, yet within his own town he was not believed, and this weighed heavily on him personally.

CHAPTER EIGHT

The Shopping Center

There was no place to buy even so much as a bottle of milk, so everything you had to do, you did by going over to Chicago Heights to shop. There was a truck that came around during the day for the construction crews that sold sandwiches and stuff, but they would also sell to housewives, so you could go over and get something from them.

—Robert Dinerstein, Oral History Recollection

I T was one of the stranger aspects of the expansion of the suburbs after the war. Americans had saved more money than at any time in their past. At the war's end they had a nest egg of personal savings worth over $136 billion in banks and government bonds. But there was little to buy. The war was over, a war that had consumed most goods and services, and now these young Americans wanted cars, washing machines, stoves, new styles, and entertainment. For the early residents of Park Forest a loaf of bread or a pot roast required a round trip of almost ten miles. Cashing a check required going to their bank, because many stores would not cash their checks. Shopping, for those who did not own a car, was an even more complicated and difficult adventure. Manilow and Klutznick knew that with Park Forest they not only had the retail market to themselves but an unprecedented demand as well. The young families moving into the village were requiring not only quality housing but also quality goods and services.

In the earliest prospectus for the community, written during the summer of 1946, there were estimates on the purchasing power of the new residents. Discussions were held on which commercial uses would be required and how they would be managed. Unlike other villages and towns, where demand was met by unguided entrepreneurial activity, new shops, and expanding stores, American Community Builder's approach was scientific and limiting. They reasoned that, if an existing town of the same size might support 125 food establishments, Park Forest could "retain the element of competitive selling and service the population more effectively, with some 5 to 8 food establishments, including several supermarkets." All that was required was sound management in selecting those establishments—selection based on demographics.

ACB hired the Real Estate Research Corporation to do an extensive survey of the present and future retail trends of the region. They projected incomes, percentage of income available for retail sales, and how far the retail market extended. Klutznick knew from the beginning that if the center were to survive it needed more support than what would come from just the new residents in Park Forest.

Real Estate Research Corporation determined that the average annual income of the new residents would be about $5,300. All but $2,000 of that amount would be spent in retail stores. Eighty percent of the total (i.e., more than $21 million) would be spent at the Park Forest shopping center. This, however, would be only half of the projected sales for the center; the remaining sales were expected to come from the Chicago southside.

To confirm this, Real Estate Research Corporation conducted three surveys to determine present shopping habits and where there were points of dissatisfaction with current shopping conditions. The first survey was a series of interviews taken in Chicago Heights (the largest retail area on the far southside) and at the shopping district at Sixty-third and Halsted (within the city limits of Chicago). At both locations they found that shoppers were already in the habit of driving to other communities for major purchases and could be drawn to Park Forest with the proper mix of stores.

Second, they mailed five thousand survey forms to consumers outside the Chicago city limits but still within the Park Forest shopping area. The survey asked where they went to purchase clothing, appliances, and furniture, how often, and how they got there. It also a asked their opinion of the current retail opportunities in the south Chicago area. They received an unexpected high number of returns from the mailing. Forty percent replied that they shopped by automobile, and only 26 percent said they shopped in the community where they lived. Real Estate Research Corporation also found that only 22 percent did any significant shopping in downtown Chicago, and another 10 percent admitted an occasional trip downtown.

The third and last survey was limited to the early residents of Park Forest. With the help of the apartment managers and the completed rental forms, they attempted to determine family composition, place of employment, income, automobile ownership, and previous residence. All three surveys were conducted to determine what commercial uses the region needed as well as what the residents wanted. These projections allowed ACB to better determine the shopping center's mix and square footage while also supplying potential store operators important demographic information many could not afford to compile on their own.[1] Later surveys conducted by the village found that the Plaza attracted shoppers from as far away as Kankakee and Joliet, over thirty miles away.

Prior to the Real Estate Research Corporation surveys, the initial study plans called for a commercial center with 250,000 square feet of leasable space. The architects, Loebl and Schlossman, were asked to prepare the conceptual plans and cost estimates for a center of this size. Even though a final location had not been set, the financial costs involved in the construction were being prepared. Elbert Peets continued developing his overall community plans, and by October 1946 the commercial center had been placed in two possible locations. The first plan placed the shopping center on the north side of the development near a proposed train station on the Elgin, Joliet & Eastern Railroad line. The second placed the shopping center further south, toward the geographic middle of the village, along Western Avenue.

Klutznick, throughout this period, was also engaged in discussions with potential commercial tenants and had submitted the two alternative plans to them for their comments. Most favored the first plan, with its greater traffic counts and easier access to Matteson and Chicago Heights. Secondary considerations in its favor were the locations of the Illinois Central Railroad, the ease of connections to existing utilities, and the possible inclusion of the industrial property. The second plan's benefits focused on the existing and future residents and the ability to expand in almost all directions. The central location of the commercial area also provided a retail center closer to the residents and, as such, reduced automobile use in the interior.

The role of Western Avenue in the town plan, according to Peets, was the subject of "infinite discussions." There were discussions about moving Western Avenue east to the edge of the Forest Preserve or west to front directly on the plaza's central location. There were discussions about tunneling under the railroads to speed traffic flow and about the addition of a median to improve its appearance. These ideas quickly passed. The money was not available, and the state would not accept moving the road.

Peets believed that Western Avenue would and should become the backbone street of the community and, as such, should have the shopping center front directly on it. The center, with this juxtaposition with Western Avenue, would be the most convenient location for both the townspeople and others in the area. The architects and Klutznick wanted the central location to make it easier to expand the center while reducing the possibility of competition. Peets always believed the central location was more aesthetically pleasing, even though he favored a more active location on Western Avenue. Peets also did not believe that the center would grow to the size that it would eventually become.[2]

The first plan, plan A as it was called, unfortunately had one serious flaw: it required the cooperation of the railroad—cooperation that was not forthcoming.

The Illinois Central Railroad did not want to get involved with the community and would not support the expansion of commuter services to either the north side or Western Avenue locations. As a result of this intransigence, the second plan's central location was selected just prior to the first public announcement on October 28, 1946.

The opportunity to integrate the village with transit would be lost forever. This unrealized concept was a central tenet of Ebenezer Howard's Garden City planning. The shopping center itself would provide the hub for the development of the village plan. Twenty-five years later the Plaza, as it was called, was seen as isolated and remote to those outside the village. The later growth and aggressiveness of the newer regional shopping centers in southern Cook County would severely impact many of the Plaza's retail tenants.

The Plaza, by February 1947, had been given a life of its own, separate and distinct from the housing issues. It would respond to the projected initial purchasing power of thirteen to eighteen million dollars in local salaries and anticipated annual sales of over ten million dollars. These projections resulted in a plan for 225,000 square feet of rentable space and a listing of over thirty-six possible uses.

Loebl and Schlossman became Loebl, Schlossman and Bennett in 1947, after Richard Bennett joined the firm as designer for the new community. Bennett planned an informal layout to the Plaza which was efficient in merchandising methods and attractive in appearance. He believed that shopping should be an adventure and a search for a bargain. "You never find a bargain straight ahead," he would later say, "you have to look around. The design curves and forces the shopper in and out and around the plaza."[3]

There was no focal point to the Plaza and no corner where everyone had to pass. The center was enclosed on three sides by parking, and the initial plan had a formal drop-off entry on the eastern side with direct access from Victory Boulevard. Six secondary entries from the parking lots provided good distribution to the shops. The interconnecting walkway was covered with a metal awning that extended in front of all the stores, providing shelter from the rain and snow. The buildings were a mix of Chicago common brick and white paint. The interior court was fully landscaped with large lawn areas, some trees, diagonal walkways, and flower beds.

The Holiday Theatre, with its eleven hundred seats and glass-enclosed baby crying room, provided the central north side anchor. The theater was opened on October 28, 1950, exactly four years after the community was first announced and three years after the first dirt was moved. The first movie that played there was called *"Tight" Little Island*, a hilarious British film about a cargo of whiskey, a

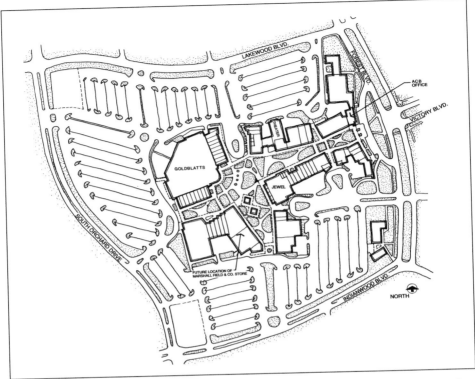

Fig. 42. The Plaza opened with a broad selection of stores surrounding an open courtyard free from cars. This scheme became typical for American shopping centers, both enclosed and open. *Source:* author's drawing.

sinking ship, and an island of thirsty Scotsmen. In many ways life in the film resembled that for the isolated residents of Park Forest and their quests for companionship and their penchant for court parties and liquor.

The Jewel Tea grocery store was the largest store in its chain and was the Plaza's south side anchor. It was modern in layout, simple in construction, but with just a twist in the ceiling design which gave it a distinctive look. It also provided its customers a convenient grocery bag pickup area, one of the first to acknowledge the use of the automobile. The store would last only a few years in this location; it was not big enough to meet the incredible growth of the village and moved further west across Orchard Drive to its own small center. Other stores in the Plaza included a S. S. Kresge Five and Dime, a liquor store, music shop, hobby store, clothing's stores, and baby shops. The biggest draws were the hardware store, barbershop, and beauty parlor.[4]

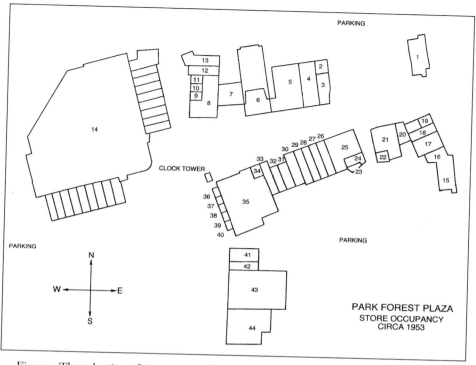

Fig. 43. The selection of stores was as diverse as in any small town in the United States. (See table 8.1 for identification of businesses.) *Source:* author's drawing.

The first tenants were concerned about the free-form nature of the center's plan and their ability to market and operate their stores effectively. They soon learned that the buildings were planned for selling, even though they were not designed to typical chain store standards. The merchant's concern may have been more relevant than it was given credit for at the time. The great number of residents and their need for goods covered many of the flaws of the design, and, until credible retail competition developed, the Plaza functioned well.

The Plaza's design and shape is based, according to Richard Bennett, on the Plaza San Marco in Venice with its large courtyard and tower. The central clock tower was supposed to be twice as high as it was built and have a broad pool and fountain at its base. It was to be seen for miles and be a visual attraction and focus for the community. But at forty feet it could hardly be seen outside of the Plaza. Sam Beber, who was in charge of the construction, stopped its height at forty feet, took the pool and fountain out, and, according to Bennett, would have eliminated it entirely if he could have. The tower was for years the symbol for the village and was used on the village vehicle sticker and on all stationery and offi-

Fig. 44. Nathan Manilow at the foot of the clock tower. Richard Bennett based the design for the Plaza and clock tower on the Plaza San Marco in Venice. *Source:* courtesy of Park Forest Public Library.

cial correspondence. Thirty five years later, on a cold January day in 1987, the tower was demolished with the swinging impact of an iron ball. The tower, like the Plaza itself, would not withstand its collision with time.[5]

In September 1953 Goldblatt's added the sixteenth store of its chain to the

TABLE 8.1

Park Forest Plaza Store List, 1953

1. Administration Building (American Community Builders)	21. Park Forest Hardware
2. Public Service Co.	22. Park Forest Water Company
3. Fran's of Park Forest (women's apparel)	23. Camera Corner
	24. Hofmann Florist
4. Park Forest Liquors	25. Drug Store
5. Siefer's of Park Forest (furniture)	26. Bakery
	27. Cleaners
6. Shapiro's Shoe Shop	28. Prince & Princess Toy Shop
7. Holiday Theater	29. Delicatessen
8. MacArnolds (women's apparel)	30. Cocktail Lounge
	31. Youngster's (infants and children) ²\AU\
9. Art Mart (gift shop)	32. Beauty Shop
10. Dr. Julian Rice (optometrist)	33. Laundromat
	34. Hickory Hill Farms (cut chicken shop)
11. McClurg's Book Shop	35. Jewel Foods
12. Vistain's News Agency (magazines and party favors)	36. Amstadter Storage & Van Co.
	37. Karmel Korn Shop
13. Park Forest TV & Record Center	38. Park Forest Jewlers
14. Goldblatts' Department Store	39. Park Forest Shoe Repair
15. Bank of Park Forest	40. Park Forest Currency Exchange
16. Entrance to Medical Arts Building	41. Fidler's for Men (clothing and accessories)
17. Post Office	42. Park Forest Insurance Co.
18. Hobby & Sports Center	43. S. S. Kresge Co.
19. Dutch Mill Candy Store	44. Pick-N-Save Food Store
20. Barber Shop	

Plaza. The 60,000 square foot store, also designed by Loebl, Schlossman and Bennett, was located west of the theater and formed the northwest corner anchor for the mall. Goldblatt's was a middle-market department store and contained softgoods such as clothing and household products. It also had an outside area selling shrubbery and garden furniture.

A wide, gold-colored canopy extended across the building's front that faced the Plaza. This structure was large enough to walk on, and in the fall of 1956 a campaigning Vice President Richard Nixon spoke to a huge gathering of Park Forest's residents from this vantage point. It was probably the largest crowd ever assembled in the history of the Plaza.

Within a year of the Goldblatt's opening, the most important store of the center would be committed to. Philip Klutznick firmly believed there must be shift in emphasis from house rentals to shopping center rentals as a major source

Fig. 45. The Plaza, with its clock tower, after Marshall Field's opened in 1955. The Plaza's design seemed to set the center for the growth of the village. *Source:* courtesy of Park Forest Public Library.

of income for ACB. To insure a continued income stream, a healthy and viable center must be maintained. The continued growth of the Plaza was paramount, and to support this end Klutznick convinced Marshall Field and Company to place their fifth store on the southern side of the Plaza.[6]

James Palmer, Marshall Field's president, had taken the advice of Ferd Kramer not to build his own store and be a landlord to himself but to find a builder to construct the store. Kramer recommended Klutznick. Ferd Kramer had been involved with Park Forest four years earlier when ACB was looking for financial backing. Kramer of Draper and Kramer, one of Chicago's largest real estate firms, put Klutznick and representatives of Northwestern Mutual and New York Life together. These two insurance firms were responsible for over $22 million of the initial mortgage of $27.2 million for the rental housing.

The two had been friends since Kramer hired Klutznick in 1941, when he, Kramer, was a key official in the federal Defense Housing department. Kramer, only four years older than Klutznick, was the administrator who called him to

Washington from Chicago. According to Kramer, Klutznick was "that young lawyer from Omaha who knows something about housing," and now, ten years later, their relationship had grown to include some of the biggest builders and commercial interests in the country.

Klutznick negotiated the placement and construction of the Marshall Field store on the southwestern corner of the Plaza. His involvement with the Marshall Field and Company would later lead to stores in three of the region's early shopping malls that he would develop: Old Orchard, Oakbrook, and River Oaks. Eventually, this alliance would lead to the inclusion of a Field's store in Klutznick's downtown Chicago Water Tower Place, built in the 1970s.

The first building, to the right of the main entry from Victory Boulevard, was occupied by American Community Builders. This two-story structure would later become the home of the Bank of Park Forest and other financial concerns. When built, it was at the eastern entry to the mall from Forest Boulevard and faced a comfortable drop-off and turnaround area. Twelve years later, in 1963, the construction of the Sears Roebuck and Company store would geographically push the ACB office building toward the center of the shopping center. This construction would damage the integrity of the Plaza and the village's internal circulation more than any other modification to the Elbert Peets plan. It was obvious that Sears wanted the exposure that the Western Avenue window provided (harkening back to the Peets's concepts), but, in doing so, it fundamentally destroyed the circulation plan of the village. The store was placed outside the eastern gateway to the Plaza and extended across Forest Boulevard and down Victory Boulevard, essentially cutting Park Forest in two.

The Sears store created a draw to the eastern end of the Plaza and helped to support the smaller stores between Marshall Fields, Goldblatt's, and itself. This triangular circulation pattern greatly helped all the retail uses. The revitalization of the Plaza and the added sales tax income offset the impact to the village circulation, but, sadly, it also lost its primary entry. Like the rental apartments, the Plaza would only be entered through its many back doors; it no longer had a "front door." Forest Boulevard relinquished its role as the primary north-to-south street in the village, and Orchard Boulevard, on the west side of the Plaza, became the dominant street.

After the completion and opening of the Marshall Field store in 1955, the Plaza continued to grow and prosper. During the recession of 1957 and 1958, when the country as a whole saw retail sales fall by almost 4 percent, Park Forest Plaza's sales increased by 17 percent. The young citizens of the suburbs, even with their mortgages and their budgets, still spent money. Washing machines needed to be purchased, cars needed to be replaced, and, of course, lawns needed to be mowed.

Fig. 46. The Plaza offered a delightfully different form of shopping from the urban store-front experience of the 1950s. *Source:* courtesy of Park Forest Public Library.

The tough economic times of the late 1950s, especially evident in the older industrial centers, seemed to pass over the suburban countryside. Most everyone lived on the edge financially, and, with hard times, they watched every dime. They told no one when fired from a job and kept up appearances until a new position could be secured. As one financial manager said, "They were all going to keep up with the Jones's . . . They do live beyond their means, but they do it in a nice, genteel way."

By the early 1960s, with the completion of the Sears store, the Plaza was booming. There was even a proposal to expand the center by removing some of the apartments to the east of the Plaza to allow the construction of a J. C. Penney Company store. Plans were shown to the village, but it never happened.

The first blow to the commercial power of the Plaza was done surprisingly by Klutznick himself. Four years after quietly selling his interest in the Plaza in 1962, he assembled a team of architects and landscape architects and built the first of the truly modern shopping centers, River Oaks. Built in Calumet City, about twelve miles from Park Forest, it began to take customers from the northeast market of the Plaza. It too was an open mall, but it was denser and more enclosed, with a brighter and more vibrant mix of stores. River Oaks, along with its earlier sisters, Old Orchard and Oak Brook, also built by Klutznick, had a profound effect on the retail market of the South and West Sides of Chicago. This effect was not to be challenged for ten years, until the massive impact of the combination of the interstate highway system and the enclosed shopping mall appeared in the region.

After the opening of the Marshall Fields store in River Oaks, the financial impact on the Plaza was immediate. The store manager for the Park Forest store reported that, after the first Christmas that the River Oaks store was open, Park Forest had negative sales. This was due in great part to returns from River Oaks being made in the Park Forest store. This seemingly minor note would eventually herald bigger problems for the Plaza. Park Forest's residents were shopping at River Oaks and were responding to newer and better stores.

From 1962 through 1973 the Plaza was still owned and operated by Nate Manilow. It managed to suffer through the impacts of the new malls and turbulent social and business times. In 1968 it was ranked fourth in retail sales among forty-eight Chicago suburbs. In the late 1960s Manilow initiated another community development immediately south of Park Forest called Park Forest South. This development was a direct result of Lyndon Johnson's Great Society program and HUD's New Communities Act of 1968. HUD made significant funds available for the development of new towns throughout the country. To get funds for his new project Manilow sold Park Forest Plaza in December 1973 to a group of 212 airline pilots seeking tax advantages and write-offs. This group was formed by a Chicago accountant Joseph Borenstein.[7]

In 1972 Lincoln Mall was built in Matteson. The region's first enclosed shopping mall included the J. C. Penney store that had not been built in Park Forest. Lincoln Mall directly fronted on Lincoln Highway and was less than a mile from the new Interstate 57 that ran from Chicago to Memphis, Tennessee. It was also about three miles from the original plan A shopping center location that had been favored by ACB in 1946.

Ownership changes of the Plaza were to continue for the next two decades. In July 1976 the property was owned by Park Forest, Ltd. Through a concerted effort to rake away all income from the center, Acquisition and Development Advisors, Inc., the management company operated by Barry S. Marlin, destroyed any remaining economic viability of the Plaza and drove the partnership that owned the center into bankruptcy. Marlin was also indicted for mail fraud and income tax evasion in California for Ponzi-type investment schemes, and he eventually went to prison. In 1977 a bankruptcy court judge approved the Plaza's sale to a Chicago real estate firm, but the transaction did not go through. Great West Life Assurance Company of Canada had held the mortgage with Nathan Manilow since 1965, and in 1977 it was still holding the property.

It was important to compete with the new enclosed malls, but Park Forest Plaza fatally hesitated. Nothing was done to compete with the changes in retail marketing, and little was done to improve its deteriorating physical condition. John Weigel, writing in the *Park Forest Reporter* on May 12, 1976, called for the public buyout of the Plaza: "The best solution to the control of the future of the Park Forest Plaza and the village is for the citizens to band together and purchase the shopping center." He suggested that the village form a corporation and offer and purchase shares of stock. Unfortunately, his proposal was only that, a proposal. There was too great a fear, at the time, about the loss of tax revenues from the center to make such a drastic, though viable, solution real.

Goldblatt's filed for bankruptcy in 1981 and closed its Park Forest store. In 1983 Great West Life Assurance sold the center to another group, Park Forest Plaza Associates, whose partners were a Chicago architect, a Philadelphia investment counselor, and Donald Levine of Munster, Indiana (a few years later Levine was murdered in what seems to have been a hired killing). The remaining stores began to move out in 1984-85. Roofs leaked, and the maintenance of the center continued to decline. The failure of the Plaza was almost at hand.

Ron Bean, the village president at the time, managed to convince the townspeople and commercial owners of the advantages of forming a tax-increment financing district (TIF) to generate more than five million dollars in public funds to rehabilitate the center. This was combined with several million dollars from another new ownership group headed by Baltimore-based Robert Embry, once director of HUD's urban development action grant program, and David Cordish, another former HUD official. The village persuaded the state to put up thirteen million dollars in low-interest state bonds for remodeling expenses. If successful, the increases in real estate tax valuations and sales revenues would pay the debt; if unsuccessful, the villagers would pay off the debt.

The Plaza was reopened on Saturday, August 29, 1987, and rechristened as "the Centre." The almost abandoned shopping center had been outwardly rehabilitated; it had lost its historic clock tower and had gained new walkways, but the interiors were not improved and the roof only patched. Dramatic facades in green copper were built, and an extensive pond and waterfall system was added to the central court from the same type of limestone the village sat upon. After the improvements were completed, an air of confidence returned to the retailers in the Centre. Unfortunately, the customers didn't.

In many ways this was like painting the inside of a house to prevent the roof from leaking. Without a strong management team, separate and independent from the involvement of the village, little could be done to improve the economic base of the Centre. It needed new stores and enticements, not a cosmetic Disneyesque face-lift. It was reported that Cordish brought in new chain stores for one-year contracts, possibly in payment for favors at other malls they owned. After the term of their short contract was up, many of the stores closed and pulled out. An improved design may encourage someone to visit, but to insure success it was incumbent on the new public-private partnership to have that visitor return time and time again. Only a great mix of permanent stores could have done that, or a mix that the community needed.

To compound the problems, in 1986, as the remodeling began, Marshall Field tried to break its lease and abandon its store. Through the grassroots efforts of the community, a six thousand–signature petition, a strong buying campaign to show their economic clout, picketers handing out informational flyers at the Loop store, and extensive media coverage, the company was persuaded to reconsider and elected to stay. The primary reason for their decision to stay was probably less than altruistic; it was more likely the village's lawsuit to collect $5.2 million in tax-increment financing bonds issued to refinance the rehabilitation.

By mid-1990 the Centre had managed to recover and sit up. There was still a weak pulse, but there was color in its cheeks. Marshall Fields and Sears were extensively renovated, and this was seen as a strong sign of confidence. The theater was reopened with five screens, and almost forty stores had returned. But it was still short, by half, the number of shops promised by the current owner for opening day.

Soon, however, the patient had a relapse. After a disappointing 1990 Christmas season, six stores moved out. Even though the village believed there were still enough retail sales in the village to support its bond payments, there was a long-term concern over the schedule of payments, and there was talk of seeking special legislation from Springfield to get relief. There was also a significant amount of finger pointing. The developer said that they were not getting the support from the village which they expected, such as scheduling festival events in the Centre. There was talk of converting to niche markets: theming for the Centre, big box retailing, home improvement centers, and outlet malls. About that time Joe Weinberg, vice president for the Cordish-Embry firm, was quoted as saying: "The market in the south suburbs has changed in that there's a lot more retail competition. We need to differentiate ourselves in the marketplace . . . The hope is that the Centre may be able to siphon off a few busloads of penny-pinching shoppers in the Chicago area that normally find themselves in Michigan City, Indiana, or Kenosha, Wisconsin, for an outlet fix." A drowning man will grasp at anything. The developer, in frustration, commented in a phrase of un-

derstatement: "I don't know how long we can sit and wait. It could become a political issue."

They did not have to sit very long. The Cordish-Embry group sold the Centre to another group of investors located in Chicago; a new business was incorporated under the name Parkside Land Company to manage the center. The
new group showed no more concern for the Centre's growth and future than the
previous owners.

By the spring of 1995 the mall was again abandoned. Only a few small, service-oriented stores managed to remain. Sears was ready to move to Lincoln Mall,
and the fate of the Marshall Fields store was yet to be determined. The only positive element for the Centre was the relocation of the Village Hall there. This was
a questionable decision. The Village Hall may entice some foot traffic to the
Centre, but it also creates negative storefront space and will hinder inevitable redevelopment of the retail core.

The village tried to stay neutral about all the changes. Barbara Berlin, a
former village planner, when asked the position of the village regarding these
changes and the ensuing problems said, "We always took the position that it was
a privately owned shopping center and not our job to do the plans." But they did
have some ideas. "First," she said, "I would have liked to face the fact that it was
not a regional shopping center, although we kept trying to make it one . . . I
would have considered demolishing some of the space. And I would bring in
housing, perhaps on the periphery of the parking lot. That would make it more
like a downtown."[8]

During the winter of 1995-96 a significant event occurred: the Centre's ownership changed again. This time the village bought the property. Using some of
the $2.6 million in funds generated by a settlement with Sears (a result of its mov-
ing to Lincoln Mall), the village bought the Centre from Parkside Land Company and paid the past-due property taxes. With the remaining funds the village
began the long process of recreating a downtown and new heart for the village.

An industrial park component was planned as an important economic element
of the community from the initial inception of the village in 1946. The original
prospectus pointed to the excellent railroad connections that were available on
the Michigan Central and the highway access to Western Avenue and Route 30.
ACB put specific limitations on these parcels from the very beginning. Klutznick
wrote, "In view of the concept of a planned and integrated community which
could be immeasurably harmed by the introduction of nuisance industries, a limitation is provided that only such industries that do not generate smoke, unconscionable noises, or emit undesirable odors, will be permitted access to this land."

At a time when heavy industry was king this was a bold and enlightened statement; it may have also severely limited the growth of the industrial lands for twenty years. ACB was also looking at the industrial area as one of the financial supports of the village. Three important purposes were defined in the ACB prospectus:

1. The establishment of industry is essential for the development of a sound tax basis for the town.
2. The presence of industry will tend to stabilize the community.
3. The industry will afford supplementary outlet for the employment needs of the residents of the community.

The only participation of ACB would be to select the industry, approve the general plan of development, and dispose of the land to approved industries.

The November 1946 plan located the industrial areas north of the railroad tracks. These parcels were extensive and extended east and west of Western Avenue up to the property's boundary with Chicago Heights and in a northerly direction up to Route 30. By the time the proposal for FHA guarantees had been completed, in the late winter of 1947, the industrial area had been set at about 475 acres.

In the early 1950s the industrial park was advertised as an excellent location for "decentralized defense production" with an ample labor supply and freedom from urban congestion. Unfortunately, ACB knew how to build commercial centers and housing, but the company could not lure the industrial users that the community needed to round out its financial makeup. By mid 1951 the plans began to show these areas as "Reserved," and any mention of industrial development was dropped from most advertisements.

Jack Rashkin, an early employee of ACB, would recall almost thirty years later that the industrial park may have never been scheduled to make a serious effort at establishing itself. He suggested that Sam Beber, through his intransigence and demeanor, may have even killed potential deals. One deal did not get away, however, and it may have been more the result of Tom McDade's workaholic attitude than anything else. McDade went to work for ACB in June 1951. He had searched out Park Forest and called Phil Klutznick at home to ask for a job, met him, and immediately got into an argument. This inauspicious beginning would result in a professional association between McDade and Klutznick which would last for over twenty-five years.

McDade was working on a Sunday in the ACB offices when his receptionist told him that a gentleman was in the lobby who would like to talk to someone about having a factory building in Industry Park. "Would I see him?" responded McDade, "How quickly can you knit a red carpet?"

Even though he was not in charge of the industrial park, McDade and the other senior ACB staff members would wear whatever hat was available and needed to be worn. The gentlemen introduced himself as George Holly, president of the Hollymatic Manufacturing Company. He lived in Olympia Fields, just across the north border of Park Forest, and was looking for a site for his new manufacturing plant. Could Park Forest help him out? He wanted to build a new manufacturing plant but wondered if the village would allow the siting of a helicopter landing site in the industrial park to help his business. The village approved the helicopter landing site, and Hollymatic opened its manufacturing plant on North Street at "Holly" Street.[9]

Hollymatic joined three other smaller industries: Donahue Sales Corporation was a distributor for Talon Zippers, Star Disposal the town's scavenger service, and Winstrom Manufacturing built windows. It would be a long time before other significant industrial facilities would join the group. Eventually, Lincolnwood and other housing developments to the north and west would claim the land originally designated for Park Forest's Industry Park. The industrial and employment center would resolve itself into a parcel of land with less than seventy acres, 15 percent of its original size—in reality too small to provide any substantive benefit for the village.

A fifty-five-acre parcel of land to the west of the industrial park was acquired by the Illinois Department of Mental Health in the late 1960s for an innovative center for developmentally handicapped children. Instead of warehousing retarded children in large, dormitory-type buildings, the center built separate houses for smaller groups of children, who would live in a family-oriented manner. In the 1980s the Michigan Central track was abandoned and removed. The right-of-way became a component of a regional hiking trail system called the Prairie Path which extends west to Joliet.

With the loss of its industrial component Park Forest would never meet the criteria established by Ebenezer Howard and his Garden Cities. Seventy acres would, at its greatest employee density, provide only about twenty-four hundred jobs, whereas the original Industrial Park might have provided over sixteen thousand jobs, a significant and community supporting number. For Park Forest this lack of industry, like the shopping center, was an opportunity lost.

CHAPTER NINE

The Single-Family Homes

We are not peas in a pod. I thought it would be like that, especially
because incomes are nearly the same. But it's amazing how different and
varied people are, likes and dislikes, attitudes and wants. I never really
knew what people were until I came here.

—Anonymous Park Forest mother

We aren't interested in houses alone. We are trying to create a better life
for people. In our view, we will have failed if all we do is produce houses.

—Philip M. Klutznick, *Collier's Magazine*, February 14, 1948

AMERICAN workers at the end of World War II, with their amassed savings and war bonds, were in a position to put 20 to 30 percent down on a new house. It was the GI who was on the short end financially, but the loan guarantees in the GI Bill of Rights enabled veterans to compete in the housing market with war workers. Whereas it was possible for the war workers to buy a $10,000 house with a down payment of from $2,000 to $4,000, the veteran could buy that house with almost nothing down. The money did not come from the Veterans' Administration or the government but from the financial institution that was making the loan. The Veterans' Administration was the guarantor on the note. The guarantee was for 40 percent of the price of the house, to a maximum of $4,000. The bill further stipulated that the rate of interest should not exceed 4 percent on any loan guaranteed by the Veterans' Administration, and, if it did exceed that rate, the guarantee would become void. To insure this valuation, the VA appraised the properties to confirm the value and the price; if approved, the loan and guarantee was granted. The only outright gift to the veteran was the first year's interest on the guaranteed portion of the loan. In the case of the $10,000 home this would amount to $160, the interest on the $4,000 guarantee. Between the massed savings and the government's support of residential loans, the potential for inflation was significant.

The banks and other financial institutions had also accumulated more cash and government bonds then they had ever held before. Considering what their financial strengths had been only a few short years before the war, their liquidity surpassed anything they could have imagined. Cut-throat competition for the home loan customer developed, and in some markets state governments were required to step in and control the excesses of some institutions.

In 1946, with the amount of money available and the willing support of the banking industry, it was not unusual to see homes that had sold in the late 1930s for $6,500 to $7,500 now selling for $10,000 and $12,000. It was estimated that in the first half of 1947 the average increase in the price of a finished house rose from 15 to 50 percent. The quality of homes suffered due to the scarcity of materials, but buyers were still willing to pay the high prices because of the lack of supply and the unprecedented demand. Veterans and workers needed new homes, regardless of the quality—homes that in many cases were considerably better than where they had been living.

In 1947 the home building industry still could not meet the demand. It continued to stumble along with a volume of new homes which was little better than halfway between the Depression low and the peak of the early 1920s. Even though the number of starts was significant, the number of finishes canceled many of the gains. To meet the demand would require home builders, essentially a cottage industry, to build twice as many houses at significantly lower prices. Home building was not monopolistic. Every town and village had its own home builders, who would put up a few homes and be responsible to no one but themselves and their buyers. In 1938 the average builder of single-family houses produced three and a half houses a year. The builder's price was based on his cost plus whatever the market would bear. Unlike in other industries, in which competition and fashion may demand changes and price adjustments, the home builder continued as he had done for years, providing a custom product for a generally undemanding clientele.

It was in this housing environment that the United States found itself at the end of the war. The existing housing industry, if it could be called one, could not supply the product that the public demanded, and, no matter how much pressure the government thought it could apply, it could not change that fact. According to a *Fortune* magazine article in 1947 on the housing industry, the disorder and snaillike speed of home builders was directly traceable to their scale. *Fortune* made the following case:

1. The housing industry's methods were archaic and inefficient. Unlike other industries, there wasn't the economy of scale and repetition that produced less-expensive products but a series of unconnected handicraft operations of masons, carpenters, electricians, plumbers, and other trades.

2. The builder passed on responsibility for the house to numerous subcontrac-

tors. As a result, the masonry contractor was at the mercy of the framing contractor, the plasterer must wait for the plumber, and so on. A day delay here
and there would add up to weeks on the final house, and time was money.

3. In metropolitan areas the building trades would limit the quantity of work,
   outlaw technological progress, keep labor productivity low, and engage in
   costly bickering among themselves. But this was as much the fault of the unorganized builders as it was the unions themselves. Neither had control of
   the demands that were required for the process.

4. The system for acquiring the materials for the house was fantastically expensive. The builder bought his materials at what was essentially a retail price.
   As an example, plywood moved through so many operations and procedures
   to get to the home site that its final price to the builder reflected every one of
   these cost increases. Unfortunately, the economies of scale came to bear; the
   builder was not buying a thousand sheets of plywood, only a few at a time,
   and could not gain the advantage those thousand sheets could give him.

5. The small builder could not pass up the opportunity to "get his when the getting is good." The builder would always price his house at whatever he could
   sell it for. He would not build when he could not sell the house at a profitable price, and he would ask and get the most when competition for his
   product was greatest.[1]

A number of studies were conducted in the 1950s which bore this cost of home
building out. Scale and quantity were in most cases the most essential aspect
needed to meet an increasing market.[2]

It become clear, from this evidence, that only through the use of large-scale
construction operations could affordable houses be built in the numbers required
to meet the demand and the market. Nate Manilow and American Community
Builders arrived at this same conclusion in the summer of 1946. Park Forest, even
after substantial changes to the initial marketing plan by the offering of apartments, would still contain a minimum of five thousand single-family detached
homes with a broad mixtures of styles and prices.

An easy criticism of the new towns built after World War II was that the
homes, placed repetitively row upon row, were occupied by people who were like
the homes: very similar socially, educationally, and culturally. They all had 2.3
children; he worked downtown; she stayed home with the kids. In many respects
the critics were correct, since outward and obvious appearances can easily be defined and presented. Like residents in so many other postwar communities, Park
Foresters were similar. Most were young families, traditional in the truest defined
sense. Most families consisted of dad, a college graduate, who worked in the
Loop; mom, also with some college, who stayed home and raised the children.

Saturdays were spent around the house doing chores such as mowing the lawn, and Sundays were for church. Outward appearances supported the stereotype; the reality was different.

The market ACB was looking at in 1946 conformed to the model American family. That family's income was about $2,750 a year, or about $230 a month. With one-fifth to one-quarter available for rent, there was a mass market for houses renting for about $60 a month or selling for about $7,000. This was exactly the base market ACB had started with, and, after constructing 3,010 apartments, that market for single-family homes was still strong in 1950. By 1952 the 15,000 people that made up Park Forest were young and comparatively well-educated, middle-income families. The average adult age was thirty, had a family income of about $5,800, and half the men and one-third of the women were college educated. And, according to the March 1952 *House & Home,* Park Forest residents "probably have more clubs, committees and service organizations per square foot—and more children—than any other town of its size in the country."

As ACB began final preparation of the first phase of homes, the Korean War began. Again, the uncertainty of materials and labor became an issue. Increased costs of steel and the allocation of that industry's output to the war would certainly drive prices up, resulting in higher home costs and a slowing of the market. In the summer of 1950 Klutznick announced that ACB intended to "produce the best house it can at the lowest cost it can." He also said that its housing program would be pursued in accordance with President Truman's directive regarding the needs of the war effort. The war may have had an impact on the housing industry, but it seemed to affect only "fringe," or marginal, builders, and the impact may have been more from their own business practices than the war.

The previous four years in the United States housing market had been extremely busy ones. After a very slow restart of the housing industry immediately after the war and the often confusing contributions by the government, approximately 3,476,200 units were built between 1946 and 1949. And during 1950 an all-time high of 1,396,000 units were built. Public opinion, and votes, was being mollified; the housing crises no longer was demanding the citizens' overriding concern.[3]

ACB was optimistic. At the same time the impacts of the war were being discussed, the company announced the start of 2,800 individual homes in the Sauk Trail area south of the Plaza Shopping Center. The homes would be conventional one-story homes on 60' x 100' lots and sell for between $12,500 and $14,000.

Phil Klutznick and Nate Manilow could not take the chance that their home designs would hinder or slow sales. When sales manager Jack Rashkin was asked how he knew he could sell the house designs, he answered: "We ought to know. We've been selling [these same designs] in Manilow's own projects for three

Fig. 47. Single-family homes along one of the village's curving streets. *Source:* courtesy of Park Forest Public Library.

years!" And, true enough, their sales elsewhere continually ran ahead of construction.

Even though the residential designs were well over three years old, they were safe and conservative, and Klutznick and Manilow were not about to experiment with the ultimate consumer product, the house. They relied on their experience with these designs. They had built them in Chicago in Jeffrey Manor and were sure of buyers' demands and the proven cost of the houses. The designs were easily stripped down to reduce the costs or embellished with stone and other architectural elements to increase their price and curb appeal.

Initially, ACB proposed one basic plan, with alternative facade elevations. This house was 24′0″ by 34′6″; it had one 20′6″ × 12′6″ living room, a small kitchen and utility room, a small bathroom, and two bedrooms. The total square footage was 828. They would later add a carport. A three-bedroom plan would eventually also be offered.

What did the buyers want in a house? They would pay more if the home had a visible roof, used traditional materials, and the windows were constructed with mullions, which reduced the large uninterrupted glass surface of the "picture" window. They wanted brick and stone facades for the look of permanence, and they wanted the appearance of a higher-cost home but without the expense.

The return to the tried-and-true sabotaged the site planning that Elbert Peets and Richard Bennett had continuously developed for three years. The earliest plans for the single-family neighborhoods reflected Peets concepts for Greendale, Wisconsin, and the other Greenbelt communities. The residential streets would either be short cul-de-sac types, with a very small turning circle serving about eight to ten homes or a loop street that returned to the primary neighborhood street. Few homes would front on the neighborhood street; most would face the loop street that served just those residents living there.

This early layout plan of the street pattern was used by ACB in its published plans throughout the development of the apartment units and was publicly displayed in articles about the community until the late spring of 1948. It was as the first plans for the single-family lot layouts went through the approval process with the new village planning commission that the pattern and the fundamental fabric of the town began to change. A sketch of the village, included in an article in *Architectural Forum* magazine in August 1948, showed a modified version of the November 12, 1946, original plan. The new plan showed the shopping center in exactly the same location, and all the rental units were shown as they were built (in fact at the time of publication the first units were being occupied), but it was the circulation that changed. A four-lane divided highway extended from the Twenty-sixth Street entry from the Chicago Heights boundary west to Sauk Trail as it entered into Matteson. This highway paralleled the railroad for about a mile before heading southwest toward Matteson. Western Avenue jogged east about five hundred feet and proceeded under this four-lane highway as well as passing under the two railroad rights-of-way. The circular loop road was modified to enclose a large lake populated with numerous small islands. An extensive area of large lots and wooded areas to the west and south of the core of the village were sketched in. The plan also made the first serious attempt at lotting out the central area of the village where it straddled Sauk Trail.

The new August 1948 plan began to evolve into a hybrid between Peets's plan, with its curving streets, which created smaller residential neighborhoods, and the more familiar grid pattern of the older city. Peets's original pattern would have created a more definitive hierarchy of streets and circulation patterns; those using the neighborhood streets would either be residents, their guests, or service people—no through traffic. The village loop streets would move residents more easily through the village and would also make it easier to locate the neighborhoods. Peets's plan also included a connective greenbelt throughout the village

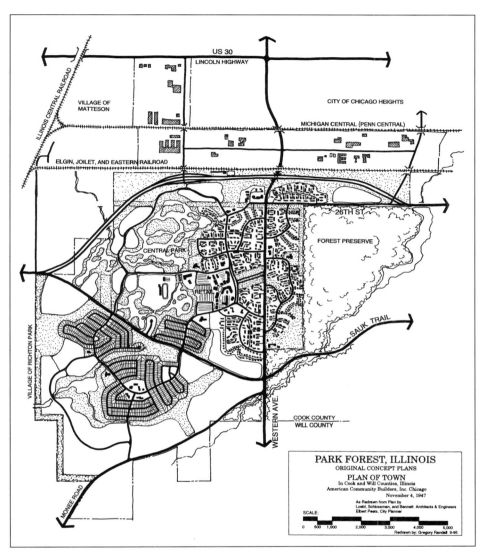

Fig. 48. *Architectural Forum* reprinted an earlier plan in August 1948 which showed Twenty-sixth Street connecting Matteson to Chicago Heights. Redrawn from a plan by Loebl, Schlossman, and Bennett, November 4, 1947.

which may have allowed the schools and commercial areas to be interconnected by walks and paths that were not along streets. In the new plan the "for sale" streets now entered and exited from at least two separate and distinct streets. There was no longer the definition of small neighborhoods within an area, and there was a loss of public parks and buffers between the neighborhoods as was found in the apartment areas.

What forced these significant changes to Peets's plan? Utilities, for one. There was the need to loop water lines to more than one mainline source; this would permit continuing service if one line needed to be shut down for repair. Streets with two outlets would also allow for more options for sewer and storm flow management. An additional change was forced on the plan by the village. The initial streets had an integral street, curb, and sidewalk, which was an efficient and common practice. Unfortunately, the design did not take into account the problems of snow removal. With an adjacent sidewalk the plowed snow was piled on the walk and had to be removed by hand. The village insisted on moving the walk away from the curb, providing a landscaped strip that softened the street, reduced its apparent width, and gave the village a place to deposit the snow. This would become a standard for the village.

The grading of the neighborhoods also may have forced the change in street patterns. The modified grid permitted easier mass grading and terracing between streets and house pads. Transitions could be taken up more easily in the back yards, whereas the alternative layout of Peets's plan may have resulted in more massive changes in grades which would have been placed in public areas and not sold to home buyers. The resulting curving grid pattern that was built was more efficient, cheaper to construct, permitted greater utility options, and was more familiar to the potential home buyers. It was not the Chicago grid pattern, but it was vaguely similar.

The most ambitious of the conceptual plans was developed in the late summer of 1950. This plan no longer showed an east-west four-lane highway but proposed an extensive lake system in the lowland area north of Lakewood Boulevard which extended all the way to the high tension tower easement. Two parkland drainage areas with their own smaller lakes extended south to Sauk Trail and west toward Matteson. The large lake would have been over eighty acres in surface area and would have been a significant recreation resource for the village. In addition to the lakes, the high school was planned for the corner of Sauk Trail and Indianwood Boulevard. It would anchor the southeast corner of the lake and park complex. The best aspect of this plan was the town center's location directly on the greenway. This plan, if constructed, would have dramatically set the village apart from others in the Chicago area. Unfortunately, due to costs, none of the lakes were built.

The plan for Park Forest, by mid-1950, had changed from a Greenbelt community into a hybrid suburban development. The extensive buffers shown in the early plans were gone, the distinctive neighborhoods were lost, and the elements that had made Riverside, Illinois, so visually inviting were excluded. The open-

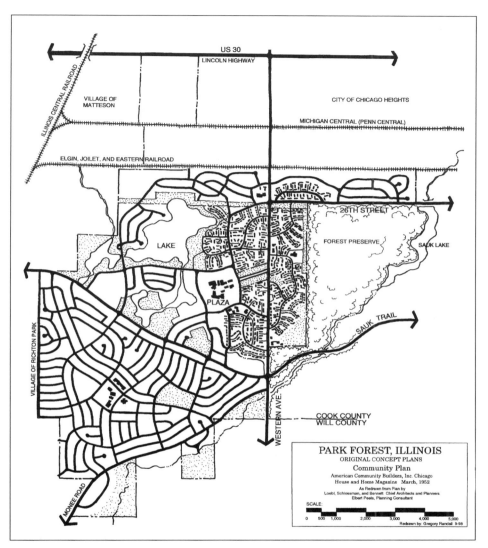

Fig. 49. By early 1952 the single-family homes and the street pattern began to change from Peets's concepts. This plan also showed a large recreational lake in the northwest corner of the community. Redrawn from a plan by Loebl, Schlossman, and Bennett, March 1952.

space delights of the apartments, even with their very low density, were not to be found or shared by the new residents in the single-family homes areas. It became a community of streets and intersections.

It was about this time that Henry S. Churchill was invited to review the sub-

Fig. 50. Aerial view of the first single-family neighborhoods, August 1955. *Source:* courtesy of Park Forest Public Library.

division plans and sketches. According to Ed Waterman, his involvement was minor and may not have significantly contributed to the final designs. What is curious, however, is why Klutznick would have invited a man so diametrically opposed to this form of planning and community design and in many respects his own personal beliefs. Waterman reflected years later that, "if Churchill was involved, it was probably that his name had value with FHA and mortgage lenders and the kind of publications in which Klutznick liked to be mentioned. Klutznick used to go in for that kind of stuff. I believe Churchill was paid a fee, but I do not think it was enough to warrant any more than a quick look and OK."

Churchill's comments may have made an impact on the planning of the for-sale area. During the previous two years a minor, but interesting, skirmish had developed between Churchill and Peets over the "neighborhood concept" in planning. During the summer of 1948 the *Journal of Housing* published a two-part paper by Reginald Isaacs which challenged the concept and use of the neighborhood in community planning. Isaacs was not comfortable with the use of neighborhood in both new communities and the revamping of the older urban areas. It seemed to be an artificial construction that was not socially supporting but was, rather, exclusionary and racist. Offering little but complaints, Isaacs's article prompted a flurry of letters, especially between Elbert Peets and Churchill. Churchill concurred with Isaacs's assessment: "I have no use for the 'neighborhood' and almost as little for those purists of zoning who would keep various land uses wholly apart. I question whether, except for the well-to-do bourgeois suburb, an unmixed residential area is even desirable."

Peets took great exception to these notions: "silly talk and make believe plans should not obscure the fact that the neighborhood—in some forms and degrees—is a very useful planning motif." Peets went on to discuss the inevitable issues of friendships and interconnections within a community and strongly believed that planning contributed little to these notions of "socialized" planning. Peets continued: "It would be relevant, perhaps, to repeat the common saying that it is not so much what you do as how you do it. If we take the word 'how' to mean in how many skillfully studied ways, each adapted to its purpose and situation—then I would say that the best 'substitute' for the neighborhood concept is newly and more intelligently designed neighborhoods. That, I think, will be the answer—quite probably under a new name, so everybody will be pleased."

Four years later Lewis Mumford weighed in with his summation of the neighborhood published in the English journal *Town Planning Review* (and republished in his book *The Urban Prospect*):

> Let me sum up. The neighborhood is a social fact; it exists in an inchoate form even when it is not articulated on a plan or provided with the institutions needed by a domestic community. By conscience design and provision the neighborhood may become an essential organ of an integrated city; and the discussion of the problems raised by neighborhood design will lead to solutions that will carry further the movement begun theoretically in [Clarence] Perry's studies, carried out concretely at Radburn, and applied on a large scale in the British New Towns. Has not the time come for a much more comprehensive canvass of the social functions of the neighborhood, for a more subtle and sympathetic interpretation of the needs of urban families at every stage in the cycle of human growth, and a more adventurous exploration of alternative solutions?[4]

It can be seen in the revised plans, three years after Churchill and Peets's letters, that Churchill's beliefs may have had an impact on Klutznick and Manilow. The plans changed to a more conservative neighborhood layout.

ACB's vice president in charge of construction was Joe Goldman, an architect by training but a hard-headed builder by experience. Goldman had watched and read about spectacular experiments and innovations in home construction and had come to the conclusion that many of the more striking departures from orthodox building methods simply did not work. He believed that it was through humdrum, undramatic corner-cutting that real savings could be accomplished — and not through the use of the more glamorous and highly mechanized "modern" procedures.

Goldman proposed and then built simple solutions to problems that, when magnified by miles and miles of roads and hundreds of residential units, amounted to substantial savings. He integrated the curb and sidewalk into one unit, eliminating the narrow parkway and easing the installation process of the walk (this was a design that the town would change). This combination moved the house closer to the street and reduced the length of utility pipes and drains, which resulted in a savings of almost twelve feet of copper pipe per household. Goldman also constructed shared sewer and water lines to the houses, again saving almost 50 percent of the installation service normally provided. But it was his management of the subcontractors which accomplished the greatest efficiency and savings.

To increase the speed the various operations took to complete, ACB got away from line production. The company started the practice of using multiple construction crews in separate areas, which created competition in both production and in quality. Each crew did one to two units per day, and the contractor who completed his quota of units first was given additional units to build, thus increasing his profit. ACB also shifted the responsibility for materials management to the crews. Instead of having centralized distribution centers where materials might be lost, wasted, or stolen, the field crews managed their own materials and ordered only what they needed for a given time. This produced the double benefit of reducing losses in stock and facilitating the job of keeping track of the exact amounts of materials bought and used in each house.

Probably the most important cost reduction was realized by handling materials only once. Suppliers were instructed to deliver lumber required for each house directly to the individual lot. It was then cut and fabricated with minimal dual handling. The savings mounted quickly. Even though there was significant support for prefabricated homes, they required the handling of the same materials over and over and ultimately cost more than conventional home construction.

ACB firmly believed in supporting their subcontractors, and, in addition to maintaining personal contact with each contractor and his crew, it tried to help solve problems and reduce losses. Goldman did not want one contractor doing all the work required for that trade. He often had eight masons instead of one and multiple substitutes for each of his other trades. This would allow for competition while also reducing his exposure to work stoppages. ACB even financed some contractors in various phases of their operations so that they could perform the best job possible. They also required the subcontractors to appreciate the work of the other subs. Proper installation of one trade's work would always make it easier for workers of subsequent trades to complete their work. As Goldman put it, "Adherence to the old fashioned standards of good labor and good working conditions, of wise purchasing, intelligent coordination and a spirit of cooperation among men and management still are the cornerstones of economical building."[5]

This standardization had its problems, however, for the more picky of the homeowners. One new homeowner, Richard Niendorf, remembered a problem with the bathroom in his new home. "We wanted blue bathroom fixtures," he recalled.

> We bought the house like many people did, when it was just a hole in the ground . . . But we saw the plans, liked the court layout, so we signed. Every weekend, we'd drive down from our apartment in Chicago to see the progress. My wife wanted blue fixtures, but we knew that they dropped the fixtures off at each house, in order, and you only got what came. So one weekend, we found out that next week the fixtures would come for the houses in our court. I went up to the construction office, found the driver of the delivery truck, and promised him a case of beer if we got blue bathroom fixtures. Next weekend, we drove down, and there were the blue fixtures installed. I went right out and bought the beer.[6]

The problems with meeting the demand for housing in postwar America forced the government—and Truman's housing expediter, Wilson W. Wyatt, in particular—into supporting ventures that were experimental and costly. Wyatt wanted the prefabricated housing industry, one that had never done over $100 million in a year, to grow into a massive industry that would build over $2.5 billion worth of prefabricated houses within one year. One of the simplest but most slashing indictments of this new housing form came from the loyal opposition in Congress. Republican Jessie Sumner, Illinois congresswoman, called Wyatt's prefabs nothing more than "glorified garbage cans." These heated discussions and rancorous partisan debates occurred while Klutznick was directly under Wyatt's control as commissioner of the Federal Public Housing Authority. The direction Truman gave to the "expediter" was simple: deal with the "short-term" housing crisis; long-term problems will be dealt with separately.

In 1946 there were no large-scale builders of homes in the United States. The Levitts and American Community Builders were still in their teenage years, and the national builders of the 1970s and 1980s were in playpens. The thought of a manufactured house fit well with the beliefs of the day. The country was gearing up to manufacture cars and washers, and a house was only larger and slightly more complex. Or at least that was the belief.

Prefabricated housing requires more than mass production. It is concerned with engineering, construction technique, materials, and transportation. The factory house was a radical change from the traditional process of house building which had developed over thousands of years. Houses were built one at a time, whether a hovel or castle, and each was a custom product. The prefabs industry had been supplying components and panelized sections of homes for a number of years, but now the industry was looking at building complete homes from roof to carpet, at a centralized plant, and then shipping them to the house sites.

This industry was not going to close down the conventional building industry but would add to the supply and help to meet the demand. Even with public disclaimers by the government, many in the home building industry felt threatened and challenged. Wyatt and his various housing authorities did little to discourage this fear. He advocated restrictions on commercial and industrial construction, gave priorities for materials to the prefabrication industry, and guaranteed a market for prefab houses. From an fledgling industry that hoped to build 30,000 housing units in 1946, Wyatt wanted 250,000 and, in turn, would provide the government's support. Those in the prefabricated housing industry were wringing their hands in anticipation.[7]

Locally, those outside the industry were also anticipating the prefab house, and they did not like what they saw and heard. Fearing the loss of jobs, the building trade unions put up a strenuous fight. Revisions to zoning codes (ordinances that they had helped put in place) which would have changed land uses and construction techniques in favor of prefabrication were fought. While this fight resulted in a massive overhaul of the Chicago zoning code, it did little to appease the unions.

Philip Klutznick said, from the inception of Park Forest, that it would be a good location for manufactured houses. The Chicago-based Lustron Corporation, a new company affiliated with the Chicago Vitreous Enamel Product Company, would be an important supplier of those houses. The company was to use the techniques learned in the steel plate and enamel coating industry and apply them to manufactured housing. Two days after the October 28, 1946, formal Park Forest announcement at the Palmer House, the Lustron company was the subject of an article in the *Chicago Tribune*. Lustron's difficulty in meeting the stringent zoning controls of Chicago and its desire to acquire the massive Dodge-Chicago plant to build homes was presented. The article noted that the national housing agency had ordered the plant turned over to Lustron, but the war assets administration had contracted to lease that same plant to the Tucker Automobile Corporation. Eventually, Lustron would lose out and would move its plant to a large surplus structure in Columbus, Ohio.

Within a few years Lustron was producing a well-designed home that was selling for nine to ten thousand dollars, and by the summer of 1949 Klutznick was significantly involved with the future of Lustron. He was anticipating placing two thousand of the prefabricated steel/porcelain Lustron homes along with five hundred conventionally built homes south of the apartments. These were to be the first for-sale homes available to the public.

To assist builders the Housing Act of 1948 included a section that allowed the Reconstruction Finance Corporation (RFC) to loan up to $50 million to produce prefabricated houses. ACB took advantage of this section and requested a loan of $5 million dollars to aid in the purchase of Lustron homes; by the time the loan was received the amount had grown to almost $6.4 million. About this same time it was announced that the RFC, under pressure from the White House, had also loaned $37 million directly to Lustron. Truman wanted Congress to appropriate $25 million to "aid the distribution and marketing of prefabricated homes," but Congress refused. The administration then loaned the Housing Act's remaining allotted funds. All told, Lustron received, directly or indirectly, $42 million of the funds.[8]

In a bizarre series of events Klutznick, Lustron, and the megalomaniacal Joseph R. McCarthy came together over the issues of public housing and prefabricated housing. McCarthy, a vocal and brash critic of public housing, used this issue as his first step to national prominence. Using tactics not wholly accepted within the Congress, McCarthy seized control of the committee that had been selected to investigate the issues of federal housing reform—including, and primarily, public housing. Using this pulpit, McCarthy, for six months, harangued and attacked those in favor of public housing and its benefits. As Richard Davies, in his book *Housing Reform during the Truman Administration*, points out, McCarthy "continually sought evidence to support his contention that public housing did not serve low-income families as much as it served families that could afford to pay the rents. When the former public housing commissioner, Philip Klutznick, testified at a hearing in Chicago, McCarthy left the room and returned only after Klutznick had finished his testimony. Apparently, McCarthy did not want to tangle with a person well-versed in the intricacies of public housing."[9]

Even though the hearings produced little that surprised those following the nationwide investigation, eighteen proposals were listed. These included 500,000 units of public housing, expansion of FHA loan activities, slum clearance directed by local authorities, and the recommendation for the acceptance of a national housing policy. McCarthy refused to sign the report, though his was the only dissenting voice. He produced a minority report that paralleled much of the final report except for its support for public housing.

McCarthy's adamant stand against public housing led to an involved scheme that helped to fund his strapped political bank account. Using his membership in the Senate Banking and Currency Committee and the joint investigation committee, he produced an article titled "A Dollar's Worth of Housing for Every Dollar Spent." Three publishing companies turned the poorly written and organized document down. Not to be turned away from the public trough, he turned to Carl Strandlund, the president of Lustron Corporation. Earlier in the year McCarthy had successfully helped Lustron obtain the loan of $37,500,000 from the RFC. McCarthy had stressed the importance of the prefabrication industry in his minority report and now used this position to help himself. He persuaded Strandlund and Lustron to buy the article hastily for ten thousand dollars. In effect, Lustron paid McCarthy out of the newly acquired federal loan it was going to use to build its facility. It would also turn out that the president of Lustron was also bankrolling McCarthy's wagers at Pimlico and Laurel racetracks.[10]

It is obvious that Klutznick and McCarthy were probably never involved directly together on this issue of prefabricated homes. While both supported the concept and program, it was for entirely different reasons. Klutznick saw the industry as one more way to produce inexpensive homes and to meet a rising demand; McCarthy saw it as a way to further his political future and his personal gain.

Lustron homes became more expensive and could not compete in the marketplace. A small builder could beat the price of the enameled home, and the bigger production builders could easily underprice the structure. Klutznick continued to believe in Lustron. He believed the whole nation had a stake in the Lustron experiment because the conventional builder only affects his own area, whereas Lustron would impact housing everywhere. Unfortunately, the marketplace did not accept this belief, and, after serious attempts by Klutznick to save the company in the late winter of 1950, it failed. The RFC foreclosed on the company's assets, and within a few months it ceased to exist. Park Forest would eventually install some prefabricated homes, but they would prove to be inconsequential to the sales and marketing of the village.

Pastor C. Charles Bachmann and his wife, Mary Lee, residents of the Park Forest apartments for fifteen months, became the first homeowners, on February 1, 1951. It would still be a few months before their home at 307 Osage was completed. As a veteran, Bachmann bought the $12,725 home with a downpayment of $1,725 and paid the remaining balance with monthly installments of $76, which was lower than his present rent. Being the first homeowner also entitled

Fig. 51. One aspect of the village which did not change with the construction of single-family homes was the number of children; they were everywhere. *Source:* courtesy of Park Forest Public Library.

the Bachmanns to become the second property taxpayers in the village behind American Community Builders.

The residents of the apartments had first choice of the houses as they were offered for sale during the winter of 1951. Hundreds of local residents had visited the model home and office at 137 Peach Street. This localized marketing proved a great success, and, by the time the first advertised public announcements and showings were made on April 1, almost 200 of the 1,525 homes available had been sold to existing residents.

In the summer of 1951 the Chicago Chapter of the American Institute of Architects presented the village and its architects with an Award of Merit, citing Park Forest as a "balanced community development with controlled architectural design." The judges were especially impressed by the integration of all elements of living which went into the master plan.[11] Late that same year Park Forest was selected as one of five U.S. communities to win a National Association of Home Builders "Award of Merit" for the planning and design of the community. The ju-

Fig. 52. Klutznick so admired the homes built by Abraham Levitt and his sons in Levit-town that he built similar designs in Park Forest. *Source:* author's photo.

rors applauded the "unusually generous" lot sizes and the "butt lots" placed at the end of the residential blocks which broke "the unsightly view down the interior of the block from homes across the street."[12]

Park Forest was still building two-bedroom homes in 1952 when most other builders in the Chicago region had started to go to larger three- and four-bed-room homes. ACB still felt there was a strong market for this size home and would continue offering this smaller house while also adding larger homes to its inventory. Within the year over 1,300 single-family homes had been built and oc-cupied. Klutznick looked at the existing market and decided to adjust the com-pany's sales program to include units for under $12,000. ACB did this by offering up to 1,250 modified versions of the popular stock two-bedroom house, stripped down to sell at $11,995. He also proposed 100 homes in the $15,000 price range with two bedrooms and attached garage which would also broaden the market and appeal to those buyers who wanted "a little more livability." It was at this time that the first custom home sites were placed on the market. Approximately sixty homes in the $20,000 to $35,000 price range were made available at the southern end of the village, just off Monee Road.[13]

Abraham Levitt and his two sons, William and Alfred, had the greatest im-pact on postwar housing in America. They would eventually build more than

140,000 houses throughout the Mid-Atlantic region and turn home building into a major manufacturing industry. Levittown in the Town of Hempstead, Long Island, New York, would encompass more than 17,400 single-family homes and eventually, at its peak, more than 82,000 residents. Unlike Park Forest, it would never stand on its own. It became a part of the existing town.

It was in Levittown that the Levitts initiated many of the procedures and standards for home construction. They broke construction into twenty-seven separate but related steps, from the pouring of the foundation to the final cleanup. Wherever possible, thy used preassembled components such as standard plumbing assemblies and door frames. This reduced the number of skilled man-hours while at the same time increasing the speed of the construction itself. They were some of the first builders to practice vertical integration of the construction process. They made their own concrete, grew and cut their own timber, and through their subsidiaries purchased appliances. At the peak of their construction they were completing over thirty homes a day.

Part of Levittown's success, like Park Forest, was the unfulfilled demand for housing and the ability to meet that demand with a simple and affordable home. Their house was a 750 square foot Cape Cod design and in fact looked very much like the house that a first-grade student would draw. It contained four ground-floor rooms and the ability to add two more rooms in the spacious attic. The floor plan was practical and spacious and would permit easy expansion outward from the rear as the demands for space increased with the growth of the family. A steeply pitched roof reduced leakage problems. There were no frills, no fireplaces, and no hallways or other "wasted" spaces. It was a simple and direct home set on a 60-by-100 foot lot.

Attacked from all sides for the repetitive look of the community and its endless advance to the horizon, Levittown was an unmitigated success. It was labeled as having "cookie cutter lots" and being "impoverished in form." Even Lewis Mumford complained about the lack of diversity among the housing designs and the incomes of the new residents. It was a middle-income ghetto. Those most impacted, the residents, didn't care what was said about the community or themselves. They loved the community and their new neighbors, who were all about their same age and had the same interests and number of children. They would stand in line for up to four days when new neighborhoods were announced; in one day, in March 1949, over fourteen hundred Levittown contracts were drawn up.[14]

Phil Klutznick readily admitted that he had "borrowed" housing plans from his friend and builder William J. Levitt. As the market for homes in Park Forest expanded, Klutznick felt that it was important to diversify the number of housing types the company offered and to expand the price range. The standard Park For-

Fig. 53. Twelve cooperative housing units were built in 1953 but failed in the marketplace. *Source:* from a plan by Loebl, Schlossman, and Bennett.

est home in 1953 was selling between $13,200 and $14,200 and was increasingly moving out of the starter home market.

ACB proposed a new subdivision in a panhandle piece of the village which abutted Chicago Heights and called it Eastgate. These 283 homes would be the lowest-priced homes ever offered in Park Forest and would be exact copies of the thousands of houses built by Levitt in his New York and New Jersey Levittowns. They were two-bedroom Cape Cod designs with an unfinished second floor. Selling for between $11,000 and $11,500, these homes were almost 25 percent lower in price than anything else in the village. They sold quickly, but, unlike Levitt's villages, they were to remain the cheapest and least desirable of the house plans built in Park Forest. The area would remain the least expensive in the village and would later be fraught with social problems brought on, in part, by the subsidized nature of the homeownerships and the conversion to rentals by owners.

House and Home magazine, in the spring of 1952, called Park Forest the largest new community ever planned by private enterprise in the United States. At the same time, Phil Klutznick announced that a thousand units had been planned which conformed to the requirements of FHA Section 213. This requirement was necessary to fill that "no man's land of housing"—the gap of 20 percent which existed in the Chicago area between the highest-income group served by public housing and the lowest-income class taken care of by private lending. It was surprising as well as significant that a builder as large as ACB was considering going into co-ops, often regarded as a risky investment and publicly unacceptable.

ACB went to great lengths in redesigning the apartment structures to correct many of the problems with the old design. Most were to be three bedrooms, and

ACB changed the floor plan to take advantage of the common area and attached carports to the units. They were going to be located within the single-family home neighborhoods along Blackhawk Drive and directly across the street from the small commercial center. Unfortunately, even with all the planning, the co-ops were not successful, and the marketplace refused the offer. Only twelve were built, and they ended up as rental units.

Throughout the rest of the decade ACB continued to offer larger and more diversified styles of homes to the marketplace. Custom home lots were offered for sale in the Osage and Oakwood areas. A more modern design was offered in the Algonquin and Talala School areas. And in 1957 the first "split-level" homes were offered at $20,000 in the Winnebago Park area.

In 1955 Thorn Creek Estates was opened for sale. This seventy-five-lot custom home subdivision was originally developed in Will County but was later annexed into the village. A few of the officers of ACB built homes in this subdivision. Philip Klutznick built a home of considerable size and stature on Monee Road which, forty years later, may still be the largest home in the village.

Also in 1955, after nearly nine months of debate and study, the village plan commission conditionally approved the preliminary plot plan for Area 15. Called Lincolnwood by Carroll Sweet Jr., Area 15 was a 350-acre tract of land between the Michigan Central tracks and Lincoln Highway and was, in the original plans, the industrial park. ACB proposed to build 1,177 homes and a half-million dollar secondary commercial center. At the time of the conditional approval, the land was not a part of the village and needed to be annexed. Annexation proved to be difficult and time-consuming. Access to the land was difficult because Orchard Boulevard crossed over two railroad tracks, which could cause a delay for emergency vehicles. Underpasses would have to be built, and the issue would be finalized only after the village and the builder had made a determination about how they would share the costs.

Just prior to his leaving ACB, Carroll Sweet Jr. named the streets in the new area after prominent people and events during the lifetime of Abraham Lincoln. A short skirmish occurred over the naming of one street after General Robert E. Lee. It seemed that ninety years later there were still Civil War battles being fought. The name remained, and, as Sweet said later, "if any name is linked everlastingly with Lincoln it is that of General Robert E. Lee."[15] Two schools would also be built, and eventually the last of the homes would be completed in the mid-1960s, for almost $35,000.

Almost 5,500 single-family homes were built in Park Forest in addition to the 3,010 apartments. ACB offered eight distinctively different home designs and showed them off with 45 model homes. Two-, three-, four-, and even five-bedroom plans were sold. They had flat roofs and steeply pitched roofs, and they sold for $10,000 to over $35,000. Considering the times, a more diverse community would be hard to find.

In the mid- to late 1950s one limiting factor to the competitiveness of the village was the shrinking house—or so it seemed. Families that started in 1948 with one small baby living in the rentals moved to a house with two small children in 1951 and by 1958 had four children, a much better income, and no place to put everyone.

The physical changes started out small. There were no prohibitions on closing off the garage, so many homeowners converted it into another bedroom, study, or even dining room. New garages were built in the backyard, for two cars this time, and connected back to the house with a screened-in porch. These porches would later be converted into a den or more bedrooms as the case warranted. The house grew outward toward the rear of the lot, usually with more bedrooms, but no one pushed the house forward. Today, fifty years later, there is a conformity to the street side of the homes which is pleasant and supportive of the other homes.

One change did affect the appearance of the street: the houses grew upward. Some of the second-story additions extended over half the house and created a comfortable balance of size and scale. Others removed the entire roof and expanded across the length of the house. In most cases a simple yet proportionally comfortable facade resulted. More critical was the impact on the street. The low, single-story houses, even with their varied facades of stone and brick, were still very repetitive. The two-story expansions help to change this rhythm and instill a better scale to the neighborhood. This upward growth along with the growth of the street trees has created delightful neighborhoods that, even after four decades, seem well prepared for four more.

Expansion of the house boded well for the village. At a time when it was easy to move to another new suburb and into a house exactly as the buyer wanted it, many Park Forest residents chose to stay and put up with the remodeling of a less-than-adequate house. This may have been a result of the connections that these people felt for the village more than a financial consideration; they stayed because of friends and time invested. For many it was impossible to consider any other alternative than Park Forest as home.

The design and planning of a new community cannot provide the social elements that naturally evolve in urban areas. The planning may provide the urban structure with schools, theaters, and public places, but it cannot provide the flesh for the bone. Only people can. Park Forest had neither history, tradition, nor established structure. It had no inherited customs, institutions, taboos, "socially important families," or rich neighborhoods. There wasn't, as American folklore and

Fig. 54. Every remodel design was unique; each family had a different idea of what their dream home should be. *Source:* author's photo.

Jerry Loebl said, a "wrong side of the tracks'" (though in Park Forest the tracks themselves proved to be a big issue in the late 1950s). The designs and layouts were the blackboard, but the residents would have to provide the chalk.

Park Forest was outwardly neither rich nor poor. It had no older people or even older children. It had no single men and, due to the requirements of the initial tenant selection, no single women. It had no blacks and very few other minorities. There were no relatives to "just stop by"; mothers and mothers-in-law generally lived hundreds of miles away. Comparisons to a prison were easily made by the critics, especially with respect to the women, who found it difficult to escape the neighborhood for even a few hours. The men went to work; the women stayed home. Suburban communities were easy targets for writers whose market was the urban apartment dweller and academician. For some reason these communities threatened them; what you do not understand can very often frighten you.

Friendships in the community were often started between children and moved on to the adults. Schools were the great connectors in Park Forest. Children went to schools that were no more than few blocks away, and, as a result, their parents were close by. Social contact was easier and was often based on an introduction by a six-year-old. In later years there were fewer children of the same age, they lived further apart, and often they were bused to schools. Maintaining friendships and other connections became more difficult.

With the start of the Lincolnwood subdivision significant changes would occur in the structure of American Community Builders which would forever change its relationship to the Village of Park Forest. ACB was beginning to separate itself from the day-to-day operations of building homes and in 1958, with the approval of the Lincolnwood plan, spun off a company that would build the homes and sell them.

Phil Klutznick had often presented to his employees the belief that there were bright things in both ACB's future and theirs. As he made money, so would they. There would be more financial opportunities as time went on. As such, he proposed to liquidate American Community Builders and distribute the assets pro-rata to the stock holders. This was primarily done as a way to minimize the tax consequences of a wholesale selling off of the company. Klutznick and Sam Beber suggested to a group of their employees that a new corporation be set up. ACB would then dissolve, and the four partners and owners of the rental properties—Klutznick, Manilow, Loebl, and Beber—would enter into an agreement with the new company to manage the rental and commercial properties. They would also rent the new company space in the Plaza to carry on real estate resales and brokerage. Lastly, they would enter into a contract to sell the new company the platted and unimproved land in Lincolnwood. The new group would then be the builder and seller of the 1,177 homes approved there. None of the rental or commercial properties would be sold to this group; it would become, in effect, a property management company.

From the beginning this turned out to be a one-sided deal. The new company was headed by Ed Waterman, a nine-year employee of ACB and the signer of the first lease for an apartment. Nine others made up the stockholders and directors; two of these were relatives of Klutznick and Beber. The complications and changes in the ownership of the properties resulted in significant profits for the partners of ACB without their relinquishing control of the properties and other assets. The new venture had to agree that all salary limits, borrowing, new ventures, and most building and marketing decisions be approved by its former employers while also giving frequent financial disclosures to them as well.

This seemingly one-sided association soured the feelings of many of the partners, and within a few short years the new company had changed radically. Waterman left in 1960, and many of the others left soon after. The effects on the village of the management and ownership changes were few, but this begins to outline the difficulty that builders have in extracting themselves from the communities they set in place. An even more difficult and divisive ownership change occurred between the developer and the village over the sale of the water company.[16]

In 1954 the village entered into negotiations with ACB to buy the water company. This purchase was a result of one of the dedication agreements negotiated with ACB in 1951 but was delayed at the suggestion of Klutznick until the village was better organized to take on such responsibilities. The village saw this purchase as an opportunity to expand its revenue sources while also gaining control of the largest single income-producing asset of the village. The income derived from the water company could go for expenses that could not normally be paid for out of tax revenues. Extensive discussions and rulings from the Illinois Commerce Commission extended the acquisition date of the system almost four years, until January 1958. The price paid to the stockholders of the water company was $3.4 million. The stockholders were the principals of ACB who arranged, prior to the sale, a tax-free distribution of the stock to themselves. The individual owners took this as a capital gain and made a handsome profit. This coincided with the liquidation of ACB later that year and the establishment of the Lincolnwood development company. All in all 1958 was a very good year financially for the principals and founders of American Community Builders.[17]

As ACB proceeded with the liquidation of its assets, many agreements and conditions that were part of various village approvals made during the previous six years came to the table for resolution. What brought this to head was the pending approval of the Lincolnwood subdivision. The village board realized that they would not have another opportunity to force ACB to meet its obligations after the approval of Lincolnwood, since this was probably the last development by ACB to be approved in the village. It was also about this time that Klutznick was elected president of B'nai B'rith, resigned as president of ACB, and became its chairman of the board. Nate Manilow assumed the presidency and took over the negotiations with the village.

Manilow was able to acquire zoning changes (most were from residential to commercial) for many small parcels throughout the village, while the village was able finally to plat the rental area so as to protect the open-space areas within the apartment areas from development. The final trust resolution required ACB to pay $306,000 to the village to cover the costs of completing the shopping list of delinquent items that the village had accumulated.

In 1962 Philip Klutznick and American Community Builders sold the rentals to the tenants. There were a number of reasons for doing this, but the primary reason was to capitalize on the gain in the value of the rentals and move forward with their other interests. Klutznick was still living in the village, but his business concerns, along with those of his partner and brother-in-law, Sam Beber, were also changing. The cash generated by the sale of the rentals would be welcome.

The nine original mortgage areas had remained separate from one another even after fifteen years. This separation was not a problem while they were under one ownership, but, with conversion, significant changes would have to take place. Each area still had its own mortgage and FHA guarantee. ACB sold five of these areas and converted them to cooperative ownerships. The remaining four areas remained rentals but were under new ownership. For the cooperative areas a 70 percent subscription rate or consent by the existing renters was needed to insure their conversion. Each was then purchased by the cooperative under a Section 213, nonsubsidized FHA mortgage. They were later turned over to a new federal program within Housing and Urban Development (HUD).

It was hoped, at the time of the conversions, that these cooperatives would later join as one and share their management and operational costs. This never happened. Each cooperative, its managers, and board of directors saw themselves as independent and only responsible to their shareholders; they became small centers of power within the village. They were also under the control of the village through strict zoning controls that had been put in place. These co-ops would eventually include 1,998 units.

The remaining rental units were either converted into condominiums or left as rental complexes, each under separate ownership. The condominiums were formed from the duplexes originally laid out for future conversion. These were not subdivided, as originally planned, into fee simple lots, but small associations were formed which grouped these buildings together. A total of 582 rentals were converted into condominiums.

The apartment areas that remained as rentals were sold to a series of owners who did little to improve the quality of the aging buildings. They also began, through HUD, to rent to subsidized renters. This reduction in cash flow, along with the increasing costs of management and operation, created problems for the village. The owners would use the losses for tax write-offs for other business interests. The buildings were allowed to deteriorate, and little was done to maintain their appearance. At the same time, the cooperatives were generally improving the condition of their structures. The separation of quality and appearance between the otherwise identical buildings would continue until the present.

Janet Muchnik, city manager in 1995 and past school board member and village trustee, believed that the conversion of the rental units into ownership housing had saved the village. The conversions occurred during a time of inexpensive home prices and no demand for rental units. The apartments had, by early 1963, a vacancy rate of 23 percent; one in four units was empty. It was possible during the mid-1960s to own a home for less than the monthly rent of one of the apartments. Social problems began to develop within the rental areas due to lowering rents. The conversions helped to maintain a strong economic element within the village, reduced the transient nature of the renters, and provided alternative housing types to those wishing to stay in the village after selling their detached homes. After conversion, the multifamily areas had a vacancy rate of less than 1 percent. The conversions even temporarily helped the remaining rental areas due to the move-overs by residents who did not want to own one of the cooperatives or condominiums. It was a logical solution to a very difficult problem.

With ownership the rentals were physically improved; additional insulation was added, as were new roofs and siding, enlarged parking areas, and new windows. These improvements helped to stabilize many of the buildings that were beginning to show their age while also fixing the basic inadequacies that the rentals had suffered from the beginning. The most important problem corrected, due to the rising cost of energy, was the lack of insulation in the buildings. Aerial surveys were even conducted using infrared and thermal photography to map the most serious problem buildings.

Two residential towers were constructed in the 1970s which would provide apartments for seniors and disabled and low-income renters. These towers signaled important changes to the community. They addressed the aging of the residents as well as the diverse economic mix of the village's citizens. In all, two hundred and fifty units were built.

In the United States, between 1946 and 1953, over ten million new homes had been built and sold. Housing had become one of the nation's four great industries (the others were food, clothing, and automobiles) and by 1954 was larger than the automobile industry. Through the demands that home construction made on other facets of the economy—such as new furniture, appliances, and schools—it was the leader of the economic recovery after World War II and would continue to keep the American economy prosperous throughout the 1950s.

What caught the experts by surprise was not that homes would be in demand but, rather, the depth and duration of that demand. People just didn't buy a house; they "needed" to buy a house. It reaffirmed their family and established roots for a generation of transients. It became a place they could call their own. This intrinsic desire had a profound impact on the building industry. This *need* was deeper than expected, and, coupled with the replacement demands of older housing, the potential market for the rest of the 1950s would be almost 1.1 million housing units a year.

Simple economic statistics began to explain the support for this growth as well. Cash income per family had risen by almost 40 percent in real dollars since the Crash of 1929, but the average value per housing unit fell during that same period by 30 percent. The costs of construction, due to the mass construction techniques employed by Park Forest and Levittown and emulated by others, were kept down while at the same time providing more home for the dollar.[18]

The greatest impact on housing construction was the partnership of the government with private builders through the use of the FHA. The FHA's commitments and the bipartisan support through three presidential administrations for guaranteeing mortgagees before the homes were built allowed for longer-term planning, construction, and marketing. These policies and support kept prices down, helped to control inflation, and met the public's demand. Most important, it kept the construction and marketing of homes in the private sector of the economy.

Park Forest, by a combination of federal guarantees and private initiatives, became a role model for home building for the rest of the century. Its planning, construction, and financial techniques were imitated around the nation. And, especially, it was a great commercial and financial success for the developer, builders, and architect.

CHAPTER TEN

The Legacy

The objective, therefore, is:

A well planned, thoroughly livable town graced by an informal—yet harmonious—atmosphere;

A place where people will breathe the wholesome spirit of our democracy;

A demonstration that all this is within the orbit of the resources of free enterprise . . .

The cornerstone of the plan is the needs of the American Family.

—Introduction, "American Community Builders," 1947

WHAT is the direction of new town planning today? A wish for the good old days when everyone knew and helped one another? A place where Jimmy Stewart would wish to hang his shingle for his building and loan? The concept of the extended village family as shown in *It's a Wonderful Life* is a tangible dream to many who are or wish to be town planners. The wish to be part of a community is as important as all other human desires. Our community, our hometown, is a place where our guardian angels watch over us and protect us—guardian angels who are friends and neighbors. It is a place where on the Fourth of July we stand on the curb with our neighbors and watch the parade. Our kids go by, in the band or on bikes, and the next-door neighbor drives his '48 Plymouth convertible, with the Village Queen of "Whatever" riding on the back seat. Our hometown marches by in front of us.

"Where ya from?" People always ask us about our hometown when we travel. Sometimes it is a place we left thirty years ago, yet we still call it our hometown. This nostalgic yearning for a hometown can be a strong emotion. It often becomes an important memory and can be built on to form a new community. It can become one of the keys to good town planning. It is as strong a principle as the layout and the architecture of the village. But it is just one of the keys to good planning; the others are more mundane: good access and internal circulation, strong market for homes, a strong economy, public involvement, private ownership of a substantial majority of homes, and inexpensive land. What is important today is that to promote this wistfulness, this nostalgia for a hometown, as the primary motivating force behind a cure for what is perceived to be wrong with current community planning is at best naive and at worst dangerous and expensive dreaming.

In 1946 community planners were not as presumptuous. There was only the need for affordable housing and a desire to capitalize on that demand. Park Forest could have easily been planned and subdivided like thousands of other parcels of land across America. It would have been easy to extend the grid pattern of Chicago, continue to number the streets based on the system that already existed to the north, and sell homes. The houses would have sold at a volume that would have met the construction and sales program eventually built in Park Forest. Demand was that great.

But, because of the vision and management of three men, Park Forest was different. To build a new town requires four things: an idea, a design, a builder, and money. Without any one of these four elements the town cannot be successfully built. The idea, or dream, of Park Forest had more than its fair share of supporters. They shared the goal of providing housing for the returning soldier and his family. This was not an uncommon objective, but it was rare to find a group that envisioned a complete community.

The planners and designers believed in Park Forest. Their backgrounds, experiences, and educations had prepared them for this opportunity, and they embraced it. The village's historical foundation was firmly established with the garden cities and the Greenbelt towns. Elbert Peets was there to direct them toward these goals and to insure that they were built into the final design. The architects, Loebl, Schlossman, and Bennett, fulfilled the dream with populist designs responsive to the demands of the market and the community.

Money and builders are bound together. Money fuels the fire of their needs, quenches their demands, and tempers their dreams. Find a good builder, and you will find a good money manager. In Park Forest a good builder, Nathan Manilow, met the dreamer Carroll Sweet and, together with the astute businessman and manager, Philip Klutznick, formed a trinity that built one of the few, if not the only, complete new town immediately after World War II. It is astounding to think that with all the opportunities through government-sponsored loans, available land, demand for housing, and other enticements, so few of these towns were built. This is not a measure of the failures but a commendation to those who persevered.

Manilow would have built five or six thousand homes immediately after the war. He would have built them somewhere in the Chicago area. He was a builder, and the opportunity that presented itself in 1946 was unprecedented. He brought construction and management skills to the project, but he was not a developer. Manilow was a builder.

A good developer sees with a broader and more encompassing perspective. Based on his intuition and experience, he understands the interrelationships that town planning offers. He understands the timing and the short- and long-term markets. Philip Klutznick may have been as much of a dreamer as Sweet, but he was more pragmatic. His experience with the designers of the Greenbelt towns and what they tried to accomplish allowed him to take the socialized programs of the New Deal and transform them into the practical privatization of community planning of the postwar era. He understood the goals of the Greenbelt towns and their problems. He was able to transform the heavy hand and excesses of government planning into the frugal and freer planning of private business.

The planning of the Greenbelt communities generated enormous staffs and bureaucracies to build a few homes at inordinately high costs. This housing required substantial subsidies that were buried in the development costs. Klutznick was not going to allow this to happen to Park Forest. At every stage of the design, development, and construction, costs were assessed and challenged. Sam Beber was often perceived as the villain, yet his proof is in the successful completion. While many others faltered, Park Forest was built substantially as it was planned.

In most respects Park Forest can be considered the fourth and last of the Greenbelt towns; almost every one of their physical aspects was incorporated into its planning. The government had established five requirements early in the process of creating and planning Greenbelt communities, including:

1. Close to industrial employment,
2. Good access by railroad and highways,
3. Large acreages of unspoiled and unbuilt land,
4. The land be easy to build on,
5. And lastly, the land must be suitable for farming.[1]

Park Forest met all these criteria. Being close to Chicago Heights and Harvey, Park Forest sat astride two of the nations most important rail lines and highways. The site's contiguous open lands drained well toward creeks and would continue to support some farming for the next fifty years.

The most important difference between the Greenbelt towns and Park Forest was that Park Forest was privately built and publically owned. It was the combination of these two opposites which made it successful. For all of the effort that ACB put into the community, the residents put a hundred times more. It was their desire to build the social community that became the Village of Park Forest which made it a success.

The planning, design, development, and construction of new towns must be left in the hands of the private builder. The government must stand on the side-

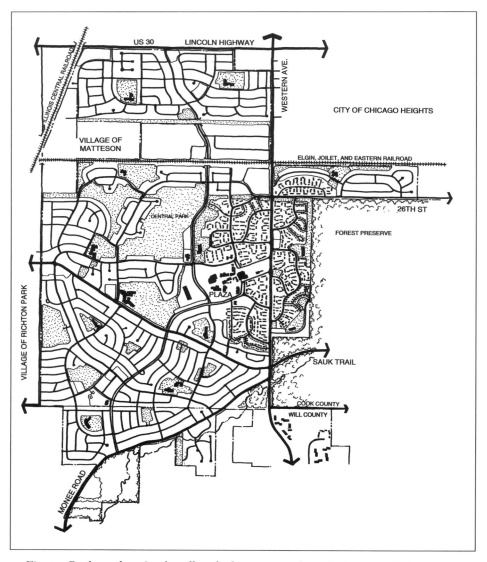

Fig. 55. By the early 1960s the village had grown to its boundaries and, with few exceptions, was complete. *Source:* redrawn from a plan by Loebl, Schlossman, and Bennett, April 1981.

lines coaching the builder, working with the team, acting as cheerleader, financier, and, when appropriate, referee. It is not the government's place to build these towns. Unfortunately, many communities and governments see themselves as surrogate builders; they want the glory of design and planning without the responsibility of the building and marketing. Many local and federal projects are financially hamstrung through excessive redesign and development demands before a spade is driven into the earth.

Significant lessons can be learned from Park Forest:

Land Selection: The site, as found in 1946, could not have been better for what the builders intended. Geographically located along both new and historic transportation routes, the property was readily accessible. Utilities were available, or their construction was manageable. The land was easily worked and, other than the irritating difficulties of the tight clay soil, proved very buildable. The lowlands and pockets of peat added to the aesthetics of the site. It was only later that the variables of regional planning and growth would significantly affect the village. The location of interstate highways would pull commercial and industrial users away from Park Forest. The south suburban area, as a whole, would suffer a slow decline after America's largest airport, O'Hare, was located on the North Side, pulling industry and higher-paying jobs away from the southern counties of Chicago. But in 1946 Park Forest was ideally located, with Midway Airport only twenty miles away and the Illinois Central Railroad, a central spine of America's heartland from Chicago to New Orleans, abutting its western boundary.

Organization: The first day of Philip Klutznick's involvement in Park Forest established the ground rules for the next fifteen years. The business end of American Community Builders would be organized, managed, and scheduled. Issues would be brought to the table and debated, decisions noted, and the process would move on. A hierarchy of management allowed matters to move forward quickly and efficiently. This was the only way that 3,010 apartments could be built in less than thirty months.

Professional Planning: Competent and experienced planning and design was critical to the short- and long-term development costs of the plan. Elbert Peets brought over thirty years of skilled and professional planning knowledge to the team. His early work with Kohler and Greendale, Wisconsin, and his wartime experience prepared him for a project of this scale. Loebl, Schlossman, and Bennett took the structure of the Peets plan and revised it as times and markets changed through the 1950s. The underlying scheme was never lost.

Flexibility: The planning of the village was continually adjusted to deal with changes in markets and site conditions. The first and most important change was reaction to the existing county zoning that forced the plan toward apartments. This bit of serendipity probably saved the fledgling community. The first co-ops were discontinued when it became clear there was not a market for them. Yet fifteen years later, with a change in the same market, two-thirds of the rentals would be converted to cooperatives and condominiums. The industrial park was reduced in size when it became apparent that no users were forthcoming. Changing horses in midstream, though not advisable, must sometimes be done.

Product Control: ACB based its apartments and homes on established criteria and experience. This was not to be a revolution in housing design or even a small skirmish. The apartments reflected designs similar to those that had been built prior to the war and were adequate in size and tenant needs. The innovation was in the layout of the buildings relative to one another and the first postwar use of the superblock. The single-family homes for sale were also based on current market products. Manilow was successfully building similar houses on Chicago's South Side, and they saw no reason to change. Some of Park Forest's homes had more elaborate facades but were fundamentally simple and affordable. When needed, ACB even borrowed from Levittown for a less expensive home design.

Construction Techniques: Joe Goldman and the ACB construction team created new systems and procedures for construction which had not been seen in the Chicago area and possibly the United States. New and innovative construction schedules between trades were created. Labor agreements, when necessary, allowed for an almost uninterrupted schedule of construction. New methods of framing, interior finishing, and utility layout would influence the construction industry for more than thirty years.

Cost Control: Every nickel, literally, was watched and managed. Sam Beber, to his credit, fought every expense that he felt was out of line or could not be justified. The economies of scale allowed greater bargaining for services as well as materials. During the early days, when materials were in short supply, builders who could demand greater quantities of materials had a stronger negotiating position than those who needed only a few pieces. This large scale need added a stabilizing element to the supply and demand cycle. In 1948 there was not a larger construction project in Chicago than Park Forest.

Marketing and Advertising: From the first *Collier's* article in October 1946 to the promotional article in February 1948, marketing was to place the village before the eyes of not only the Chicago region but the whole country. As the village grew, social themes were invoked and used to advertise the quality of life which was a part of Park Forest. The community, its organizations, churches and parks, ease of shopping, and the direct connection to Chicago on the train were all themes in the advertising that brought people to the village. By today's standards these techniques may seem old and timeworn, but in 1950 they were fresh and enticing. Advertising was a recent and bold enterprise, and ACB was a master at understanding its promise.

Self-Government and the Sharing of Responsibilities: Philip Klutznick's goal, from the first day of his involvement, was to have Park Forest become a "healthy and self-governed town." Klutznick's experience with the difficulties and management problems of the New Deal Greenbelt towns forced him to understand the need for not only a community based on ownership but, along with that ownership, the responsibilities of self-government and control. He was not going to create a village that was fundamentally no more than a tenement community.

In 1967 the village contracted with a planning firm, Tech-Search, Inc., from Wilmette, Illinois, to catalog the village and plan for the future of Park Forest. *The Comprehensive Plan*, as it was called, was a detailed and thorough analysis of the state of the village: housing areas were assessed and future trends noted; commercial expectations were diagrammed and adjustments to the retail core mapped; expansions into the "fringe" areas to the south were planned and projected. Unfortunately, many of the most important impacts of the next twenty-five years were not even addressed by *The Comprehensive Plan*, this oversight would prove to be significant to the financial health of the village.

The impact of the regional mall in Matteson was not anticipated or even proffered. Tech-Search reported in *The Comprehensive Plan* that the Plaza developers were looking to increase the shopping center to over 1.5 million square feet by expanding into some of the residential areas. The plan projected sales of almost a quarter-billion dollars by 1985. They projected significant residential growth for the whole area but "were doubtful that another regional center would become feasible by 1985." This mistake in crystal ball gazing would cost the village dearly. Within five years of the report Lincoln Mall was opened.[2]

The Plan also projected areas for redevelopment starting in 1980 which included replacing the aging rental units and cooperatives with denser complexes. It neglected to present a strong program about how this was to be accomplished. With over nineteen hundred individual owners, acquiring and then clearing these properties would prove to be more difficult then building the original community. And, due to the government's loans on the conversion, which would run for almost forty more years, these changes could not soon happen. The plan pointed out obvious issues but provided little tangible reality.

An extensive and detailed analysis that mapped the southern lands abutting the village was also undertaken in the plan. These fringe areas were projected with residential densities and other land uses, and their annexation would have effectively doubled the size of the village and probably permitted a more aggressive and expansive look to the future of the village. Unfortunately, with the acquisition of the core parcels of this fringe area by Nathan Manilow and his establishment of Park Forest South (later renamed University Park) in the late 1960s, this expansion program was effectively stopped. It had been the village's best opportunity to enervate the maturing community. *The Comprehensive Plan* represented an excellent benchmark, but it was also a menu of opportunities that, while promising, were never served.

As communities continue to grow and mature, issues that had been less important can move to the front, and others, once critical, may no longer be a concern. A community can be considered like a machine; over time parts wear out and need replacement. The machine needs to be oiled and occasionally polished and shown off, and often its original use changes over time. Significant developments in the fundamental commercial and office machinery need to be adjusted for.

These changes have occurred in the Garden Cities outside of London as well as the Greenbelt communities of the New Deal. Letchworth has rebuilt its commercial core, added shopping arcades, and upgraded its walkways and street furniture. Welwyn has closed one end of its commercial care by adding an enclosed mall of shops that would rival those of the best of America's small centers. Both are active and dynamic commercial centers that are easily accessible by walkways and sidewalks.

In Park Forest zoning, perimeter control, economic growth, move-up housing, the aging of the citizens, changes in the social structure, and reuse of outdated facilities were challenges the village had to meet during the first fifty years. The disposition of the shopping center continues to vex the community today.

Zoning: As a community matures, the need for additional land has to be acknowledged and, if possible, new land placed within its boundaries. Changing the zoning requirements to accommodate the Sears store also allowed the conversion of many of the apartments into cooperative townhomes. Seniors were housed in higher-density residential towers within existing apartment areas. Each of these developments, at the time, strengthened the village.

Beginning in 2004, after the cooperative debts to the federal government generated by the conversion to private ownership are paid off, substantial changes within the cooperatives can begin. Additional units may be added. A program for removal and rehabilitation can get under way. Units can be joined together, providing larger and more valuable properties that benefit the village as a whole. Garages and additional parking can be provided. Competition within the regional housing market is strong and demanding, and Park Forest can contribute to this need.

Perimeter Control of the Community: The Comprehensive Plan was an early attempt to understand the growth of the village. Since then the village seems to react to developments instead of being an initiator, as it had been in the early 1950s. Today the village must look not only inward but outward. The northern, eastern, and western edges are fairly well defined, but the southern reaches need to be protected. This may included aggressive annexations and even joining with

University Park. This union would substantially strengthen both villages while also expanding the potential for each into the next century. After all, fifty years does go by quickly.

Move-up Housing: The initial plans and subsequent additions did little to stem the continued out-migration of the successful and "upwardly mobile" family. Many left after contributing substantially to the quality of the community. Others saw Park Forest as a way-stop on the corporate ladder. But the greatest number left because the value of the homes was not sufficient to meet their social and economic expectations. Many only moved four or five miles away, to the more affluent villages of Flossmoor, Olympia Fields, and Homewood. It was not the region or the village itself; it was economics. Unfortunately for many, moving up required moving out. The village lost their industry and their income. Many were important to the social fabric of the village, and each loss could not but hinder its growth. The initial planning may have been able to anticipate this need if it had been a more critical element of the design. A broader and more diverse housing mixture—as there was in communities such as Shaker Heights in Cleveland—if phased properly, would have strengthened the evolution of Park Forest.

The village is beginning to address this problem through the recent development of more expensive homes to the southwest around the new golf course. Although the number of these homes is not yet significant, it is a step in the direction of a more diverse economic mix of housing types and values. Larger units in the cooperative areas will create a newer, more urbane market and again expand the types of homes available. Every expansion, accomplished with quality homes within a broad range of values, aids the village and supports and broadens the economic structure.

Changing Demographics and the Aging of Citizens: One element of community planning which is more easily integrated into an existing city is the creation of denser senior neighborhoods. Higher densities are possible with high-rises and townhome complexes. Since the demands for family yards and multiple-car garages are gone, Park Forest has placed these new facilities where they have the best value and effect. The townhomes, both rentals and cooperatives, continue to provide for seniors, encouraging many to stay where old friendships run deep and others to move back into the village. Strengthening and expanding this market would again help the village. Throughout the country significant numbers of private developers have moved into the senior market. Developments range from small clusters of units to extensive communities of apartments and houses which provide a range of social activities. Encouraging an operator of this type of community into the village is a possible consideration.

Reuse of Outdated Facilities: The reuse of school sites would encourage and support growth of the village. School sites can be used for senior residential

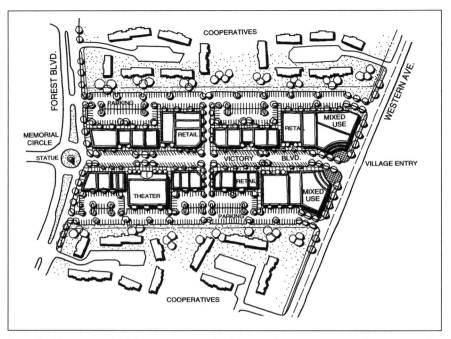

Fig. 56. The removal of the vacant Sears building and reconstruction of Victory Boule-vard will restore the center of the village. *Source:* author's drawing.

neighborhoods or higher density housing. These properties could either be sold or extended long-term leases. The leasing option would allow the district to gen-erate income without losing the property. As the last fifty years have shown, deci-sions made in the past can haunt the community forever. Economic and social changes in the future may require the land for schools once again. Retaining this land could be considered long-term insurance.

The basic physical structure of the existing mall is incompatible in today's re-tail market. It has a poor reputation, and its glory days are long gone and far away. Few remember the vibrant center that it was in the 1950s and 1960s. Fundamen-tal and important changes must be made to the perception and use of the retail portion, and most of all there must be a more enlightened use of the land under the mall itself.

The Centre can no longer function as an introverted retail mechanism that turns its back on the village. Stores and shops must be readily available to the community and provide a familiar and cohesive experience to the citizen. The Sears store is by now at least thirty years old, and most of the other buildings are almost forty-five years old. Their age, coupled with the dysfunctional layout, requires them to be removed, releasing the land for more profitable and more appropriate uses.

The Sears store and attendant parking area should be demolished and Victory Boulevard restored to its original location. Forest Boulevard can then be rebuilt to unify the north and south parts of the village. This intersection would provide a focus and center for the community. Victory Boulevard would again extend from Western Avenue to Forest Boulevard and create a new main street with over nine hundred lineal feet of stores, shops, theaters, restaurants, and upstairs offices. Parking would be in front of shops such as the cleaners and the delicatessen, and longer-term parking could be made available behind the stores for the tenants, shoppers, and office personnel.

Elbert Peets's original circulation plan provided for the classic unencumbered boulevard entry to the village, which fifty years ago may have been proper. Today, synergies must be created, so that, by letting different land uses interact, they support one another. Victory Boulevard would become the center for the village. These new stores are not the big box retailers like Sears and Marshall Fields but smaller, more service-oriented establishments such as drug stores, small specialty retailers, and service providers. The comparison stores were left to places like Lincoln Mall. The stores along Victory Boulevard are the same as those found on every main street in older American communities and those that have been relegated to strip malls. Coffee shops, travel agencies, barbers, small restaurants, cleaners, shoe stores, music stores, book stores, and specialty clothing stores for men and women should face the street and customers. Upstairs, over some of the buildings, small office spaces for tax accountants, architects, and real estate and insurance people can be made be available. The theater must move to this new street to serve as the afternoon and evening "anchor" that theaters have provided for over seventy years in America's small towns. It should have at least six smaller theaters within it in order to extend variety to all age groups.

It would be important to control the number and types of ground-floor offices, since they will subtract from the vitality of the street. Banks should be limited because of their relatively high frontage demands. Corners are critical; restaurants and other businesses that grab the attention of the passerby should be located here.

Most important, the street should be built through entrepreneurial growth and construction. The street frontage would be subdivided into lots that are typically twenty-five to thirty feet wide and about eighty feet deep. These lots would then be sold to individual buyers, who could combine two, three, or four lots, build a retail/office building under stringent design controls, and then rent that space to an approved list of retail establishments. Critical to this suggestion is that

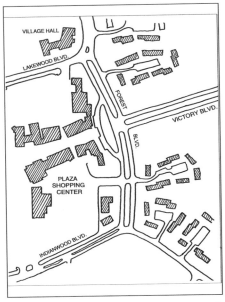

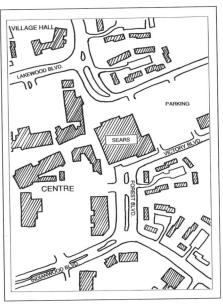

Fig. 57. The removal of the Sears store and reconstruction of Victory Boulevard will strengthen the Plaza's grasp on Western Avenue and reconnect the north and south sides of the village, ca. 1959. *Source:* author's drawing.

Fig. 58. Same as fig. 57, ca. 1970. *Source:* author's drawing.

numerous investors and retailers absorb the costs and variabilities of the commercial market. The stores would be built out as the market and need expands, with no empty buildings needing tenants. Builders only commit to construction when they have tenants. In effect this is similar to the way strip malls in the community operate but with a fundamental difference: with numerous builders competing for tenants, rents are more negotiable. This same process also applies to land for offices.

Control of the street should be through zoning and design regulations. An association of building owners and tenants would work with the village to insure the continued maintenance and mix of tenants. Parking and all land outside the building envelope should be owned and managed by the village. Having parking meters in the lots provides a policing mechanism and insures a good turnover. Office workers and shop owners can use window permits for long-term parking.

The street should have a strong sense of scale and permanence. Brick and windows should dominate the street, with trees and high-quality furnishings giving it charm and character. There is a great heritage of brick commercial facades

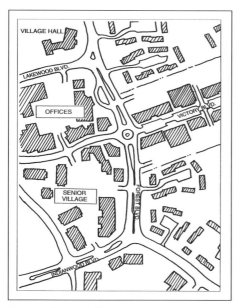

Fig. 59. Same as fig. 57, ca. 2010. *Source:* author's drawing.

throughout the Chicago region, and building the main street in Park Forest would provide an opportunity to continue that tradition. Structures must be kept simple to keep costs and rents within manageable limits, yet they should extend to the visitor a welcome feeling.

Victory Boulevard would become the front door to the village. It would extend west as the new main street, and, where it crosses Forest Boulevard, the village's heart would be recreated. A circular island could manage the traffic and provide a place for heroic commercial art, possibly honoring the GI's who built the town. New office buildings could enclose the intersection on the west side, reflecting the architecture and shops of the retail side to the east. Residents from both the south and north sides of the village would be directed here before they entered the retail side.

Victory Boulevard would then extend gently downhill to the west, slicing the old Centre property in two, then intersect with Orchard Drive, in front of the Jewel Tea grocery store. About halfway between Forest and Orchard the old Centre property would again be crossed and quartered by an extension of Lester Road which extends to Lakewood Boulevard. The four quarters of the old center are now more manageable and phaseable for alternative land uses. The northeast corner could still have the bowling alley and some of the existing buildings, but

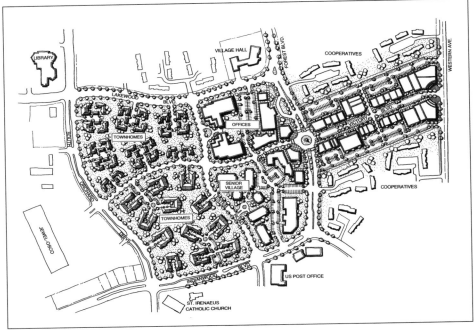

Fig. 60. The redesign and reuse of the old Plaza site would support the new Main Street and reinforce the center of the village. *Source:* author.

behind those buildings and fronting on Lester there could be taller high-rises for seniors and other more dependent renters. On the east side of Lester and south of Victory additional ten- to twelve-story multiuse high-rises with offices, or a mix of offices and apartments or condominiums, could be built. These denser towers would help to support the retailers to the east. An expanded village hall and civic center could be located within this area.

On the west side of Lester and on both sides of Victory Boulevard there could be townhomes and garden apartments with densities approaching fifteen units per acre. At this density parking can still be reasonably accommodated on the ground without requiring more expensive structures. The character of the street frontage could resemble that of the existing apartments and cooperatives to the east. Comfortable setbacks, lawn areas, and street trees would integrate these new neighborhoods into the existing visual fabric of the village. Pedestrian sidewalks would connect the retail main street to the residents, and the village hall, post office, and library would be arranged along this pedestrian diagonal, for convenience.

By destroying the physical and emotional structure of the old Centre, the remaining properties would become more manageable and phaseable. Housing markets currently do not exist for a thousand housing units built in one phase, but they do exist for neighborhoods of one hundred to two hundred homes. This same tenet holds for the commercial main street as well. The blocks of buildings can stand alone and be built as the demand and competition for space expands. It is important to reaffirm the village's connection to the regional highway, Western Avenue. By drawing villagers and visitors from the north and the south, the core of Park Forest is supported. In addition, the villagers no longer have to go onto Western Avenue to travel about their town. Victory Boulevard also becomes a great place for the Fourth of July Parade. And, as proposed in the first plans by Peets, Western Avenue again is the key to the community.

Long-Term Economic Growth: Such growth can be anticipated but not assured. The common traps are easily seen in the predictions made by *The Comprehensive Plan*. Zoning can anticipate growth and can encourage it. The village must be flexible and not turn away from the future. Above all, it must be able to react quickly to the fortunes of opportunity. Builders, developers, business owners, and manufactures do not take years or even months to make decisions; it is too expensive. Communities must be able to react just as quickly.

Can "Park Forest" happen again? Simply, no. The social and economic conditions will probably never reappear in a form that would dam growth to the magnitude that occurred from 1930 to 1945. Can communities similar to Park Forest be built? Probably, yes. But the time frames and planning must take into account extended development patterns and be able to weather economic changes. A village the size of Park Forest may take at least ten to fifteen years to build and market. The planning and approval process may take almost as long as the construction. There are few developers with the resources to last that long.

Community planners and developers must understand that there is a fundamental difference in the perception of the community between the resident and the planner. For the resident the perception extends outward from their bedroom to the world as a whole. For planners the perception is the reverse; it is from the outside, toward the center. Thus, conflicts can, and often do, result. Residents seek security, safety, and economic protection. They want security for their houses and families and the sense that they are safe in their own beds; likewise, they seek safety on the streets and in public facilities. That is often why, sadly, school bond issues are voted down, but seldom are funds for police and fire protection.

The last desire may be the most important: economic protection. For most people their home and personal property are their only assets—their savings account. The perceived growth of that asset, their equity, is a retirement fund, a college fund, and their future. They pick properties based on the protection of that equity. That is why inexpensive properties in quality neighborhoods seldom sit for long and why a similar-priced property may go begging in a less desirable neighborhood. People understand the protection of value by the quality of adjacent properties. Residents can lose their equity, and neighborhoods can gain an unfavorable reputation when values drop. The inherent and perceived values of property are not identical. Like with inflation, this instability can be an insidious destroyer of wealth and equity.

Good community planning must address these issues. Security and safety can be built into the design of the community. The reinforcement of the neighborhood through buffers, parks, recreational uses, and open-space areas establishes the fundamental basis and structure of the village. An organized collection of these neighborhoods, interconnected by parkways and avenues, allows for a hierarchy of values and densities and the necessary phasing. Proper transportation design provides safe passage for children and adults while at the same time permitting timely travel within the village. Bikeways, underpasses, sidewalks separated from busy roadways, and narrow streets all add to the safety of the community.

Current "neotraditional" planning tends toward an egalitarian concept of mixed residential values, all within the same neighborhood, putting apartments next to a small single-family home next to a large house next to a cooperative townhome complex, all in the name of diversity and example—diversity because it justifies a social position taken in land-use planning and example because it represents what can be found in older, traditionally planned communities. What is sometimes forgotten is that most of the neighborhoods did not start this way but, rather, evolved into their condition. For the new neighborhood there is little protection of equity, security is often compromised, and safety suffers.

Park Forest for the last fifty years has protected itself from these pressures. Unfortunately, the measures undertaken may have also stifled the economic growth that was seen in other communities in the Chicago area. Studies have shown that many corporate locations are based not on "real" issues such as their proximity to available employees and affordable housing but on where the boss lives. In the Chicago area the bosses tended to prefer to live on the North Side and built their new facilities there. That decision, coupled with the airport and interstate highways, supported the growth to the north and west. Chicago's southern Cook County suffered and continues to suffer today.

One wonders what might have happened if a broader range of housing values were built initially in Park Forest and what that legacy would be now for the village. Would the resident CEO have built his plant in the community, like George Holly did? Would the idea of a more affluent village have reinforced the economic structure of the Plaza? Would the village have become a catalyst for growth in the area?

William H. Whyte Jr., in 1968, twelve years after his detailed social study of Park Forest, challenged the community planners of his day. He said, "Listening to some new town discussions, one gets the feeling that the end object is not a workable community so much as the untrammeled exercise in planning it."[3] This statement was a strong follow-up to his observation in *The Organization Man* that planners shouldn't necessarily be maligned for becoming interested in sociology, "but a little sociology (applied to planning) can be a dangerous weapon, for it seems so objective that it is easy to forget the questions of value involved."[4]

This exercise in social planning may come from the desire not only to create but to do good—from the belief that if the planning strives to meet some social standard or goal, whether by providing front porches, narrower streets, or other element of design, the residents will live better and happier lives. This burden rests squarely on the shoulders of the designers, and they placed it there themselves.

The reality is far more simple. A town is more than sticks and stones, and the best towns have evolved or, in any case, have been forced to deal with change. It is arrogant to believe that communities are like movie sets that, if properly constructed, will form new villages like Frank Capra's Bedford Falls. Too often the new paradigms of planning tend toward costly subdivisions too expensive for most people and too inflexible to be able to change and grow. They become like an elegant house that can't have an extra bedroom added on because the design and structure won't allow it.

Planners and architects of the new towns of today seem focused on appearances and form, not social structures and government. They are destined to design and then bequeath to local governments expensive facilities that can over time become unmanageable. These communities often come about as result of the hodgepodge of local community requirements and approvals made up of existing land-use plans and zonings that cannot respond to the flexibility that new communities demand. The builder frequently finds that the huge infrastructure facilities and costs generated early in the process garner little governmental support and in some cases foster outright antagonism. The new resident is often the one to bear the costs of these improvements, while the community at large benefits.

Many regions faced with residential expansion limit, if not ban, the potential for the establishment of whole new towns. Regional governments, commissions, and councils, created by states to oversee growth, are disdained by existing towns. But, when these towns have questions of self-serving influence or need to raise revenue, they seek out these same councils. Communities fight for the right to annex areas as large or larger than Park Forest so that they can include the new residents and their properties on community tax rolls—a chance that Park Forest had, and missed, with the lands to the south.

These new towns, like Park Forest in its early days, are dynamic and proud. They often push the surrounding towns and villages forward. If they are denied opportunities to create new and flexible governments, however, they are lost to the staid old communities. Their new residents, when swallowed up by the existing community, are often left out of important issues and are politically, physically, and economically isolated from the older village as well.

The new residents typically lack political power, and, unless there is a binding issue, a Klutznick as it were, they seldom challenge the existing political structure. Being economically isolated, because their properties are often significantly higher or lower in value than the existing community average, they are seen as a threat. This can be seen in new higher-density neighborhoods, where a cheapening of existing property values is perceived. Realistically speaking, this is a pattern that will probably never change. The existing communities will continue to grow until they butt up against the expansions of their neighbors. At this point any additional growth will be from within and will begin to tax infrastructure systems that were not designed for this growth.

New towns, to be successful, must be formed from a partnership between the builder and the residents. Too often the builder is forced to design and develop the community from a defensive position. This is the direct result of the plethora of lawsuits and changing market conditions—lawsuits involving traffic, design flaws, homeowners' associations, assumed promises, real promises not kept, misunderstandings, and loss of assets when the residential market drops. The tension between builder and resident has now evolved to the point of not providing a community center with meeting rooms because the builder fears it would be too convenient a place for his customers to gather and scheme against him. This is planning by paranoia.

New homeowners, on the other hand, expects everything to be complete and perfect the day they arrive. They are excited about their new home and fail to understand the complexities of the development. They have the right to expect a properly built community, but they also must contribute to the process. Too often they accept what is placed before them without question. The young residents of Park Forest, after adjusting to their new role within the community, began to question what was proposed and then worked closely with the builder—the loyal opposition, if you will. It was through this participation and cooperation that the community grew and prospered.

Planning today must include not only the builder but, at the correct time, the residents and users. In existing communities these functions are designated to town planning staffs and city councils, but in newly planned and isolated developments new residents should be sought out and brought into the process. An association between the builder and the resident will create a stronger community.

The process of community planning is incredibly complex. It is a mixture of history, economics, sociology, and art. It requires community planners, architects, developers, city officials, attorneys, and involved residents. It needs land, roads, buildings, time, and money—lots of money. And, to be as successful as Park Forest, it needs luck. For the young men and women who returned from a war of such magnitude and unimaginable horror, luck walked with them across Europe and the Pacific and then sat with them at their dinner tables as they built their new lives.

Creating new towns is a continually evolving process, and how we plan communities in the future will be very different from how the GI town Park Forest was built. But one reality is simple and universal whenever these new communities are planned and built. Every town starts with one home built for one family. Everything else built afterward is support.

Epilogue

One might say that a small town ceases to be one as soon as someone who has lived in it for a number of years finds unfamiliar faces as he walks down the street and is not moved to discover who they are and how they got there.

—Max Lerner, *America as Civilization*

MUCH has changed in the Village of Park Forest since I completed this manuscript in the summer of 1997. Sears is gone, the new Main Street passes by the storefronts of the old plaza, and you can now stop at the curb and run into the old Holiday Theater (now called the Centre Cinema) and get a ticket for the next show. The Centre has been split down its middle, and a new spine has been created that connects Western Avenue on the east to Orchard Drive on the west. Along this spine new stores are opening that are easily accessed and present their doors easily to customers. A traditional village main street has been created from the seminal plaza of fifty years before. New housing has been proposed on the old Sears site and parking lot; someone's new home is now a short walk to the center of the town. The Village Hall has been relocated to the old Marshall Field store and has become the village hub. There is a new Village Green—in almost the same location where Bennett's homage to Venice, the old village clock tower, stood for over forty years and Nixon stood and spoke on Goldblatt's roof.

The new owners of the Centre, the Village of Park Forest, expect to create or recreate almost 250,000 square feet of retail, service, restaurant, office, or institutional space and approximately four hundred housing units. To support these goals the village has announced a pro-business program to promote the Centre's growth.

The view of the village retail core by its residents has changed. No longer competitive on a regional or even subregional basis, the Centre has turned toward what its primary focus should be—serving its residents. It has become a village center with shops and stores that serve the day-to-day needs of the community. It is a rebirth of the concept of a small-town center, possibly a village like

Frank Capra's Bedford Falls. When this is accomplished the village can move on to expansion and growth, assuming that it wants to. A critical and difficult point will come if the village is successful with its redevelopment; it may actually become too successful. Success will be seen when there is pressure on leasable office space (where people want to work), existing stores wish to expand (keep their location—expand their shelf space), other businesses want in, and there is a substantial increase in the number of workers coming into the village center compared to the number who leave.

In the noncompetitive environment of the 1950s the Park Forest Plaza was successful in creating a similar village center. It evolved, grew, aged, came close to dying, and is now being reborn. But rebirth in these difficult and competitive times has its scary moments. The most important has to do with land—will there be enough to satisfy the future demand? The next will be momentum or its corollary, inertia; if a village or town center is perceived as static, with no potential for growth, outside investors will move their money elsewhere. As such, the village must be able to expand its conceptual program far beyond the expectations shown in its master plan for 1997. This does not mean that the plan must be implemented along a straight line of growth and investment; it must, however, be able to accommodate the changes in fortune and demand.

Simple questions must be explored and understood as the village moves into the next century. Where can growth occur? Have we excluded the potential for dynamic changes? Will the village be able to protect its core? Will it be able to deal with the independent forces of builders and developers, or will the Village fail to understand their motives and needs?

The village core plan itself should be able to absorb significantly more square footage of use: offices, retail space, and even residential units. But this growth will only occur if the value of the underlying land is increased, justifying the incredible increase in costs from the existing one- and two-story village center to parking structures and high-rise buildings. Is this in the cards for the Village of Park Forest? Only time will tell. But few other towns have the fifty years of modern economic experience that Park Forest has. The village's history is based on the hard realities of the shifting value, demand, growth, and inattention. Inattention stunted growth in the Centre, and, most important, blinded the community to the changes taking place in America's retail dynamic.

But this growth can be daunting and, for many people, frightening. This retail dynamic changed the local hardware store to Home Depot; it changed the local coffee shop to a McDonalds or Starbucks. These changes eliminated hundreds of small shops and combined them into more convenient, larger stores. The history of downtowns is ever changing and fluid, and to gain something you may lose something. Often a change is not right or wrong but is simply uncom-

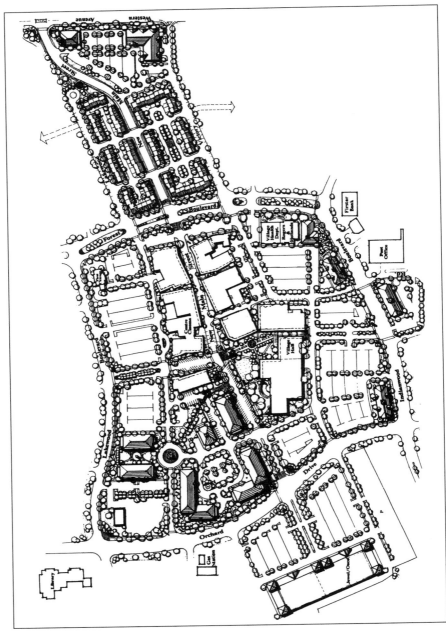

Fig. 61. The Lakota Group's redevelopment plan for the downtown area of Park Forest.

fortable for being a change—one we may dislike but in time grow to tolerate. Perhaps our children will accept what we challenged, but they will probably dislike some of the changes that take place on their watch.

The era of the small town has returned. Reactions to growth and financial uncertainty range from avoidance to fear, and people seem to prefer what is familiar and comfortable. The reconstruction of the village center might help to satisfy the community's need for a viable focus, a "hometown." Over time Park Forest became complacent, not outwardly and vocally but passively, and this allowed things to stagnate. Almost fifty years earlier Al Engelhard referred to Philip Klutznick as the "monster, someone we can whisper about, conspire about, hang in effigy." The members of the village focused their ire and dislike on Klutznick, and this propelled them to heights of community fellowship which few other villages were able to achieve. Such is what seems to have happened with the old Plaza. After years of neglect, chicanery, and deception, the village had had enough and took back the Plaza—took back its heart. The people of Park Forest are still arguing over street names—what should they call the new "Main Street"? should it be renamed Victory Boulevard?—but these are arguments of concern, not debates at a postmortem.

The new planners for the village, the Lakota Group, a Chicago urban design and landscape architectural firm headed by John LaMotte, are continuing the process started over one hundred years ago with Riverside, Illinois. Like the village itself, the revitalization is an extension of the process of change and experimentation in which there may be no right or wrong, only success or failure. Through the efforts of the current village board and village manager, Janet Muchnik, properties are being sold to return them to the tax base. The village has also received state funds in support of its efforts. In the summer of 1998 Willis Johnson and his Tivoli Enterprises acquired the theater and thirteen other properties. Johnson had operated the Centre theater for the past few years and now has the opportunity to recreate the dynamic of the Plaza's past. William H. Whyte Jr. noted over forty years ago, "Park Forest swallows up more civic energy per hundred people than any other community in the country." This is still true today, on the eve of the village's fiftieth birthday.

Elbert Peets's Correspondence with Walter Blucher

In the late spring of 1950 a series of letters were exchanged between Elbert Peets, the planner of Park Forest, and Walter H. Blucher, executive director of the American Society of Planning Officials. The first one, preceding this letter by Peets, has not been located, though here Peets presents its primary premise.

May 25, 1950

Dear Mr. [Walter] Blucher:

Jake Crane [Jacob Crane co-designer of Greendale, Wisconsin, with Peets] has sent me your letter of the 16th. In spite of the shock it gave me, I couldn't help smiling at the ironic perfection of your reply to my old friend Jake's perhaps-too-complimentary letter!

I'm afraid that few of Park Forest's faults can be ascribed to any butchering of my work. The plans of the housing and the streets serving it were incorporated in signed contracts. It happens that Norman Schlossman recently warned me that I'd have some sad surprises next time I visited the job (I have not seen it since June, '48) but he must have referred to bad construction and divergences from our grading and location plans.

I am sending you prints of a tracing I made recently of the central part of our final development plan, also a photostat of that plan. (And, since there was room in the envelope, a print of one of my Greendale studies.)

Here are a few random facts and comments:

1. Without having inside knowledge of the financial situation, I worked on the assumption that housing projects can't afford (right off) to be good towns. I thought that PF would barely squeak through and that all reasonable economies should be made. For example, I connected all 12 service and parking courts with Western Ave., in order to save land and pavement enough to allow for widening pavements.
2. For economy, also, we used minimum pavement widths (except in the twin-house cul-de-sacs, where FHA insisted on greater width that was necessary) but made the rights-of-way wide enough to allow for widening pavements.

3. One bad spot, the dog-leg alignment of 26th Street, west of Western Ave., is due to the fact that the power company reversed its earlier approval of a smooth route across its right of way and asked for a perpendicular crossing. (This was after all the contracts and mortgages had been signed. We secured the compromise shown in the plan.)

4. My first study for PF (June, '46) showed Western Ave. widened, with a median strip. This could not have been done by the project, not only because of the cost but also because it was off-site. There was much talk about widening the pavement (by the State) and I left a study for a widening, east of the existing pavement.

5. The role of Western Ave. in the town plan and regional plan was the subject of infinite discussion—and some very careful study. So far as I know, every person and organization consulted agreed that the street would never carry a large amount of regional traffic. The architects and the company real estate people had various ideas about shifting it to the east (to take it around the town) or to the west (to bring it through traffic close to the commercial group). I let these ideas die of their own weight, knowing that the necessary road building and underpasses could not be financed or carried out before the housing was built. It is my belief that within a few years the Western Ave. pavement will be widened and that for the mile and a quarter that is within the built-up area it will perform satisfactorily the function of a slow-traffic collector street.

6. There were many differences of opinion in the designing and managing group. In most matters related to planning I had pretty good luck. I was even lucky, I think, in the one case where Klutznick ruled against me. From my first studies, I favored locating the commercial center on Western Ave.—on the west side. The architects, after some wild guesses, favored the present site, or a location somewhat south of it. My argument was that Western would and should become the back-bone street of the layout and that this location was the most convenient for both the townspeople and outsiders, also for servicing.

   There was, however, a more basic difference of opinion—I did not feel that the shopping center would grow as large as Jerry Loebl and Phil thought it would. When Phil insisted on the larger area my favored location was ruled out. The present site has the advantage of permitting and indefinite growth of buildings and parking. And I always agreed that it was aesthetically the more desirable.

7. Concerning the "system" of the housing—the grouping, servicing, rear courts, front malls, etc.: the change from a sale to a rental program was made in late 1946 at a time when I happened to be spending a week in Washington. The basic determination as to the types and the arrangement of the housing were made largely by Klutznick and reflect his admiration of Baldwin Hills [a high-density apartment complex built just prior to World War II in Los Angeles]. Phil even ruled out walks paralleling the edges of the parking lots, though the architects and I argued strongly for them. We made some pretense of allowing future garages, but I wouldn't want the job of fitting them in. Phil insisted that the little play places be in the rear [parking] courts; I wanted them in the [landscaped] malls.

[At this point in the correspondence a page seems to be missing.]
expression of residential use and scale) would have led to the preservation of many old streets or parts of them—perhaps as playgrounds or parking areas or simply as utility routes. Good trees would have been marked and saved, and some of the scattered good houses—it is just these impediments to unrestricted paper planning that bind a design to the ground and give it visual and sentimental articulation . . . All of which it is impossible to do, naturally, in a hundred scale model or in six weeks.

All this is not criticism—it is just (confidentially) my long apology for being a bit slow-thinking when a lot of people are looking at me!

Cordially,
Elbert Peets

American Society of Planning Officials
1313 East Sixtieth Street
Chicago 37, Illinois

May 29, 1950

Mr. Elbert Peets
1613 Riggs Place
Washington 9, D.C.

Dear Mr. Peets:

I very much appreciate your informative letter about your plan for Park Forest.

I have a very great interest in this development because all of us concerned with planning are interested in any new town developments; because I live in Flossmoor [a village about 5 miles north] and have had an opportunity to watch Park Forest rather carefully; because of a number of residents of Park Forest who work here in the building—including the President of the village (Dennis O'Harrow), who is my assistant. I have been in close touch with the planning commission and the board of education in Park Forest and I, perhaps, have heard more criticism of it than most people.

In the earliest stages of development I warned that they would have trouble with their basements as they were being constructed (that trouble developed with a vengeance). Some of the things that happened were inevitable. Some of the shortcomings could not, by any stretch of the imagination, be attributed to the site-planner.

I did have in mind such things as the inadequate parking compounds which in some instances do not provide space for the residents, much less for visitors. I am interested to know what your recommendation was with respect to the Tot-Lots now constructed adjacent to the parking compounds. There has been criticism of the fact that no garages are provided (except carports in a very few instances) in a development of this kind where there are many new automobiles which are exposed to our hard winter weather. There has been criticism of inadequate school sites. It has been reported that when the village officials met with the developers to discuss a community building, the village officials were advised that no site had yet been selected for that purpose. It was hard to believe that a community of 30,000 could be designed without an advance determination of where the municipal center would be.

I think sometimes that this development suffers from too much being claimed for it. Modest claims and even understatements would, in my opinion, be more effective.

I look forward to the receipt of the prints and I look forward even more eagerly to an opportunity to discuss this matter with you. I hope, sometime when you are in Chicago, Park Forest can be discussed with some of the village officials, including the president, the Planning Commission and the Board of Education. Incidentally, one of the members of the Board of Education, Bill Slayton, is now in Washington, working for the Housing and Home Finance Agency in Urban Redevelopment field services. I think it would be exceedingly interesting for you to talk with him to get the impressions of some of the school officials and the residents.

Sincerely,
Walter H. Blucher
Executive Director

[Response]
1613 Riggs Pl Wash 9, 6/6/50

Dear Mr. Blucher:

Picking up our discussion of the Park Forest plan, I can well imagine that your friend who is president of the village was astonished when he was told there was no site marked for a municipal building. The site shown on the plan had the immediate approval of Phil Klutznick. It's not impossible that he was influenced by the fact that the land was of little value. If so, I agreed with him, because I don't think a small town can afford an expensive building or a valuable site for its town hall. The architects' earlier studies placed the town hall near or in the commercial center, one argument being the proximity of parking space. But when I set out to show as much parking as Phil and his store expert wanted, I found it necessary to trim off the essentials. But a stronger motive for choosing a perimeter location was this: at Greendale, for diverse reasons which seemed good at the time, we managed to get the municipal service scattered all over the landscape. Sherry Reader [identification unknown] wrote me a caustic letter on the subject once; I could answer many of his charges, the matter has been a sore one to me ever since.

So at Park Forest (I hate the name—they chose it while I was in Puerto Rico and insisted that it was just a temporary name) I wanted to emphasize the housekeeping aspect of the municipal center. The site I proposed is conveniently located, a semi-portal site, visible from the shopping center—picturesquely, at least; the connecting street is convex in profile, which is why I curved it. It will be convenient to the future industrial area. It is a good place for the (first) fire station, near main circulating streets, yet away from excessive street parking and traffic congestion. The area of the site is sufficient for public works yards, etc., and if necessary these can be spread toward the water plant. In fact, I think the public service company might let the Village use parts of its right of way for fenced storage. The site is low (the construction people promised to fill a strip just north of the street) and I had in mind a building with fully exposed basement at the rear. (Please tell your presidential friend that I intended his office to be in the second story, with an elegant view south along Main Street, or whatever they called it, and another over the domain of the wild ducks. So you see, whether the site is right or wrong, it wasn't chosen without a good deal of thought!)

You used the expression "community building." That, of course, may be a very different thing from the town hall. In a general way I thought of cultural facilities, such as the library, as being associated with the high school. I did not try to program this kind of construction in detail, but tried to provide an ample amount of vacant space around the commercial center. I wanted Phil to dedicate to the town the strips of land along the short street that connects the shopping group with Western Avenue, but he merely smiled. The school sites are just as large as I could get, and you will notice that all of them have an open side. In the case of the one at the east boundary I assumed, on the basis of reports from Charley Waldman after a cordial interview with the president of the utility company, that the right of way land, about three acres, could be used for play purposes.

Thank you for mentioning Mr. Slayton; I have not looked him up yet, but will. I am frequently at the DSCUR offices because I wrote two applications for advance of preliminary funds while I was in Puerto Rico in March and April, and they are now being processed.

Enough for now!

Cordially,
Elbert Peets

Preliminary Prospectus for the Community, July 25, 1946

On July 25, 1946, during the initial formation of the company that was to become American Community Builders, a prospectus was written which formulated the scope of what the village of Park Forest was to become. It has been provided as written.

Preliminary Prospectus

Objective

The goal is to provide a fully integrated and liveable community. The aim is to capture all of the advantages of country living in an urban atmosphere within the economic reach of those that will live in the town. In its full realization a harmonious variety of homes will be blended into a simple, but artistic, abundantly green landscape.

Location

The town site is to the south of the City of Chicago with the north terminus at about Lincoln Highway, Route 30, and commonly described as 211th Street. The area consists of approximately 2,200 acres, nearly all of which is located in Cook County. It is bordered on the east, in a south-easterly direction by the Forest Preserve. To the east are located Chicago Heights and South Chicago Heights. To the west is the little village of Matteson.

Transportation

Existing transportation is of two types. The Illinois Central, fastest commuting serviced in the Chicago vicinity, has its tracks immediately to the west of the town site. The estimated traveling time on the I.C. to its existing stations and with the present type of service is fifty minutes from the Loop. Much less traveling time is required to reach the heavy industrial area in south Chicago and surrounding areas. Easy access is available by motor vehicular travel by way of Western Avenue. It proposed to establish a station on the I.C. within the boundaries of the town site itself. In addition it is contemplated that feeder bus service will be provided within the town proper in order to reach the I.C. station and to facilitate communication within the town itself. Wide and safe large scale arterials are projected to ease and facilitate the flow of motor vehicular traffic around the town and within the heart of its development.

Residential Construction

The town plan calls for 5,000 plus dwelling units of all types. It is presently anticipated that 20% to 24% of these units will be row houses and garden type apartments—the remainder are scheduled to be free standing two and three bedroom houses. The projected price range is in the $7,000 to $10,000 class. It is hoped to be able to attain the $7,000 figure through the sale of row or twin houses although at this writing the objective is still not clearly ascertainable. The garden apartments are to be developed in small groups and will rent at or about the $7,000 sale price equivalent.

Public Facilities

Three elementary schools and one high school are projected. It is the aim of the planners to revolve three distinct neighborhoods and around the elementary schools providing in connection with each adequate extra space for recreation and play for adults as well as children. In connection with the high school, stadium and other facilities are planned to provide the meeting place for community wide observances and activity. The physical center of the town will be occupied by a large scale park which will provide not only a wide open vista but a natural center for the community's outdoor life, as well.

The municipal service buildings such as town hall, fire and police departments, are planned for the downtown area and will be made an integral part of the shopping center. The substation of the fire department will be provided in an outlying section of the town.

Areas are being set aside for churches. Any denomination will be provided with required land at little or no cost, but its plans for a structure will be subject to the approval of the town's architectural advisors. The aim, of course, is to maintain reasonable architectural standards.

Commercial Facilities

The present plan provides a large scale downtown shopping district. At present it would appear the range of purchasing power might well be from $13,000,000 to $18,000,000 per annum at 1945 prices. The acreage covered by the town, therefore, suggests that in addition to the central shopping center an outlying auxiliary center is essential. By executing the plan for an integrated community, it is possible to eliminate the wasteful extravagance of excessive duplication of commercial facility and yet retain the element of competition which is indispensable to a sound shopping center. For example, the average community of the size of the projected town will be found to have anywhere from 70 to 125 or 150 food establishments. It would appear that a community of the size properly developed can retain the element of competitive selling and service the population more effectively, with some 5 to 8 establishments, including several supermarkets. The same, of course, applies with respect to other shopping and service facilities. The number of filling stations that dot the horizon of the average town is anywhere from 8 to 10 times as many are needed to properly service the inhabitants of a town this size. The conclusion seems to be that approximately 50 to 60 stories including theatres, bank facilities, and office facilities should be reasonably adequate to provide maximum service on a competitive basis to the community residents and at the same time afford a reasonable return to the owners. The commercial areas will be developed by the owning company and will be leased to the operators.

Industrial

The location of the town provides a logical belt for industrial development. The north extremity has an outlet to Lincoln Highway, provided trackage on the Michigan Central and some 1,500 feet to the south of that trackage Belt Line trackage is also available. In view of the concept of a planned and integrated community which could be immeasurably harmed by the introduction of nuisance industries, a limitation is provided that only such industries that do not generate smoke, unconscionable noises, or emit undesirable odors, will be permitted access to this land. Within this limitation an active effort will be made to secure industries which will erect their own buildings consistent with a broad architectural plan. There are several purposes served by this provision:

A.   The establishment of industry is essential for the development of a sound tax basis for the town.
B.   The presence of industry will tend to stabilize the community.
C.   The industry will afford a supplementary outlet for the employment needs of the residents of the community.

The only participation of the developers of the program will be to (a) select industry, (b) approve the general plan of development, and (c) dispose of the land to approved industries.

Utility System

The plans call for a new and independent utility system to be owned by the developers of the town. The power plant will either generate its own power or purchase power at wholesale from the Public Service Company of Northern Illinois and redistribute it at retail. The water pumping and distribution system will be developed anew. A sewage disposal plant is projected to accommodate the needs of the entire community and to provide for possible expansion. Consideration is being given to the development of steam at the site of the power plant and to sell and distribute to the industries and commercial enterprises which require it such service. It is the intention to eliminate the use of coal for heating purposes in the town at large in order to maintain a clean environment and to eliminate the smoke nuisance.

Notes

Chapter One: The Builders

Epigraph: The Best Years of Our Lives, directed by William Wyler, is one of the best post-war movies to show the hopes and expectations of returning veterans and the impact on their families.

1. Gwendolyn Wright, *Building the Dream: A Social History of Housing in America* (Cambridge: MIT Press, 1981), 217–22.

2. David McCullough, *Truman* (New York: Simon and Schuster, 1992), 470.

3. A series of articles were written for *House and Garden* magazine in 1943 by the future architect of Park Forest, Richard Bennett. These articles describe a community so like Park Forest that it is understandable why Bennett was brought on board the team by Loebl and Schlossman.

4. McCullough, *Truman*, 468.

5. Barton J. Bernstein and Allen J. Matusow, *The Truman Administration: A Document History* (New York: Harper and Row), 92.

6. Philip Klutznick, with Sidney Hyman, *Angles of Vision: A Memoir of My Lives* (Chicago: Ivan Dee, 1991), 16–19.

7. The Bureau of Labor Statistics reports 662,500 "starts" of private dwellings in 1946, 845,600 in 1947, and more than 913,000 in 1948; it wasn't until 1949 that over one million non-farm homes were built.

8. Elaine Tyler May, *Homeward Bound: American Families in the Cold War Era* (New York: Basic Books, 1988), 23–24.

9. William H. Whyte Jr., *The Organization Man* (New York: Simon and Schuster, 1956), 268.

10. John P. Dean, "Don't Get Stuck with a House," *Harper's*, July 1945, 90–96. This is an interesting article that attacks home ownership in favor of more federally aided or constructed housing. This series of articles is mentioned in Henry Churchill's book *The City Is the People*, which has a similar view point and which proposes the municipal ownership of land and long-term leasing.

11. Lestern Velie, "Housing: The Chicago Racket," *Collier's Magazine*, October 26, 1946, 16.

12. Klutznick and Hyman, *Angles of Vision*, 31.

13. John P. Dean, "Home Ownership: Is It Sound?" *Harper's*, 1945.

14. "Building: He Owns a Town," *Newsweek*, May 25, 1953, 71–72.

Chapter Two: The Beginning

1. Harry Henderson and Sam Shaw, "City to Order," *Collier's Magazine*, February 14, 1948, 16–17.

2. Philip Klutznick with Sidney Hyman, *Angles of Vision: A Memoir of My Lives* (Chicago: Ivan Dee, 1991), 22.

3. "Mr. Wyatt's Shortage," *Fortune Magazine*, April 1946, 107.

4. Gurney Breckenfeld, *Columbia and the New Cities* (New York: Ives Washburn, 1971), 119–20.

5. Olmsted, Vaux and Co., "Preliminary Report upon the Proposed Suburban Village at Riverside, Near Chicago"; reprinted in *Landscape Architecture*, July 1931, 268 — a thorough presentation, in Olmsted's words, regarding the village of Riverside and his philosophy of suburban development.

6. Ibid., 262.

7. Dugald MacFadyen, *Sir Ebenezer Howard and the Town Planning Movement* (1933; rpt., Manchester: Manchester University Press, 1970), 11.

8. Ibid., 12.

9. Ibid., 11.

10. Norman T. Newton, *Design on the Land* (Cambridge: Belknap Press of Harvard University Press, 1971), 454–56.

11. Lewis Mumford, "The Garden City Idea and Modern Planning," preface to the 1946 edition of *Garden Cities of To-Morrow* (1946; rpt, London: Faber and Faber, 1970), 29.

12. Donald L. Miller, ed., *The Lewis Mumford Reader* (Athens: University of Georgia Press, 1995), 169. This essay was originally titled *The Modern City in Forms and Functions of Twentieth Century Architecture*, vol. 4: *Building Types*, ed. Talbot Hamlin (New York: Columbia University Press, 1952), 775–819.

13. Clarence S. Stein, *Toward New Towns for America* (Cambridge: MIT Press, 1966), 21.

14. MacFadyen, *Sir Ebenezer Howard*, 164.

15. Stein, *Toward New Towns for America*, 27.

16. Ibid., 34.

17. Daniel Schaffer, *Garden Cities for America: The Radburn Experience* (Philadelphia: Temple University Press, 1982), 153.

18. Stein, *Toward New Towns for America*, 35.

19. Ibid., 72.

20. Ibid., 119.

21. Henry S. Churchill, *The City Is the People* (New York: Reynal and Hitchcock, 1945), 80.

22. Arthur M. Schlesinger Jr., *The Age of Roosevelt: The Coming of the New Deal* (Boston: Riverside Press Cambridge, 1958), 370–72.

23. Diane Ghirardo, *Building New Communities: New Deal America and Fascist Italy* (Princeton: Princeton University Press, 1989), 118–19.

24. Henry S. Churchill, "America's Town Planning Begins," *New Republic*, June 3, 1936, 96.

25. Ibid., 176. (Churchill firmly believed, as seen in his writings, that private ownership of land was not an acceptable concept.)

26. Arnold R. Alanen and Joseph A. Eden, *Main Street Ready-Made* (Madison: State Historical Society of Wisconsin, 1987), 13.

27. Ibid., 32.

28. Joseph L. Arnold, *The New Deal in the Suburbs* (Columbus: Ohio State University Press, 1971), 92.

29. Breckenfeld, *Columbia and the New Cities*, 120.

30. Alanen and Eden, *Main Street Ready-Made*, 40.

31. Arnold, *New Deal in the Suburbs*, 99.

32. Breckenfeld, *Columbia and the New Cities*, 120.

33. Philip Klutznick, "Memorandum re: Protective Ownership," July 24, 1946. This is found in the original meeting minutes for American Community Builders for the summer and fall of 1946.

34. Lewis Mumford, *The Culture of Cities* (New York: Harcourt, Brace and Company, 1938), 401.

35. Alanen and Eden, *Main Street Ready-Made*, 37.

Chapter Three: Acquiring the Site and Other Players

1. Herbert Emmerich, "NAHO's President Pays Tribute to Mr. Klutznick," *Journal of Housing*, July 1946, 133. Klutznick would later hold offices in the United Nations and as secretary of commerce in the Carter Administration.

2. Philip Klutznick, with Sidney Hyman, *Angles of Vision: A Memoir of My Lives* (Chicago: Ivan Dee, 1991), 135.

3. Elbert Peets, *On the Art of Designing Cities: Selected Essays of Elbert Peets*, ed. Paul D. Speiregen (Cambridge: MIT Press, 1968), 204.

Chapter Four: The Planning

1. Contract between Loebl and Schlossman and Elbert Peets, May 14, 1946.

2. A full reprint of the original July 1946 prospectus is included in appendix B.

3. Philip Kluznick, "Prospectus," American Community Builders, July 25, 1946, 1.

4. Richard Bennett, *The Oral History of Park Forest: OH! Park Forest*, recorded August 28, 1980, 9.

5. Carroll F. Sweet Jr., *Park Forest—The Early Years*, vol. 4 (unpublished autobiography, 1987), 10.

6. Philip Kluznick, with Sidney Hyman, *Angles of Vision: A Memoir of My Lives* (Chicago: Ivan Dee, 1991), 137–38.

7. Sweet, *Park Forest*, 12–13.

8. Ibid., 12.

9. "Plan Home Colony in Chicago Suburb," *New York Times*, October 29, 1946, 43.

10. Elbert Peets, *On the Art of Designing Cities: Selected Essays of Elbert Peets*, ed. Paul D. Speiregen (Cambridge: MIT Press, 1968), 211.

11. Elbert Peets, "Post-War Use of Temporary Housing Sites," *American City*, November 1943, 49–50.

12. Ibid., 211.

13. Sweet, *Park Forest*, 11.

14. Marc A. Weiss, *The Rise of the Community Builders*, (New York: Columbia University Press, 1987), 146–48.

15. Ibid., 149.

16. Ibid., 152.

17. Ibid., 157.

18. The architects for Baldwin Hills Village were Reginald D. Johnson and the associated firm of Wilson, Merrill, and Alexander. They called in Clarence S. Stein as planning consultant. The landscape architect was Fred Barlow Jr. of Los Angeles.

19. Clarence S. Stein, *Toward New Towns for America* (Cambridge: MIT Press, 1966), 198.

20. Richard Marsh Bennett, FAIA, *Chicago Architects Oral History Project* (Chicago: Art Institute of Chicago, 1991), interviewed by Betty J. Blum, 63.

21. David McCullough, *Truman* (New York: Simon and Schuster, 1992), 523.

22. "Senators Taft, Ellender, Wagner Introduce General Housing Bill on March 10," *Journal of Housing*, March 1947, 59–62.

23. McCullough, *Truman*, 532.

24. "The Housing Mess," *Fortune*, January 1947, 81.

25. Sweet, *Park Forest*, 9.

26. Harry Henderson and Sam Shaw, "City to Order," *Collier's Magazine*, February 14, 1948, 52.

27. This comment appears in a letter Elbert Peets wrote to Walter H. Blucher, executive director of the American Society of Planning Officials—one of a series of correspondences between the two in May and June 1950; the original is in the Cornell University archives. See appendix A for reproductions of three letters between Peets and Blucher which describe Peets's reactions to the work of ACB during the the the two years (1948–50) he was not involved in the planning.

28. Sweet, *Park Forest*, 20.

29. Ibid., 22.

30. Ibid., 24.

31. "American Community Builders," *Architectural Forum*, August 1948, 74.

Chapter Five: The Construction

1. Carroll F. Sweet Jr., *Park Forest—The Early Years*, vol. 4 (unpublished autobiography, 1987), 15.

2. Ibid., 16.

3. Ibid., 14; and FHA prospectus submittal for community plan approval, February 1947.

4. Sweet, *Park Forest*, 19.

Chapter Six: The First Residents

Epigraph: Harry Henderson and Sam Shaw, "City to Order," *Collier's Magazine*, February 14, 1948, 54.

1. Magne Olson, extracted from a talk on "Park Forest before 1949," July 20, 1989.

2. Ibid.

3. James Gilbert, *Perfect Cities: Chicago's Utopias of 1893* (Chicago: University of Chicago Press, 1991), 192.

4. Henderson and Shaw, "City to Order," 52.

5. Ibid., 53.

6. Ibid., 54.

7. Edward Waterman, *The Oral History of Park Forest: OH! Park Forest*, recorded November 15, 1980, 1.

8. Robert Dinerstein, *The Oral History of Park Forest: OH! Park Forest*, recorded October 4–5, 11, 1980, 5.

9. Waterman, *Oral History of Park Forest*, 9.

10. Judge Henry X. Dietch, *The Oral History of Park Forest: OH! Park Forest*, recorded September 6, 1980, 6–9.

11. Carroll F. Sweet Jr., *Park Forest—The Early Years*, vol. 4 (unpublished autobiography, 1987), 29.

12. "Philip Klutznick Resigns as FPHA Commissioner," *Journal of Housing*, July 1946, 131–32. This is a reproduction of Klutznick's farewell speech to his staff at the Federal Public Housing Authority.

13. "Mayor's Conference Devotes Full Session to Housing," *Journal of Housing*, February 1947; and *Journal of Housing*, "Personals," April 1949.

14. Philip M. Klutznick, *The Oral History of Park Forest: OH! Park Forest*, recorded February 5, 1981, 37.

Chapter Seven: America Reborn

1. Thomas H. Reed, Doris D. Reed, with Murray Teigh Bloom, "Does Your City Suffer from Suburbanitis?" *Collier's Magazine*, October 11, 1952, 18–20.

2. William Zeckendorf, "Cities versus Suburbs," *Atlantic. Monthly*, June 1952, 24.

3. Philip M. Klutznick, *The Oral History of Park Forest: OH! Park Forest*, recorded February 5, 1981, 22.

4. Dennis O'Harrow, "Growing Pains of a Village Government," *American City*, January 1950, 80.

5. Jack Rashkin, *The Oral History of Park Forest: OH! Park Forest*, recorded December 9, 1980, 29–30.

6. Edward Waterman, *The Oral History of Park Forest: OH! Park Forest*, recorded November 15, 1980, 36.

7. Ibid., 7.

8. William H. Whyte Jr., "The Future, c/o Park Forest," *Fortune*, June 1953, 128.

9. William H. Whyte Jr., *The Last Landscape* (Garden City, N.Y.: Doubleday and Company, 1968), 241.

10. William H. Whyte Jr., *Organization Man* (New York: Simon and Schuster, 1956), 287.

11. Harry Henderson and Sam Shaw, "City to Order," *Collier's Magazine*, February 14, 1948, 16.

12. Robert Dinerstein, *The Oral History of Park Forest: OH! Park Forest*, recorded October 4, 1980, 17–25.

13. Anthony Monahan, "Park Forest at 20," *Midwest Magazine, Chicago Sunday Sun Times*, May 11, 1969, 42.

14. Whyte, *Organization Man*, 293.

15. Correspondence and comments in a letter to the author by Alfred Van Horn III, April 1996, regarding the Homesteaders and their importance and involvement in the community.

16. Whyte, *Organization Man*, 367.

17. Ibid., 367.

18. For a detailed article and for insight into the difficulties of establishing the Jewish congregation in Park Forest, see Herbert J. Gans, "Park Forest: Birth of a Jewish Community," *Commentary Magazine*, April 1951, 330–39.

19. Whyte, *Organization Man*, 370.

20. Harry Henderson, "The Mass-Produced Suburbs," *Harper's Magazine* (two-part article), November and December, 1953, 1:30.

21. O'Harrow, "Growing Pains of a Village Government," 80–81.

Chapter Eight: The Shopping Center

1. Geoffrey Baker and Bruno Funaro, *Shopping Centers: Design and Operation* (New York: Reinhold, 1951), 267–69.

2. Correspondence, Elbert Peets to Walter H. Blucher, May 25, 1950; see appendix for reproductions of these letters.

3. Richard Bennett, *The Oral History of Park Forest, OH! Park Forest*, recorded August 28, 1980, 7.

4. For a complete list of the original tenants in 1953, see table 4.

5. Bennett, *Oral History of Park Forest*, 6.

6. Al Chase, "Field to Build Big Store in Park Forest," *Chicago Tribune*, December 5, 1953.

7. This controversy was covered extensively in the *Park Forest Reporter*, July 7 and July 21, 1976.

8. Ann Keating and Ruth Knack, "Shopping in the Planned Community: Evolution of the Park Forest Town Center," MS, 1992, 13.

9. Thomas McDade, *The Oral History of Park Forest, OH! Park Forest*, recorded October 21, 1980, 4–5.

Chapter Nine: The Single-Family Homes

Epigraph: Anonymous woman qtd. in Harry Henderson, "The Mass Produced Suburbs," *Harper's Magazine* (two-part article), November and December 1953, 1:26.

1. "The Industry Capitalism Forgot," *Fortune*, August 1947, 65.

2. Gilbert Burck and Sanford S. Parker, "The Insatiable Market for Housing," *Fortune*, February 1954, 107. Sherman J. Maisel, an associate professor of business administration at the University of California, published a book in the early 1950s which seemed to confirm the belief that the greater the number of homes built at one time the lower the price. His book, *Homebuilding in Transition*, estimated the cost of constructing a house with 1,000 square feet of floor space by a small builder (one to twenty-five units), by a medium-sized builder (twenty-five to ninety-nine units), and a large builder (100 units or more). Before overhead and profit, Maisel figured, the house would costs the small builder $8,759, the medium-sized builder $7,916, and the large builder $7,142. The small builder, after allowing less than $750 for overhead and profit, would have to charge $9,500 for the house. But the large home builder could have charged nearly $1,000 less and still have nearly twice as much for overhead and profit.

3. Richard O. Davies, *Housing Reform during the Truman Administration* (Columbia: University of Missouri Press, 1966), 117.

4. Lewis Mumford, "The Neighborhood and the Neighborhood Unit," *Town Planning Review* (Liverpool) 24 (January 1954); reprinted in *The Urban Prospect* (New York: Harcourt Brace and World, 1968), 77–78.

5. Joseph Goldman, "Cost Cutting Construction," *Journal of Housing*, May 1953, 164.

6. Anthony Monahan, "Park Forest at 20," *Midwest Magazine, Chicago Sunday Sun Times*, May 11, 1969, 23.

7. "Mr. Wyatt's Shortage," *Fortune*, April 1946, 105.

8. The Lustron Homes collapse is a strong argument for the government to stay directly out of markets where supply and demand are a critical factor, especially when the market may not want the product or it can be produced cheaper on site. Articles in *Fortune* magazine in June 1947 and newspaper accounts in the *Chicago Tribune* in the late 1940s, by Al Chase, begin to present the problems faced by these prefab manufacturers and their almost insatiable need for government funding.

9. Davies, *Housing Reform*, 69–71.

10. Richard H. Rovere, *Senator Joe McCarthy* (1959; rpt., New York: Harper and Row, 1973), 108.

11. "Village Design Wins Award for Architects," *Park Forest Reporter,* June 15, 1951.

12. "NAHB Awards Won by Five in Neighborhood Contest," *House and Home,* January 1952, 59.

13. "Park Forest Moves into 1952," *House and Home,* March 1952, 114–16.

14. Kenneth Jackson, *Crabgrass Frontier* (New York: Oxford University Press, 1985), 234–37.

15. Carroll F. Sweet Jr., *Park Forest—The Early Years* (unpublished autobiography, 1987), 4:54.

16. Edward Waterman, *The Oral History of Park Forest: OH! Park Forest,* recorded November 15, 1980.

17. Robert Dinerstein, *The Oral History of Park Forest: OH! Park Forest,* Oct. 11 and 18, 1980, 19–45.

18. Burck and Parker, "The Insatiable Market for Housing," 102.

Chapter Ten: The Legacy

1. Albert Mayer, "The Greenbelt Towns: What and Why," *American City,* May 1936, 59–61.

2. *Comprehensive Plan, Park Forest, Illinois* (Wilmette, Ill.: Tech-Search, 1967), 2–30 to 2–33. This is an in-depth report on the economic conditions in and around Park Forest at a given moment in time. Unfortunately, most of its predictions fell far short of their mark.

3. William H. Whyte Jr., *The Last Landscape* (Garden City, N.Y.: Doubleday and Company, 1968), 243.

4. William H. Whyte Jr., *The Organization Man* (New York: Simon and Schuster, 1956), 349.

Bibliography

Alanen, Arnold R., and Joseph A. Eden. *Main Street Ready-Made: The New Deal Community of Greendale, Wisconsin.* Madison: State Historical Society of Wisconsin, 1987.

"American Community Builders." *Architectural Forum,* August 1948.

Arnold, Joseph L. *The New Deal in the Suburbs.* Columbus: Ohio State University Press, 1971.

Baker, Geoffrey, and Bruno Funaro. *Shopping Centers, Design and Operation.* New York: Reinhold, 1951.

Bellamy, Edward. *Looking Backward.* London: W. Reeves, ca. 1887.

Bernstein, Barton J., and Allen J. Matusow. *The Truman Administration: A Document History.* New York: Harper and Row, 1956.

Breckenfeld, Gurney. *Columbia and the New Cities.* New York: Ives Washburn, 1971.

Burchell, Robert W., ed. *Frontiers of Planned Unit Development: A Synthesis of Expert Opinion.* New Brunswick, N.J.: Center for Urban Policy Research, 1973.

"Building: He Owns a Town," *Newsweek,* May 25, 1953.

Burck, Gilbert, and Sanford S. Parker. "The Insatiable Market for Housing." *Fortune,* February 1954.

Carrier, Lois A. *Illinois, Crossroads of a Continent.* Urbana: University of Illinois Press, 1993.

Chase, Al. "Field to Build Big Store in Park Forest." *Chicago Tribune,* December 5, 1953.

Churchill, Henry S. "America's Town Planning Begins." *New Republic,* June 3, 1936.

———. *The City Is the People.* New York: Reynal and Hitchcock, 1945.

Comprehensive Plan, Park Forest, Illinois. Wilmette, Ill.: Tech-Search, 1967.

Davies, Richard O. *Housing Reform during the Truman Administration.* Columbia: University of Missouri Press, 1966.

Dedmon, Emmet. *Fabulous Chicago.* New York: Random House, 1953.

Dean, John P. "Home Ownership, Is It Sound?" *Harper's,* August 1945.

———. "Don't Get Stuck with a House." *Harper's,* July 1945.

Emmerich, Herbert. "NAHO's President Pays Tribute to Mr. Klutznick." *Journal of Housing,* July 1946.

Ehrenhalt, Alan. *The Lost City: The Forgotten Virtues of Community in America.* New York: Basic Books, 1995.

Fein, Albert. *Frederick Law Olmsted and the American Environmental Tradition.* New York: George Braziller, 1972.

Fishman, Robert. *Bourgeois Utopias: The Rise and Fall of Suburbia.* New York: Basic Books, 1987.

Gans, Herbert J. "Park Forest: Birth of a Jewish Community." *Commentary Magazine,* April 1951.

Ghirardo, Diane. *Building New Communities: New Deal America and Fascist Italy.* Princeton: Princeton University Press, 1989.

Gilbert, James. *Perfect Cities: Chicago's Utopias of 1893*. Chicago: University of Chicago Press, 1991.

Goldman, Joseph. "Cost Cutting Construction." *Journal of Housing*, May 1953.

Hall, Peter. *Cities of Tomorrow*. Oxford: Blackwell, 1988.

Hamlin, Talbot, ed. *The Modern City in Forms and Functions of Twentieth Century Architecture.* vol. 4: *Building Types*. New York: Columbia University Press, 1952.

Henderson, Harry. "The Mass-Produced Suburbs." *Harper's Magazine* (two-part article), November and December 1953.

Henderson, Harry, and Sam Shaw. "City to Order." *Colliers Magazine*, February 14, 1948.

"The Housing Mess." *Fortune*, January 1947.

Howard, Ebenezer. *Garden Cities of To-Morrow*. Reprint. London, Faber and Faber Ltd., 1970, First Published in 1898 as "To-Morrow: A Peaceful Path to Real Reform" and in 1902 as *Garden Cities of To-Morrow*.

Huxley, Julian. *TVA, Adventure in Planning*. Surrey: Architectural Press, 1943.

"The Industry Capitalism Forgot." *Fortune*, August 1947.

Jackson, Kenneth. *Crabgrass Frontier: The Suburbanization of the United States*. New York: Oxford University Press, 1985.

Jacobs, Jane. *The Death and Life of Great American Cities*. New York: Random House, 1961.

———. *The Economy of Cities*. New York: Random House, 1969.

Keating, Ann, and Ruth Knack. "Shopping in the Planned Community: Evolution of the Park Forest Town Center." MS, 1992.

Klutznick, Philip M., with Sidney Hyman. *Angles of Vision: A Memoir of My Lives*. Chicago: Ivan Dee, 1991.

Krueckeberg, Donald A. *The American Planner: Biographies and Recollections*. New York: Methuen, 1983.

Langdon, Philip. *A Better Place to Live: Reshaping the American Suburb*. Amherst: University of Massachusetts Press, 1994.

Lerner, Max. *America as Civilization*, vol. 1. New York: Simon and Schuster, Clarion Books, 1957.

Lingeman, Richard. *Small Town America*. New York: G. P. Putnam's Sons, 1980.

May, Elaine Tyler. *Homeward Bound: American Families in the Cold War Era*. New York: Basic Books, 1988.

"Mayor's Conference Devotes Full Session to Housing." *Journal of Housing*, February 1947.

Mayer, Albert. "The Greenbelt Towns: What and Why?" *American City*, May 1936.

MacFadyen, Dugald. *Sir Ebenezer Howard and the Town Planning Movement*. 1933. Reprint. Manchester: Manchester University Press, 1970.

McCullough, David. *Truman*, New York: Simon and Schuster, 1992.

Miller, Donald L., ed. *The Lewis Mumford Reader*. Athens: University of Georgia Press, 1995.

Monahan, Anthony. "Park Forest at 20." *Midwest Magazine, Chicago Sunday Sun Times*, May 11, 1969.

"Mr. Wyatt's Shortage." *Fortune Magazine*, April 1946.

Mumford, Lewis. *The City in History*. New York: Harcourt Brace and World, 1961.

———. *The Culture of Cities*. New York: Harcourt, Brace and Company, 1938.

———. *The Urban Prospect*. New York: Harcourt Brace and World, 1968.

———. "The Neighborhood and the Neighborhood Unit." *Town Planning Review* (Liverpool) 24: January 1954.

"NAHB Awards Won by Five in Neighborhood Contest." *House and Home*, January 1952.

National Conference on Planning. Proceedings of the Conference Held at Indianapolis, Indiana, May 25–27, 1942. Chicago: American Society of Planning Officials, 1942.

Newman, Elmer S. *Lewis Mumford: A Bibliography, 1914–1970.* New York: Harcourt Brace Jovanovich, 1971.

Newton, Norman T. *Design on the Land.* Cambridge: Belknap Press of Harvard University Press, 1971.

O'Harrow, Dennis. "Growing Pains of a Village Government," *American City,* January 1950.

Olmsted, Vaux and Co. "Preliminary Report upon the Proposed Suburban Village at Riverside, near Chicago." Reprinted in *Landscape Architecture,* July 1931.

Osborn, F. J. *New Towns after the War.* London: J. M. Dent and Sons Ltd., 1918.

"Park Forest Moves into 1952." *House and Home,* March 1952.

Peets, Elbert. "Post-War Use of Temporary Housing Sites." *American City,* November 1943.

"Philip Klutznick Resigns as FPHA Commissioner." *Journal of Housing,* July 1946.

"Plan Home Colony in Chicago Suburb." *New York Times,* October 29, 1946.

Purdom, C. B. *The Building of Satellite Towns.* 1925. Reprint. London: J. M. Dent and Sons Ltd., 1949.

Reed, Thomas H., Doris D. Reed, with Murray Teigh Bloom. "Does Your City Suffer from Suburbanitis?" *Collier's Magazine,* October 11, 1952.

Rovere, Richard H. *Senator Joe McCarthy.* New York: Harper and Row, 1973.

"Senators Taft, Ellender, Wagner Introduce General Housing Bill on March 10." *Journal of Housing,* March 1947.

Schaffer, Daniel. *Garden Cities for America: The Radburn Experience.* Philadelphia: Temple University Press, 1982.

Schlesinger, Arthur M., Jr. *The Age of Roosevelt: The Coming of the New Deal.* Boston: Riverside Press Cambridge, 1958.

Spreiregen, Paul D. ed. *On the Art of Designing Cities: Selected Essays of Elbert Peets.* Cambridge: MIT Press, 1968.

Stein, Clarence S. *Toward New Towns for America.* Cambridge: MIT Press, 1966.

Stilgoe, John R. *Borderland: Origins of the American Suburb, 1820–1939.* New Haven: Yale University Press, 1988.

Sweet. Carroll F., Jr. *Park Forest — The Early Years,* vol. 4. Unpublished autobiography, 1987.

Waitley, Douglas. *Portrait of the Midwest: From the Ice Age to the Industrial Era.* New York: Abelard-Schuman, 1963.

Weiss, Marc A. *The Rise of the Community Builders.* New York: Columbia University Press, 1987.

Whyte, William H., Jr. *The Last Landscape.* Garden City, N.Y.: Doubleday and Co., 1968.

———. *The Organization Man.* New York: Simon and Schuster, 1956.

———. "The Future, c/o Park Forest." *Fortune,* June 1953.

Wright, Gwendolyn. *Building the Dream: A Social History of Housing in America.* Cambridge: MIT Press, 1981.

Velie, Lestern. "Housing: The Chicago Racket." *Colliers Magazine,* October 26, 1946.

"Village Design Wins Award for Architects." *Park Forest Reporter,* June 15, 1951.

Zeckendorf, William. "Cities versus Suburbs." *Atlantic. Monthly,* June 1952.

Oral Histories

Bennett, Richard Marsh, FAIA (Fellow American Institute of Architects). Chicago Architects Oral History Project. Chicago: Art Institute of Chicago, 1991.

———. *The Oral History of Park Forest: OH! Park Forest.* Recorded August 28, 1980.

Judge Henry X. Dietch. *The Oral History of Park Forest: OH! Park Forest.* Recorded September 6, 1980.

Dinerstein, Robert. *The Oral History of Park Forest: OH! Park Forest.* Recorded October 4–5, 11, 1980.

Klutznick, Philip M. *The Oral History of Park Forest: OH! Park Forest.* Recorded February 5, 1981.

McDade, Thomas. *The Oral History of Park Forest, OH! Park Forest.* Recorded October 21, 1980.

Rashkin, Jack. *The Oral History of Park Forest: OH! Park Forest.* Recorded December 9, 1980.

Waterman, Edward. *The Oral History of Park Forest: OH! Park Forest.* Recorded November 15, 1980.

INDEX

ABOUT THE AUTHOR

Gregory C. Randall was born in 1949 in Traverse City, Michigan, and moved as a child to Park Forest, Illinois, where he was raised. He studied architectural and industrial design at Kent State University and completed a B.S. degree in landscape architecture, with honors, at Michigan State University. From 1971 until 1993 he worked first as a designer and then as a senior principal and project manager with two planning and design firms in San Francisco (Anthony M. Guzzardo and Associates and Brown-Heldt Associates). His work in the Bay Area included many of the largest planned residential communities in California as well as corporate office campuses, retail centers, and high-density residential complexes, for which they received numerous awards. Since 1993 he has served as principal and president of Randall Planning and Design, of Walnut Creek, California, a landscape and architectural planning firm that specializes in large-scale residential communities. He has had a lifelong interest in the history of planned communities in the United States.

RELATED TITLES IN THE SERIES

Library of Congress Cataloging-in-Publication Data

Randall, Gregory C.
    America's original GI town : Park Forest, Illinois / Gregory C. Randall.
        p.   cm. — (Creating the North American landscape)
    Includes bibliographical references and index.
    ISBN 0-8018-6207-8 (acid-free paper)
    1. Park Forest (Ill.) — History — 20th century.   2. Park Forest (Ill.) — Social conditions —
20th century.   3. New towns — United States Case studies.   I. Title.   II. Series.
F549.P23R36 2000
977.3´1 — dc21   99-26762
                                                                                                          CIP